Changing Habits of Mind

Changing Habits of Mind presents a theory of personality that integrates homeostatic dynamics of the brain with self-processes, emotionality, cultural adaptation, and personal reality.

Informed by the author's brain-based, relational psychotherapeutic practice, the book discusses the brain's evolutionary growth, the four information-processing areas of the brain, and the cortex in relationship to the limbic system. Integrating the different experiences of sensory and non-sensory processes in the brain, the text introduces a theory of personality currently lacking in psychotherapy research that integrates neurobiology and psychology for the first time. Readers will learn how to integrate psychodynamic processes with cognitive behavioral techniques, while clinical vignettes exemplify the interaction of neurophysiological process with a range of psychological variables including homeostasis, developmental family dynamics, and culture.

Changing Habits of Mind expands the psychotherapist's perspective, exploring the important links between an integrated theory of personality and effective clinical practice.

Zoltan Gross has been practicing long-term intensive psychotherapy with adults since 1954. He has consulted and taught as an assistant clinical professor at UCLA Medical School and served as director of research for two hospitals and clinical director at a mental health center. At age 100, he continues to train psychotherapists in his innovative brain-based theory of personality, within the context of psychotherapy.

"A marvelous book, filled with clinical wisdom accumulated over almost a century of life. Zoltan Gross brings the difference between content and process to a whole new level, bridging emotion process and personality process, integrating state with trace work beautifully and elegantly. He picks a sufficient amount of brain-related evidence and offers a (missing) theory of emotionality, complex at first, then dazzlingly illuminating. The work of this psychology genius still at work is finally here to stay."
—**Nuno Conceição, PhD,** *Faculty of Psychology, University of Lisbon, Portugal; past president of Society for the Exploration of Psychotherapy Integration*

"This is indispensable reading not only in psychology but also in all of the human and behavioral sciences in which mind, thoughts, feelings, emotions, and behaviors are the subject of study. The book is a fascinating account of how a professional of human behavior came to the realization that popular conceptions of the mind are incorrect and how he arrived at a clearer understanding of the problem."
—**Jeffrey Bortz, PhD,** *professor of history, Appalachian State University*

"I am a clinical neurologist specializing in pain/headache. While many patients experience symptoms as manifestations of structural/functional disorders, many others have no identifiable pathology. The author's neurophysiological-based theory of personality helps me understand how better to approach my patients' suffering. Allowing me to consider a patient's behavior in a language I understand improves my ability to understand their suffering. So, from the perspective of a non-therapist (who inadvertently engages in a therapeutic relationship during the practice of neurology) the theories outlined in this book are of great relevance and importance to me."
—**Dr. David Kudrow,** *Santa Monica, California*

Changing Habits of Mind

A Brain-Based Theory of Psychotherapy

Zoltan Gross

Routledge
Taylor & Francis Group
NEW YORK AND LONDON

First published 2021
by Routledge
52 Vanderbilt Avenue, New York, NY 10017

and by Routledge
2 Park Square, Milton Park, Abingdon, Oxon, OX14 4RN

Routledge is an imprint of the Taylor & Francis Group, an informa business

© 2021 Zoltan Gross

The right of Zoltan Gross to be identified as author of this work has been asserted by him in accordance with sections 77 and 78 of the Copyright, Designs and Patents Act 1988.

The Open Access version of this book, available at www.taylorfrancis.com, has been made available under a Creative Commons Attribution-Non Commercial-No Derivatives 4.0 license

Trademark notice: Product or corporate names may be trademarks or registered trademarks, and are used only for identification and explanation without intent to infringe.

Library of Congress Cataloging-in-Publication Data
Names: Gross, Zoltan, author.
Title: Changing habits of mind : a brain-based theory of psychotherapy / Zoltan Gross.
Description: New York, NY : Routledge, 2021. | Includes bibliographical references and index.
Identifiers: LCCN 2020015202 (print) | LCCN 2020015203 (ebook) | ISBN 9780367417369 (hbk) | ISBN 9780367824150 (ebk)
Subjects: LCSH: Personality change. | Psychotherapy. | Thought and thinking—Physiological aspects.
Classification: LCC BF698.2 .G76 2021 (print) | LCC BF698.2 (ebook) | DDC 616.89/14—dc23
LC record available at https://lccn.loc.gov/2020015202
LC ebook record available at https://lccn.loc.gov/2020015203

ISBN: 978-0-367-41736-9 (hbk)
ISBN: 978-0-367-82415-0 (ebk)

Typeset in Bembo
by Apex CoVantage, LLC

Contents

Preface		vi
Acknowledgments		viii
1	The Dyad: Adventures in Psychotherapy's Wonderland	1
2	The Paradigmatic Shift: The Tyranny of Habits of Mind	26
3	A Theory of the Mind	44
4	The Ghost in the Machine	75
5	The "I" and Its Psychological Selves: Without Our Navigator We Can't Be Sure of Where We Are Going	93
6	What Emotions and Feelings Really Are!	116
7	Emotions and Feelings	129
8	A Portrait of the Person	159
9	The Art of Psychotherapy	180
	Appendix	210
	Bibliography	212
	Index	226

Preface

This book has been inspired by two major events in my professional life. First, my mind was primed with information about the brain in my doctoral dissertation on the effects of the lobotomy operation on learning. While I was intrigued by the results of the experiment and their implications for neuroscience, I remained dedicated to becoming a psychotherapist.

Second, in the early phase of my psychotherapy practice, I consulted with Hellmuth Kaiser, a member of the International Psychoanalytic Association, who called my attention to the clinical significance of the text and subtext of conversation that happens in conventional conversations, including psychotherapy ones. Hellmuth showed me how to use the subtext of psychotherapeutic dialogue to improve my therapeutic skills. His consultation was personally and professionally life altering.

It turned me into a relational therapist. It was, also, theoretically enticing. The duality of therapeutic dialogue drew my attention to the left–right duality of the brain's hemispheres. As I became more comfortable in my practice, I began asking questions about subtext and what made it so emotional. I have spent the rest of my life pursuing this question, both in my practice and my ways of thinking about the relationships between the brain, personality, and psychotherapy.

My dissertation encouraged me to learn more about the brain, which resulted in the theory explained in this book. Like all good theories, it asks more questions than it answers. In addition to addressing the complexity of the brain, I found myself wandering through epistemological issues, evolutionary, cultural, and, of course, psychological ways of thinking before I could theoretically integrate the mind with its body into a coherent functional relationship. It has been a compelling and exciting adventure.

The practices of psychotherapy and psychotherapy research have suffered from the absence of a theory of personality. Psychotherapists and psychotherapy researchers speak different theoretical languages and confuse themselves and their colleagues in the other camp by using the same words to describe different phenomena. My book opens a way to overcome this source of confusion.

The book, in the first chapter, begins with my recognition that by integrating brain dynamics with personality, I needed to make a paradigmatic shift in the way I would be describing the personality with the brain dynamics. The paradigmatic shift is described in the second chapter by describing cognition as being organized with linear/nonlinear and sensory/non-sensory formats. This called for a theory of the mind. In the third chapter the mind is described as emerging from the interaction of three biological functions of the brain: orientation (self-process), simplification (cognition), and display (consciousness). The fourth chapter explores the neurological literature where the biological functions of the mind are located in the brain.

The first half of the book, which is theoretical description of the mind/brain relationship, helped me write the second half, that describes how the mind—a process that evolved to stabilize the brain's growing complexity—creates a personality with an "I" and its selves (Chapter 5), emotion, and feelings (Chapters 6 and 7). Chapter 8 integrates all of them to describe the person, which is shaped by homeostasis, developmental family dynamics, and culture.

My theoretical descriptions of psychological variables are exemplified with clinical vignettes: stories. I have taken care to conceal the identities of clients whose personalities illustrated the dynamics I describe. None of their names are true and for some I've changed their gender because it was irrelevant to the clinical issue I was describing.

Finally, in Chapter 9, I discuss the art of psychotherapy. In it, I describe how and why the therapist's person is of prime importance in the therapeutic process since so much psychotherapeutic work can and should be done in the here-and-now interplay of the session. From the early beginnings of psychotherapy in the nineteenth century, therapists have been encouraged to avoid emotional contact with the people they serve—an impossible demand. Therefore, it is important for therapists to learn how to use their feelings therapeutically. Intensive long-term psychotherapy is an emotionally difficult but loving process.

Over the years, I have made presentations at conferences of the Society for the Exploration of Psychotherapy Integration that focused on the importance of integrating different psychotherapies. At some of their annual meetings, therapists have asked to see videos of my work with clients. You may be interested in seeing how I work. From time to time, samples will be added to my website: https://zoltangross.com.

Acknowledgments

This book could not have been written without my psychotherapy practice, which showed me a way to escape many of the common-sense falsehoods that exist about human nature. It has been a wonderful love affair. My childhood friend, Fred Nicholas, has always been a source of encouragement and warmth. I also cherish the encouragement of David Kudrow, M.D., a distinguished neurologist. I am indebted to George Stricker, Ph.D., Marvin Goldfried, Ph.D., and Paul Wachtel, Ph.D., cofounders of the Society for the Exploration of Psychotherapy Integration (SEPI), for creating an intellectual home for a lonely, private practicing psychotherapist and for encouraging my devotion to integrating homeostasis with personality dynamics. Nuno Conceição, Ph.D., Shigeru Iwakabe, Ph.D., two of my SEPI colleagues greatly helped with encouragement and enthusiasm. Helpful edits were suggested by Susan Harris, Ph.D., Jeff Bortz, Ph.D., Jeanne Robson, Ph.D., and three friends who are no longer with us, Michael Mahoney, Ph.D., James Rosenau, Ph.D., and Herb Turman. I am most deeply indebted to Peter Gelfan, who was the editor who taught me how to escape from writing ideas to myself to writing to my readers and to think in an orderly way. Those were important pieces of learning for me. And Jane Ryder, who is my guide, consultant, and emotional support as I have been learning how to get this book published. Susan Hoyt, an eagle-eyed copy editor, cleaned the copy of this book. And Fidelia Sillas, whose keen intellect and computer skills taught me much about that strange tool. She also relieved me of much detailed, but necessary, work which I abhor.

My sons, Jonathan, Richard, and Andrew, have for years read drafts of chapters, discussed the theory, and encouraged me to pursue this adventure. And finally, I love my wife, Pat, whose love, understanding, and grammatical excellence helped me through my most difficult confusions.

Chapter 1

The Dyad
Adventures in Psychotherapy's Wonderland

The Whole Is More Than the Sum of Its Parts

About a year after my resignation from the United States Army Air Corps, where I served as a celestial navigator in the Air Transport Command during World War II, I fell in love with psychotherapy. That startling moment happened when I was a student in Grace Fernald's Reading Clinic at UCLA. I was interviewing the mother of a six-year-old boy with whom I worked at the clinic. It was my first professional interview. We talked about her son, who was having difficulty learning to read, and about her worries about his future well-being. She left the interview relieved and I felt wonderful. I knew where I was headed in life.

When the war ended, I returned to UCLA to finish the doctoral program I interrupted to enlist in the Army Air Corps. In my doctoral dissertation, I hypothesized that lobotomized patients would suffer a learning deficit (Gross, 1952). At that time, there were no psychological tests that showed psychological impairment resulting from the lobotomy operation. My dissertation clearly showed that lobotomized patients had been seriously impaired by the operation. The research primed my mind to think about brain dynamics. I could have used my dissertation as a way of becoming a research neuropsychologist, but by that time I was hooked on becoming a psychotherapist where for over the past 60 years I have been enriched by that devotion.

At the beginning of my private practice, I went into my own psychoanalysis, which was then regarded as the most effective psychotherapy in the marketplace. Times have changed. Psychoanalysis has lost much of its almost religious beliefs. I went into it to resolve my own emotional difficulties and to learn more about psychotherapy by being in it myself. Early in my practice, patients would lie on my couch and *free associate*. I would interpret their associations and dreams and try to be a *blank screen*. I wasn't too successful at that. My patients teased me about being the *great stone face*. Try as I might, I was unable to totally keep my person out of my psychotherapeutic work with patients. I am now convinced that it is impossible for any therapist, of

2 The Dyad

any stripe, to keep his or her person out of the therapeutic relationship. Nor do I believe that it is therapeutically desirable to do so.

In pursuit of my efforts to unravel the mysterious emotionality of my practice, I turned to Josef Breuer's[1] report of his work with Anna O.: the first psychoanalytic case study. To my great surprise, I discovered that it was not the *talking cure* it was reputed to be. This study triggered the birth of psychoanalysis. And it is the source of the many misunderstandings about the nature of *cure*, the nature of the therapeutic relationship, and the nature of what is meaningful in that relationship.

As I pursued my interest in the Breuer/Anna O. relationship, I found that there are two very different literatures about it (Jones, 1953; Gay, 1988; Breger, 2009; Skues, 2006). The conventional one describes it as the inspiration of psychoanalysis. The other one, more recently published, disputes the claim that it was a *talking cure*. The Breuer/Anna O. relationship is a sadly misunderstood infatuation that dramatically affected both of their lives and shaped the course of psychoanalytic thinking.

In this chapter we will see that the *curing* of Anna O.'s symptoms, which were celebrated as the effects of the *talking cure*, arising from her enchanted relationship with Dr. Josef Breuer. Reading Breuer's report of his treatment of Anna O. confirmed my belief that the personality changing power of their psychotherapeutic relationship happened within the therapeutic relationship itself instead of Anna O./Breuer's and Freud's explanations of it.

I will describe the reasons for my conclusions as I present evidence for them in the following discussion. We will also see how difficult it was for them to acknowledge the therapeutic meaningfulness of the relationship that enthralled them.

They had a truly playful collaborative relationship. With much pleasure, they came up with explanations of what caused her personality changes. Not only were their explanations fun, they enabled Anna O. and Breuer to be blind to the infatuation that magically dispelled her grief and madness.

Many of Breuer's explanations are still thought to be meaningful in psychotherapeutic thinking. Understanding, catharsis, interpretation, and insight are still strongly held beliefs about the nature of what Anna O. called her *talking cure*. My re-examination of Breuer's case study validated the misgivings I had at the beginning of my practice about the therapeutic meaningfulness of these explanations.

Many years ago, I had the good fortune to have dinner with Rollo May, with whom I shared my theoretical misgivings about psychoanalytic personality theory. He agreed, saying that "Freud was a genius in asking all the right questions. Unfortunately, he came up with the wrong answers." At that time, I didn't know enough to understand this paradoxical agreement. Now I understand that Freud did ask brilliant questions and because of the limitations of understanding about personality and neurology 130 years ago, he could not come up with the right answers. His answers may have been wrong, but by applying a Darwinian metatheory to what he saw clinically, he made profound contributions to the creation of psychotherapy and he opened up new ways of thinking about human nature.

Looking at the Breuer/Anna O. relationship from today's perspective we can see the power of their emotional relationship in what they called a *cure*. A re-examination of their relationship sets the stage for a contemporary description of interpersonal relationships which is paradigmatically different from those currently used to describe the therapeutic relationship.

The Breuer/Anna O. Relationship Revisited

In 1880, on nightlong vigils, Anna O. cared for her dearly loved dying father. Finally, exhausted with excruciating grief, she developed a variety of *hysterical* symptoms, which prompted her mother to call Dr. Josef Breuer, a highly regarded Viennese physician. In the course of his treatment of Anna O., Dr. Breuer generated concepts about catharsis/abreaction, repression, and interpretation that inspired Freud to give birth to psychoanalysis. For many therapists they are still thought to be meaningful explanations about the nature of *cure* (symptom removal): which was the goal of his medical treatment. It was not psychotherapy as we know it these days.

Looking back at it from today's perspective will give us a better understanding of the nature of intimate relationships; especially the relationship that occurs in intensive emotionally oriented psychotherapy. We will see that their relationship ameliorated her suffering and the *symptoms* that plagued her. It also illuminates our human devotion to explanation and why we have overvalued it as a psychological change technique.

And, finally, it raised questions about the nature of and duration of personality change. The Breuer/Anna O. relationship vividly highlights the difference between psychotherapies that help people feel better and psychotherapies that help people escape from the characterological prisons of their childhoods. It is the difference between relieving the ache of loneliness by making emotional contact and the painful work of changing habituated character structures and creating more stable age-appropriate ones.

On hot summer nights, Breuer described his treatment of Anna O. to his dear friend, Freud, who was fascinated by Breuer's account of Anna O.'s *cure* from her painful *illness*. He told Freud that, when Anna recalled repressed painful or disagreeable emotional experiences, which, he believed, caused her symptoms, the symptom was either alleviated or it disappeared. Within the tradition of the time, if the doctor relieved a patient of a symptom, he believed she had been cured.

This was the beginning of the belief that *returning the repressed to consciousness* was curative. Fifteen years after treatment was terminated, Freud persuaded Breuer to publish his case study of Anna O.; Breuer did so with some reluctance. Here, I will present parts of Breuer's account of his relationship

4 The Dyad

with Anna O., which reveal the close loving relationship they had with one another. I will conclude my description of their relationship by showing how the denial of their love led them to change the ways they lived the rest of their lives.

From my reading of Breuer's description of her condition and his treatment of her, it was clear that he and his patient had different unacknowledged and nonconscious personal agendas about the purposes of their relationship. The following quotations from Breuer's report highlight the emotionality of their relationship.

> On December 11, [1880] the patient took to her bed and remained there until April 1. . . . There developed in rapid succession a series of severe disturbances which were apparently quite new.
>
> It was while the patient was in this condition that I undertook her treatment, and I at once recognized the seriousness of the psychical disturbance with which I had to deal. . . . For two weeks she became completely dumb and in spite of making great and continuous efforts to speak she was unable to say a syllable. And for the first time the psychical mechanism of the disorder became clear. As I knew, she had felt very much offended over something and had determined not to speak about it. When I guessed this and obliged her to speak about it, the inhibition, which had made any other kind of utterance as well, disappeared. . . . thenceforward she spoke only in English. . . . At times when she was at her best and most free, she talked French and Italian. There was complete amnesia between these times and those at which she talked English.
>
> (p. 23–24)

Shortly after she left her sick bed, her father died. About his death, Breuer said,

> This was the most severe psychical trauma that she could possibly have experienced. A violent outburst of excitement was succeeded by profound stupor which lasted about two days and she emerged in a greatly changed state.
>
> (p. 26)

When she recovered from the trauma of her father's death, her physical symptoms improved. However, her relations with others changed dramatically. She could or would not recognize people who displeased her and her tolerance for people, even those she liked, were short lived. Breuer went on to say,

> I was the only one whom she always recognized when I came in; so long as I was talking to her she was always in contact with things and

lively, . . . She had eaten extremely little previously, but now she refused nourishment all together. However, she allowed me to feed her.

(p. 26)

During this period, he introduced her to another physician to care for her while he would be gone for a short period of time, "whom like all strangers, she completely ignored while I demonstrated all her peculiarities to him" (p. 27). The cigar-smoking visiting physician tried to get her attention but to no avail.

> [Until] he succeeded in breaking through [her dismissal of him] by blowing smoke in her face. Suddenly she saw a stranger before her . . . and fell unconscious to the ground. There followed a short fit of anger and then a severe attack of anxiety. . . . Unluckily I had to leave Vienna . . . when I came back several days later, I found the patient much worse. She had gone entirely without food . . . and her hallucinatory absences [psychotic episodes] were filled with terrifying figures, death's heads and skeletons.
>
> (p. 27)

I have been quoting these sections of Breuer's case study to call attention to four aspects of his report; his presence was the most reliable condition that led to *symptom* removal. In essence, the warmth of their relationship was disregarded by Breuer. It was their warmth with one another that probably had its beginnings when he unsuccessfully tried to hypnotize her in an effort to reduce her anguish by suggesting it out of existence. Despite his failure to hypnotize her, the gentleness of the hypnosis induction procedure likely eased the pain of her grief and was the beginning of a loving relationship that created difficulties for both Anna O. and Dr. Breuer.

He describes her hostile and distant emotionality toward others, but he does not discuss the emotionality of their relationship, which is evident in her positive feelings toward him and the nightly devoted attention he gave to her.

His caring for Anna eventually caused his wife to complain about the amount of time he was away from home attending to Anna O. Breuer calms Anna O.'s anxiety. She lets him feed her. And she is "in contact and lively" when he talks to her. As treatment progressed, she calmed herself by insisting on telling him "stories." In the following quote, he says:

> The stories were always sad and some of them very charming, in the style of Hans Andersen's Picture-book without Pictures. . . . If for any reason she was unable to tell me the story during the evening hypnosis[2] she failed to calm down afterwards, and on the following day she had to tell me two stories in order for this to happen. . . . I used to visit

her in the evening, when I knew I should find her in her hypnosis, and I then relieved her of the whole stock of imaginative products which she had accumulated since my last visit. It was essential that this should be affected completely if good results were to follow. . . . She aptly described this procedure, speaking seriously, as a "talking cure," which she referred to it jokingly as "chimney sweeping" . . . she would never begin to talk until she had satisfied herself of my identity by carefully feeling my hands. . . . When I was present this state [her emotional condition] was euphoric, but in my absence, it was highly disagreeable and characterized by anxiety as well as excitement.

(p. 29–30)

Breuer vacationed for several weeks and returned to find

the most convincing evidence of the pathogenic and exciting effect brought about by the ideational complexes [in Anna while he was on vacation] . . . During this interval no "talking cure" had been carried out, for it was impossible to persuade her to confide what she had to say to anyone but me—not even to Dr. B. to whom she had in other respects become devoted. . . . The situation only became tolerable [when] . . . evening after evening [I] made her tell me three to five stories. When I had accomplished this, everything that had accumulated during the weeks of my absence had been worked off.

(p. 31–32)

After a time, her "stories" were added to the *talking cure* which removed the symptoms from which she was suffering. Breuer describes this as follows:

Each individual symptom . . . was taken separately in hand; all the occasions on which it appeared were described in reverse order, starting before the time when the patient became bed-ridden and going back to the event which had led to its first appearance. When this had been described the symptom was permanently removed. In this way her paralytic contractures and anaesthesias, disorders of vision and hearing of every sort, neuralgias, coughing, tremors, etc., and finally her disturbances of speech were "talked away."

(p. 35)

It appeared to Anna O. and Dr. Breuer that when she repressed her emotional reactions to external events, the repressed emotional reactions were transformed into physical or psychological symptoms. They also believed that when the repressed emotional experiences were restored to consciousness by recalling them, the symptoms disappeared. For example, Breuer recorded over 300 hearing disturbances that were *talked away*.

In the course of their work, she would also experience delusions or hallucinations.

Finally, in June 1882, Anna O. brought treatment to a close. Breuer was satisfied with her recovery.

Unfortunately, treatment did not end as simply or positively as he stated it. There are two dramatically different versions of what happened when treatment ended. The classic version is the one told to Ernest Jones by Freud, a very close colleague. Lucy Freeman describes his final encounter with Anna in the following fictionalized paragraph.

> On the evening, after what he thought was his last visit with Anna O., she fell into such great distress that her mother summoned him to her side again. As he entered her bedroom. . . .
>
> Suddenly she started to thrash about on the bed, seemingly gripped by acute pain. And out of her lips came the words, "Now Dr. Breuer's baby is coming! It is coming!" writhing all the while as though giving birth. This account is consistent with Jones' (1953) and Gay's (1988) description of that fateful evening in their biographies of Freud. Jones describes Breuer's reaction to Anna's pseudocyesis in the following quote.
>
> Though profoundly shocked, he managed to calm her down by hypnotizing her, and then fled the house in a cold sweat. The next day he and his wife left for Venice to spend a second honeymoon, which resulted in the conception of a daughter.
>
> (p. 225)

Other versions (Skues, 2006; Breger, 2009) tell of Dr. Breuer returning to his practice where he treated some patients with his cathartic method. They dispute the story of the false pregnancy and suggest that Freud told Jones about it. By that time, Freud had vigorously rejected Breuer. There is an implication that Freud's story resulted from his everlasting anger toward Breuer. After spending some six years in a Swiss sanitarium, Anna O. moved to Frankfurt with her mother and embarked upon a brilliant and renowned career as one of the founders of Jewish social welfare in Europe.

Another View from the Bridge

There is another explanation about Anna's recovery from her *symptoms*. I will briefly describe it here using a theory about the equilibratory (stabilizing) nature of emotionality to describe the here-and-now dynamics of the Breuer/Anna O. relationship. From the beginning of their relationship it was clear they were attracted to one another. They were in the confusing condition of infatuation when its sexuality was denied. Although the questionable pseudocyesis, at the end of her treatment, was seen as an oedipal transference phenomenon, it can also be seen as a way of accommodating the sexual arousal she experienced in an intimate, but very unconventional relationship. Vienna, at that time, was a sexually active community (Skues, 2006). And upper-class Jewish women, Anna O.'s age, were discouraged from pursuing any venture outside of marriage and motherhood. As a result, it is likely that they were sexually, impatiently waiting for their fathers to marry them off to suitable Jewish bachelors. I suspect that this was not true of Anna O. There is no evidence that she was sexually interested or active. She was, however, vigorously antagonistic to the Jewish chauvinism that discouraged her intellectual pursuits.

The emotional contact she had with Dr. Breuer relieved her grief about the death of her father and the loneliness of her life. Loneliness was a constant presence throughout Anna O.'s life. Being in the presence of a warm interested man, Dr. Breuer, who wanted to help her and who clearly enjoyed being with her gave her great comfort. But the relationship he offered was unusual and unfamiliar. There was nothing familial in it. Unlike the familial Jewish tradition, Breuer respected and encouraged the participation of her brilliant intellect. Nor was it professional in the ordinary sense of medical treatment. She was not the passive recipient of medical or physical treatments. She actively contributed to the theory that recovering repressed feelings led to the cure of distressing symptoms. The phrase *talking cure* was her description of their treatment. She felt free to discuss her feelings with Dr. Breuer, which he treated with unaccustomed interest, respect, and appreciation. In some ways, they had a conversation that resembled Martin Buber's (1958) "I-Thou" dialogue.[3] Aside from Buber's description of it, there is experimental evidence that I-Thou dialogue is emotionally arousing. I-Thou dialogue occurs when the primary topic of conversation is about the feelings that the conversants have about one another.

She and her symptoms were the primary subjects of their dialogue. Aside from that, they also enjoyed one another when they were talking about other things. When Anna O. told Breuer "Andersen-like" stories, he was pleased, and his pleasure with her assuaged her grief and anxiety. He partially replaced the love and affection she lost when her father became ill and died.

However, neither Breuer nor Anna O. were able to directly talk about their affection for one another, which probably was tinged with a sexuality which neither of them could admit. They could only enjoy the cause and effect explanations that to them looked like the cathartic effects of symptom cure. It can also be argued that her false pregnancy, if it actually happened, was a way of expressing the love and affection she felt for him but could not declare.

The rules of the psychotherapeutic relationship are so different from ordinary intimate relationships that not infrequently sexuality is sometimes simplistically and erroneously used to accommodate the complexity of the loving experience that exists between adults in a productive psychotherapeutic relationship or any creative activity, like football. I will discuss this more fully in Chapter 9.

This way of thinking about the emotionality of the therapeutic relationship is a way of integrating transferential process with the here-and-now effects of their relationship. There is no doubt Anna O. loved her father and his death was a painful loss. It is also true that her infatuation with Breuer was a tension-reducing outlet for the repression of her sexuality which existed prior to the onset of her breakdown. At the beginning of his treatment of Anna O., Breuer (while they were friends) remarked to Freud, with some surprise and relief, about the unusual absence of sexuality in her presentation or discussion. As a dedicated family man, he had the freedom of enjoying her without being burdened by the guilt-producing experience of sexuality between them. He was also uncomfortable with discussing sex openly and disagreed with Freud's theory that repressed sexuality was the cause of emotional disturbance. This led to Freud's unending rejection of him. I believe that Breuer and Anna O.'s repressed sexuality made their collaboration much easier for them. She was a very bright, attractive young woman. She spoke German, English, French, and Italian. It is interesting to note that most of her discussion with Breuer was in English. In this way her conversations with him could be private in her German-speaking home, where treatment occurred.

His attention and admiration fed her need for relief from the loneliness of her existence in Vienna. Her relationship with her mother was conflicted. Her brother was of small comfort to her. As a young woman in a wealthy, orthodox Jewish family, she was denied the ability go to the university and enrich her intelligence and find a professional occupation. Furthermore, she had little or no control over who would be chosen to be her husband. She was socially at ease with her female contemporaries. Freud's fiancée, Martha, was one of her friends. But her active and socially conventional life did not assuage the loneliness caused by the absence of a loving relationship with a sexual partner or the estrangement that existed in her family. It is easy to understand that Breuer's kind caring presence was a relief from the grief laden, emotionally impoverished and frustrating life she was living.

As their relationship progressed the *discovery* of the talking cure enabled them to experience unintended, *innocent* delight with one another. Their mutual pleasure was the curative experience. She was relieved of symptoms when Breuer was present. They returned when he was absent for periods of time and when he stopped treating her. There is a dispute about whether, or not, she suffered with a false pregnancy. There are, however, suggestions in the literature that she was a sexually attractive young woman. Breuer for the rest of his life recognized his discomfort with discussions about sex. His continued disagreement with Freud about repressed sexuality as the primary source of neurosis led to the eventual breakup of their friendship.

Anna O., on the other hand, after six years in a Swiss sanitarium was rehabilitated. After her sojourn at the sanitarium, Anna O. devoted the rest of her life to the company of women. She became a tough passionate feminist and social worker helping unfortunate Jewish women who were deprived of the ability to live independent lives and who had fallen victim to poverty and sexual abuse. She trained her wealthy female friends to raise funds and help her administer institutions she created to rehabilitate abused Jewish prostitutes and unwed mothers. To my knowledge, there were only two men in her life with whom she had an intimate relationship: her father and Breuer.

I had a therapeutic relationship that was similar to the Anna O./Breuer relationship. In the third year of my private practice, with pleasure and pain, I worked with a depressed young woman who made great progress in the initial phases of our work. Like Breuer and Anna O., we were delighted with one another. Unlike Breuer, I raced between my supervisor and analyst trying to fathom and extinguish my infatuated *countertransference* to her. In the course of our work, she repeatedly told me of dreams that sounded more like memories than dreams.

After I made the suggestion that they might be memories, she recalled, that when she was three years old, she had witnessed the murder of her mother and father by his brother with whom her mother was having an affair. She also saw her uncle commit suicide. At first, we were suspicious and doubted the reality of this recovered memory. In her search for evidence of the truth of these experiences, she went back to her hometown and to its newspaper's morgue and brought back copies of the newspaper describing the murders and suicide in very much the same way she had described them to me.

At the very beginning of my practice I thought I had been blessed. Here, within the first years of my practice I had the good fortune to participate in a psychotherapeutic *cure*. At that time, *returning the repressed* trauma, memory, or experience into an immediate, emotional experience in the consultation room was the *gold* of psychotherapeutic cure.

I was jubilant. I thought that within a few months she would no longer need treatment. We worked enthusiastically in these months dissecting the memory of witnessing the murder of her parents and other memories, which were less traumatic, but nonetheless very painful: all in the hope that these remembrances would cure her depression. Yet, except for the excitement and hope associated with the recovery of those dramatic memories, depression continued to torment her life. Finally, after two more years of fruitless effort she gave up and left our work.

Some five years after her departure, she called and made an appointment to see me. When we met, she told me of the variety of therapies she had tried after seeing me; all to no avail. I asked why she had made this appointment with me, hoping that she would tell me that she wanted to return to work with me again. She didn't. She just wanted to talk to me. She wasn't interested in psychotherapy. She had given up on that. At the end of the interview, I escorted her to her car debating with myself about asking a question that had plagued me ever since she left our work. Finally, after she was seated behind the steering wheel of her car, I could hold it in no longer. I blurted out my question, "How did recovering the memory of witnessing the murders of your parents and your uncle's suicide affect you?" She looked at me sadly and said, "I did it for you. You wanted me to remember. So, I did." With that, she drove off.

Five years later, I was told that she had committed suicide. I felt terrible about her pain and my not being able to work effectively with her. I also gave up believing that *returning the repressed* was an important therapeutic goal. Something more was needed to make psychotherapy more effective.

While I had given up belief in a, then, widely believed psychoanalytic theory, I continued practicing psychoanalytic oriented psychotherapy and seeking psychoanalytic consultation. For me, it was a one-legged search. I found clinical supervision with experienced analysts helpful. But learning more about psychoanalytic theory did not enrich the way I practiced. There, still, is no direct theoretical link between psychoanalytic theory and its practice.

At that time, psychologists were not admitted into psychoanalytic institutes, so I bootlegged psychoanalytic consultation from analysts to continue my learning. About six years after I opened my private practice, I heard that an analyst, who was a member of the International Psychoanalytic Institute, was in town and willing to train psychologists. I, of course, sought him out and spent six months working with him. Hellmuth Kaiser was the last and most influential of my consultants.

I was delighted to learn that he, too, didn't have a medical degree. He had a doctorate in mathematics. Before he became an analyst, he worked as an actuary in Germany. There he had been in psychoanalysis with Wilhelm Reich, one of the early psychoanalytic giants. Hellmuth was admitted into the International Psychoanalytic Association by Freud because he was impressed by a psychoanalytic paper Hellmuth wrote about Heinrich Heine's poetry. His early career was interrupted when he fled Nazi Germany. He wound up in Mallorca as a woodcarver and analyst to an American heiress. From there he escaped to Israel and then went to the Menninger Foundation in Kansas, where he did not fit well into the psychoanalytic community, of that time. Finally, much to my benefit he came to Los Angeles in 1962. He was one of the very early relational psychotherapists.

I was in the last months of my own analysis when I began working with Hellmuth. Consultation with him confronted me with my own unfinished personal emotional work. He called my attention to the dual process that exists in all dyadic conversations. He did it clinically. At that time, I had a speech tic. I would automatically intersperse my conversation with the phrase "you know." After listening to me for a bit, he called my attention to my "you know" with the suggestion that I was repeating it in the hope that he would agree that he knew what I was talking about. Then I would not have to try to explain what it was that I did not know. I flushed with embarrassment. A dash of adrenaline zipped through my chest. And I stopped talking. I had been caught covertly trying to convince him I was clinically brilliant.

He suggested that I listen not only to what my patients were talking about but to attend to how I was feeling about them as they were talking to me. The words were about things, interesting events, or troubling relationships that hurt, confused, or puzzled them. My feelings were aroused by the emotional ways they were presenting themselves to me. When I focused on my feelings, I realized that, as their therapist, I could choose which part of our conversation was most therapeutically meaningful. Responding to the emotional messages of the subtext surprised my people and, most often they were emotionally aroused when I responded to their emotionality rather than the content of their discussion.

Using my reactions to my patients' personal presentations changed my relationship with my patients. From that point, I thought of them as my clients, a less medically oriented term. It changed the nature of my practice from a psychoanalytically based therapy to a relational one. With Kaiser's counsel, I no longer sat, trying to be a blank screen, behind the couch making insightful interpretations based on the free associations of my patients. I confess, in the psychoanalytic period of my practice, I had moments of poetic pleasure when an interpretation of mine *hit the mark* and my patient saw something about herself that was important to her. But much of the time being a blank screen was boring and unproductively repetitious. And most importantly, much of the time I failed to see its therapeutic value. I recalled that in my own analysis, I spent many expensive hours behind a glaze saying nothing meaningful to my analyst.

In essence, Kaiser recognized the significance of the emotional presentations of his patients as an important part of what they were telling him. He suggested that their presentations were ways of eliciting a validating reaction from him. He called it the *fusion delusion*. By eliciting validation, I mean people seek to get feedback that matches a part of their personalities that are in need of a strengthening kind of exercise that stabilizes and strengthens that part of their personalities.

He explained the *fusion delusion* (Fierman, 1965) as the *universal symptom* to be treated in psychotherapy. He believed his patients try to create a feeling of fusion in the therapeutic relationship. Helping a patient see his nonconscious manipulation was similar to helping him have an emotional insight into the here-and-now movement of his character. He believed that the fusion delusion was one person's attempt to get the other person to agree with, validate, and join his or her reality to avoid the dreadful experience of being alone. He went on to suggest that when a therapist's attention was distracted by the patient's presentation, there was a strong possibility that the patient was being fusional and wanted the therapist to be congruent with her emotional need. If the therapist got in touch with his own emotional reaction to his patient, there was a strong possibility that the therapist would know what she wanted him to feel.

While I didn't fully accept Hellmuth's explanation, my emotional reaction to his observation of my tic was so vivid I did not dismiss the meaningfulness of what had happened to me. As I grew in my practice, I came to see that for many people the experience of being alone was indeed dreadful and that people do need people.

Dyadic conversation contains both text and subtext. Text is the subject matter that members of the dyad attend to in the center of awareness. Subtext is the emotional way the subject is discussed, which is presented in the background of awareness. This is well known in the theater. Actors are taught to respond to the subtext of dialogue with other actors on the stage or on a movie set. Hellmuth taught me how therapeutically meaningful the subtext of dialogue could be. As a therapist, I had the choice of responding directly to the dialogue of the subtext, which frequently varies from the text of what a person is telling me. Dialogue is like people singing to one another. Text is the words of the song and subtext is the emotional music of the relationship engaged in dialogue.

Much to my embarrassment, Kaiser showed me, in our consultations, that I, too, sang my *song* with him. In the weeks that followed my embarrassing consultation with Hellmuth Kaiser, I practiced observing and calling attention to the presentations of my patients and coping with their reactions to me. My clients had an experience similar to mine, except they reacted emotionally to me for what I said to them. These experiences convinced me that there was more than transference in our relationship. I also realized that I needed to be more emotionally skillful with the use of my feelings in my practice and, of course, in my everyday emotional life.

Recognizing the subtle behavioral, usually nonverbal, messages that people send to one another, in conversation, has long been recognized as an important but difficult to explain process. Theodor Reik (1948), in his "Listening with the Third Ear," says "[What] . . . Freud meant when he said that the capacity of the unconscious [the third ear] for fine hearing was one of the requisites for the psychoanalyst" (p. 146).

Therapeutically responding to the client's covert nonverbal communication creates a startling conversation, which resembles Martin Buber's (1958), emotional I-Thou dialogue. He was a nineteenth-century Zionist and Jewish theologian, who recognized the difference between text and subtext. Like actors and my own emotional experience, he found the emotionality of subtextual dialogue, within a theological context, *awesome*. Seeing dyadic duality in these different contexts made it obvious that it needed explanation.

When I spoke to their emotional presentations, my clients reacted to me in a way that enabled me to be more therapeutically useful than sitting behind my couch making insightful explanations. In responding to the emotional presentations of my people, I became a real person.

It was a relief to escape from the blank screen, behind which I had been instructed to hide. At first, I found that I had much to learn about my own emotionality to become therapeutically effective. Hellmuth's consultation and the way it changed my work as a therapist helped me understand what I missed in my failed treatment of the depressed young woman. It has been a continuing source of learning for me.

The emotional engagement I had with my clients called my attention to emotionality—mine, theirs, and the limitations of the existing theories of emotionality. Three other interrelated dilemmas confronted me, when I changed from a psychoanalytically oriented practice to a relational one.

First, from the beginning of this adventure, it became clear that my person is in the midst of the psychotherapeutic work. I questioned my ability to responsibly be there. I, like Freud, wasn't confident that I could respond to the emotionality that would follow from the use of my person as an important part of the therapeutic process. Yet from the beginning of this practice, I discovered that I could say things to my clients that evoked intense emotional responses, which persuaded me that I was being useful.

With this realization, I pursued both my practice and the search for an explanation of this dramatic phenomenon. Both efforts helped me become more skillful with my feelings and less anxious with the people with whom I worked. This work took us to places I never reached when I sat behind a patient lying on my couch. There were times, I made a mistake that was not useful to my client. I was able to rescue our relationship by being honest and acknowledging my mistake. I still do. When I was and sometimes still am hurt, it becomes an opportunity for me to learn more about myself and my work.

Second, by taking the position that using my feelings psychotherapeutically was a responsible way of working, I was violating the scientific tradition in which I had been trained to be a psychologist, not a psychotherapist. The theoretical atmosphere of both psychotherapy and academic psychology are very different.

They are heavily influenced by nineteenth-century empiricism. Visual observation is believed to be more reliable as information about things than feelings are as observations about interpersonal process. This is true. But it took time and practice for me to understand and learn the meaningfulness of this dilemma. It is the difference between scientific research and art. This is a major issue with which this book is concerned.

This dilemma creates an enormous difficulty for psychology and especially psychotherapy where we engage with personality, which is composed of nonsensory and nonlinear processes that never sit still. Personality is not processed by sensory systems of the brain. Our brains are in constant movement stabilizing themselves and managing our relationship to the complexity of the world in which we live and the complexity of our brains.

This brought me to my third dilemma. It was the realization that mechanistic empiricism didn't work as a theoretical ground upon which an understanding of psychotherapy could grow. As I was beginning to write about the relationship of the brain to personality, I became aware that I had to change my allegiance from science to art. Today there is a growing integration of scientific metatheory with the nonlinear traditions of the humanities (Bronowski, 1956).

The double duality of dialogue turned my brain brain-primed to the duality of information processing systems in the brain. This book, in large part, speaks to the theoretical dilemmas created by the different ways the left and right hemispheres and the anterior and posterior areas of our brains homeostatically manage information. To this point, I have told the story about how I arrived at a theory about dyadic dialogue, which I will now describe.

A Structural Description of the Theory of Dyadic Interaction

Dialogue is really *quadrilogue*. When two people speak to one another, they are simultaneously engaged in two very different conversations. Dialogue reflects the inner and outer nature of human existence. One conversation transports facts and ideas about the outer world. The other manages the internal emotional needs of the members of the dyad and of the dyad itself. For the most part, we are unaware of how complex this universal human duality is in our lives.

In my mind's eye I saw the quadruple communication of the dyad as a triangle. In Figure 1.1, I and Thou, the individuals of the dyad, are designated at the base angles of the triangle. My use of "I" and "Thou" acknowledges Martin Buber's (1958) contribution to my understanding of dyadic interaction. Lines of communication connect I and Thou to one another through the subject at the apex of the triangle (I-It communication) and directly to one another along the baseline of the triangle (I-Thou communication).

The dyad discusses matters at the apex of the triangle about something other than their feelings about one another. The subject at the apex of the dyadic triangle can be about anything: last night's dinner, who did or did not do the dishes, events at work, plans for a vacation or the ideas being presented here, or anything that is of mutual interest residing outside of their personal relationship. It is not about how the members of the dyad experience one another. It is primarily a left hemisphere of the brain process about the physical things, events, and/or interpersonal relationships.

In apical, I-It (objective) communication, the subject matter being discussed is primarily irrelevant to the emotionality of the relationship.

However, it is not unusual for the *subject* at the apex to be used metaphorically to manage the emotionality of the dyadic relationship. A mother and her teenaged daughter might be fighting furiously about doing the nightly dishes, while the central issue between them is pain about the daughter's approaching adulthood and departure from her home. A person in therapy may criticize the therapist for being five minutes late as a way of expressing her hurt feelings about something the therapist said at their last session. In both cases, attention is directed toward an external something rather than engaging the other person in painful baseline dialogue, where the lack of emotional skill and personal invalidation frequently confound both members of the dyad.

Apical communication, generally, follows the conventions of common-sense and axiomatic cultural understanding (left-hemisphere information processing). It is dialogue experienced with familiarity and ease. Here, the persons of the dyad have a sense of understanding one another. When both members of the dyad provide one another with enough validating feedback on the baseline to maintain attention to the subject, they have no difficulty keeping the subject in focal awareness. They are in *contact* and are engaged in normal conversation.

Contact is the condition in which there is sufficient mutual relevant interpersonal validation between members of the dyad to keep the same subject in their center of attention. In ordinary conversations, the presence or absence of contact resides in the background of awareness. When persons in a dyad are emotionally relevant to one another, contact is present, and their attention remains focused on the subject of their conversation. The absence of contact occurs when one or both conversants find their attention wandering or are feeling bored with the discussion.

In psychotherapy, contact between the therapist and the person seeking help is of central importance. When contact is lost, nothing much psychotherapeutically occurs. However, if the therapist asks her client about how contact got lost, baseline dialogue in the therapeutic dyad is usually resumed. This kind of dialogue is, for the most part, therapeutically illuminating.

When the therapist finds himself bored or his mind wandering, and therefore out of contact with his help-seeker, he can search his feelings about his client to find out if there is anything therapeutically meaningful in his becoming bored. For example, while I was listening, during a first interview, to a tall, handsome man in his late fifties talking about his marital difficulties, I found my mind wandering. I turned my attention to the man and saw why I lost contact with him. He was telling me a story that he had told many times before to other therapists. He was boring. But I noticed how kind and considerate he was in his complaints about his wife. I interrupted his complaints about his marriage by saying, "You are a very nice man." He was as startled as I had been with Hellmuth Kaiser. The man stopped complaining and told me in a very interesting way about his furious father and

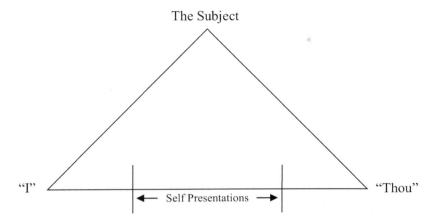

Figure 1.1 The Dyadic Triangle

how he protected himself in his childhood by being very nice and being out of contact, which contributed to his marital difficulties.

When a therapist is distracted by any feeling that interrupts her attention, she can use it as an opportunity to question what is happening in the background of their relationship or within herself. If the interruption of her awareness is a covert message from the person with whom she is working, the covert emotion can be used therapeutically.

Baseline Communication

Baseline communication occurs when the attention of both members of the dyad is focused on one another and they are telling the other how they are feeling about and experiencing the other. Examples of this are conversations between lovers when they are making love or angrily breaking up. When lovers are being affectionate with one another, they are in contact and experience varieties of pleasure. When baseline contact is ruptured by insufficient validation, dialogue becomes strained, though the dyad is in contact. In fact, I have seen couples start fights to break the anomie that exists within their dyad. Mistakes are made, alienation occurs, and sexuality, where it is a regular part of the dyad, becomes markedly diminished when baseline process is ruptured.

Even though the dyad's attention may be focused on the subject, each member of the dyad is usually nonconsciously seeking, with her personal presentation, validational feedback of some kind from the other member of the dyad. With Hellmuth Kaiser, I was unintentionally doing it, I wanted a simple smile of approval; I wanted a part of my character to be validated. The search for validation operates, for the most part, automatically, as nonconscious habits, such as smiles, nods, and ahas. Each person develops characterologically consistent habits designed to elicit validational feedback.

Baseline dialogue is invariably emotional. The moment either member of the dyad experiences its operations in conversation, its automaticity is interrupted. When family members are fighting or lovers are making love, they tell one another what they are feeling about the other. Since this is an infrequent way of talking to one another, members of the dyad have less skill processing this information. For most of us, I-Thou conversation is not processed automatically. Emotionality is evidence that the limbic system of the brain is disequilibrated. This has important implications for the therapeutic dyad, where the therapist is trained to remain invisible and anonymous. However, in relational therapy, where the therapist is visible and present, the dyad itself has an opportunity to engage in productive therapeutic work.

Furthermore, I-Thou dialogue is about the relationship as it is occurring in the moment (Gross, 1992; Stern, 2004; Hill et al., 2008). Unlike ordinary conversations, which usually are logical, linear, and sensory, it is nonlinear, nonsensory, and emotional. It is a right-brained information processing system (Schore, 2003).

Baseline dialogue, as Buber discovered, is very difficult for adults. He found it to be awe inspiring. From childhood, people are discouraged from engaging in baseline dialogue. It is common practice for very young children to be actively discouraged from embarrassing adults by telling them how they feel about them.

Times are changing. There are now pre-schools where children are encouraged to express their feelings and become skilled with their use. However, many children are trained to be *good* and to be *nice*—in other words, to validate the personal presentations of others without regard to their own feelings. Unless children are encouraged to use their feelings as meaningful ways of engaging others, they will have difficulty with the emotionality of baseline dialogue in their adulthood. It is easier to learn the benefits of being socially conforming along with other aspects of socialization a little bit later in their emotional development than it is to unlearn the early responses of their real feelings in order to be *nice*.[4]

Most dyads become emotionally aroused when their persons are confronted with unexpected information with which they are emotionally unskilled (Morris, 1977; Cotton, 1974; Buber in Kaufmann, 1970; Gross, 1992). At this point, baseline communication is displayed in the center of attention. Reactions to baseline communication are highly varied. The diversity of these reactions varies with the nature of the habituated emotionalities of the members of the dyad. The variety ranges from a folie à deux, where one member of the pair supports the madness of his partner, to a couple that lives in constructive, growing, loving harmony.

The social context within which a dialogue occurs also influences the ways the dyad reacts to baseline interaction. One of the most dramatic examples of this occurred, when a woman with whom I had been working entered one of my therapy groups. In ordinary social situations, she was an extraordinarily gracious woman, who enjoyed the warmth she received in her daily routine encounters with people she met in shops and markets. In my groups, members are encouraged to engage one another with their feelings about the way they speak to each other. In other words, the group experience is dominated by the members' emotional reactions to one another. Clearly, the group's rules of conduct were very different from the ones operating in a shopping mall. As the new member of the group recognized this, she withdrew. Her Grande Dame disappeared and was replaced with a frightened little girl.

And finally, the emotional condition of each person at the moment of engagement determines the ways in which baseline feedback is interpreted. A person awakening in a bad mood will react with greater negative intensity to something going wrong than she would if she awakened to sunshine in her soul. If a person is unskilled with the experience and expression of feelings in the moment of disruption, he is likely to automatically regress and use a childhood habituated emotionality. Validating feedback is not simply pleasure-inducing information. Validation for the individual can also occur in situations which convention defines as negative, i.e., pain or fights (Swann et al., 1992). The kind of emotional validation a person seeks depends upon his character structure and personal identity. Some are nourished by smiles, others with a good fight.

In stable, functional, secondary relationships, baseline process rarely emerges into mutual awareness. A member of a secondary dyad may at any given moment have a reaction to his partner, but it is rarely expressed. When strangers meet, they almost never directly tell one another how they feel about the other. They show superficial acceptance with automated pleasantness in their self-presentations.

Casual secondary relationships have relatively little personal meaning. In these relationships, baseline process is almost never the subject of conversation. Telling a person how you feel about her in a secondary relationship violates the conventional social contract people have with one another. In other words, ordinarily, one usually does not tell a clerk in a department store how offended he is when the clerk ignores his question. The social contract of secondary relationships is designed to facilitate focal awareness on some subject matter (I-It communication) while avoiding the embarrassment or disruption that could ensue if attention was focused on the self-presentations of the persons comprising the dyad (Goffman, 1959).

Self-Presentations

When we talk about *saving face*, we are referring to an aspect of self-presentation. A person loses face when he/she is insulted and or humiliated. The idea of *self-presentation* is more than protection from the pain if being treated badly. Self-presentation includes protection and much more. It is our way of asking others to validate some aspect of our personality. It is not true that everyone wants to be liked, but those who wish to be liked have self-presentations that elicit a liking reaction from others. The efforts of self-presentations are ubiquitous. Personality styles are created and elaborated from early childhood to old age to nourish not the souls of people but their brains. It occurred to me that if this is automatic behavior then probably it is a part of the brain's dynamics. This became a central part of my theory. I called it affect hunger. It is the brain's need for exercise in ways that resemble muscular need for exercise.

From the tales of what happens to sailors stranded on desert islands without human contact to the terrible effects of solitary confinement in prisons, there is clear evidence that *people need people*. Human beings require constant validation from other human being or when they do not receive it over long periods of time, they suffer pangs of loneliness that have severe deteriorations of psychological or physical health.

In the above diagram, the lines perpendicular to and intersecting the baseline of the dyadic triangle designate the self-presentations of the members of the pair. Self-presentations are behavioral expressions of an individual's character structure and personal identity, a face. They are signal systems of the persons engaged in conversation, signals seeking validating nonverbal feedback from the other person with whom they are speaking.

The characteristic nonverbal ways persons hold themselves, look at others, walk, and smile, and the prosody of their conversation, illuminate the emotionality of what they are saying to one another. When self-presentations are invalidated, the limbic system is disequilibrated and activates automatic self-stabilizing processes, triggering emotionality. Invalidation occurs when the feedback information disrupts the automatic flow of the person's limbic process. The processes actively solicit feedback from others to stabilize the neurological underpinning of the person and the limbic system. They are right hemisphere information-seeking systems.

The emotionality of this aspect of dyadic interaction occurs when self-presentations of the participants are disequilibrated either by invalidation or novel confrontations.

Attachments to the Dyadic Triangle

The visual stability of the lines of communication should not be construed to mean that the persons of the dyad maintain constant attention to either kind of dialogue. In conversation, the stabilizing stream of consciousness of persons fluctuates to different thoughts or perceptions to accommodate the equilibratory needs of their persons triggered by the dialogue.

The uniqueness of the dyadic character of conversation is defined by the nature of the validating systems each person brings to the dyad. Under ideal circumstances, the sweetness of a young girl's smile will delight her boyfriend, who returns the favor by melting with her adorableness. In this situation they are mutually validating one another. With repetition, this mutual validation can lead to an attachment to one another. Dyads themselves become self-perpetuating systems with the practice and rehearsal of mutually validating information about its individuals and about the dyad itself.

It is important to emphasize that validating information does not necessarily mean *pleasure* or *love*. Of course, it can have that meaning for some people, but a more reliable criterion for recognizing the source of attachment is familiarity.

Familiarity is experienced when cerebral structures are able to automatically process information that matches their structural characteristics. Processing information automatically validates and reinforces the integrity of the neurological systems that are operating automatically. It is not unusual to see a marriage where both members are dreadfully miserable with one another but are unable to separate. A dyad engaged in a folie à deux is a dramatic example of the dyad keeping its individuals bound to one another in madness and pain by being trapped in painfully habituated emotionally validating exercises. They may be excruciatingly painful but nevertheless that contributes to the durability of the relationship.

The structural dynamics of dyadic interaction are based on the equilibratory imperative of the persons of members of the dyad. Persons have character structures that determine whether or not another person will be congruent with his or her emotionality. Dating behaviors of adults exemplify this. I recall working with a young man just beginning to engage in his sexuality. He met a woman who enthusiastically joined him in that pleasure. After a few months, he found himself falling in love with her—whereupon she rejected him with the explanation, "It's a lot easier to fuck you than it is to love you." Obviously their equilibratory dynamics were very different. Some people feel anguish when they experience being loved.

The Dynamics of the Psychotherapeutic Dyad

At the center of psychotherapeutic work are the dynamics of dyadic interaction, which rest on self-perpetuating and functionally autonomous personality structures operating automatically outside of intentional control and awareness. They are habituated systems residing in the background of awareness. Addressing the efforts of personal presentations interrupts the automaticity of these efforts. It also activates consciousness: the interrupted person becomes self-conscious. As in the figure-ground illusion of Gestalt psychology, in dyadic communication, baseline and apical dialogue can be alternated. When I-Thou communication, which usually resides in the background of awareness, is moved into the center of attention, conversation becomes therapeutically more meaningful.

Listening to a song is the same kind of experience. One can focus on the lyrics or switch attention to the music. In my practice, I have found listening to the "music" when people talk to me is therapeutically useful. Working in this way enabled me to engage a client's emotionality in ways that interrupted age-inappropriate emotional habits that defeated their adult aspirations. This approach circumvented searches for logical explanations that impair emotional learning. This position is similar to Westen's (2007) description of the need to engage the emotionality of the electorate instead of relying upon logical explanation. Rosenthal (2003) concludes the retrospective of his more than 40 years of research on the effects of unintentional or covert communication with the following comment:

> In sum, then, we have learned a great deal about the importance of subtle processes of nonverbal communication, but a great deal more has yet to be learned about these processes as they occur in the relatively sheltered context of laboratories and classrooms and in the rough-and-tumble of the truly real world.
>
> (p. 151)

My theory of dyadic interaction is applicable to both the *sheltered* and *rough-and-tumble* worlds Rosenthal has explored.

Self-presentations can enable the client to avoid experiencing self-concepts that cause anxiety. Some people hide behind their personal presentations. Sometimes this takes the form of a person saying that they are *afraid* that they will be *seen*. At other times, a self-presentation enables a person to avoid experiencing painful feelings. A very successful man once told me that a stranger called him for advice in his field and said that she had been told he was the "nicest man in Hollywood." He was very pleased by the compliment and went on to enumerate several talents that contributed to his reputation. When he finished with his inventory of personal assets, I commented that it was also true that he was extraordinarily excellent and creative in his field. Tears came to his eyes and he said that that was much more difficult to hear than being told he was the nicest man in Hollywood, an image he hid behind.

Piaget's (1970) definition of a psychological structure as a *self-perpetuating wholeness* is the idea which underlies the durability of stable dyads and the change resistant nature of personality systems. This definition underscores the stability and habituated nature of personality structures. The *self-perpetuating* part reflects Piaget's biological education. It presumes a kind of biological growth similar to that which occurs in neurological systems. It requires exercise on invariant feedback and the freedom to grow to accommodate the increasing amounts of information accumulated during the course of life.

I no longer see the primary task of psychotherapy as aiding in the achievement of emotional insight. Instead, I describe psychotherapy as aiding clients to escape from habituated nonlinear emotional cognitive structures created in childhood by interrupting their automaticity and helping them create new age-appropriate personality structures.

The Wonders of Wonderland

When I began relating to my people in this way, I found myself in Alice's Wonderland. The words we used to denote feelings didn't have stable meanings, the Pleasure Principle didn't operate the way it was supposed to, and Reality took on different shapes and functions. These experiences set me to wondering where personality dynamics were located.

The emotional power and therapeutic usefulness of using therapeutic conversation in this way was fascinating and puzzling. The ubiquity of dual dialogue turned my attention to the duality of the cerebral hemispheres. The linearity of the left hemisphere and the nonlinearity of the right hemisphere fit the duality of dialogue. It struck me that the duality of conversation could be a form of the famous *figure ground* illusion of Gestalt psychology. The figural focus of attention was on a subject of conversation (the words) and the emotional needs (the music) of the dyad were displayed in the background of awareness. When I became aware of this as a possibility, it was easy for me to think that this could be a connection between the brain and personality.

Ever since 1848, when an iron bar was driven through Phineas Gage's left frontal cerebral lobe, which seriously changed his personality, we have known there must be a brain/personality relationship. Freud (1895), who started out as a neurologist studying the then recently discovered nerve cell, hoped to create a relationship between the brain and personality to complete his theory of psychoanalysis. There was not enough known about the brain when he tried and failed to complete his project. There is now!

While he opened up new ways of thinking about human nature, there is still no dynamic theory of personality that relates it to the dynamics of the brain. But now we know enough about the brain to begin thinking about a brain-based personality theory that can contribute to the work of psychotherapy.

The Power of the Therapeutic Relationship

That's where the magic began for me. First, I had to learn not to respond to my people as I might respond to my friends or family. When I could *hear* what their music is telling me and I could *sing* back to them, then I became more therapeutically relevant. This did not mean explaining what they are doing to me. But by emotionally addressing what I experienced was happening between us I was able to help them to experience and discuss the emotionality that was therapeutically meaningful to them.

The first meeting I had with a young actress I'll call Naomi exemplifies this way of working therapeutically. When I opened the door to the waiting room to meet her, I was greeted by a brisk, cheery vitality. She dazzled me with a brilliant smile. She whisked past me into my consultation room, seated herself, and expectantly waited for me. I asked her what I could do for her.

Without hesitation she told me that she was having difficulty getting work as an actress, although she had been fairly successful in the past ten years. She worried about getting older. She was going to be 35 on her next birthday. She realized that she could no longer be cast as an ingénue. Furthermore, she wanted to get married and have a child. Getting older was a problem. All of this was conveyed in a no-nonsense businesslike manner.

She paused and waited for me to respond to what she had told me. I said that I was terribly impressed by how pretty and talented she was and that if I were a TV or movie producer, I'd cast her in a quick minute. She blushed with pleasure and then got annoyed with me. She imperiously instructed me to listen to her and discover what was impeding her desires. I was, then, supposed to tell her how to correct her deficiencies. She said she knew that she had a set of problems that could be rationally understood and, therefore, should be logically explained and solved.

She was so precise, orderly, and charming that I again chose to respond to her presentation rather than her instructions. I told her how impressed I was by her ability to see issues and to state them with delightful effectiveness. She again flushed with embarrassment. Then she pouted and tearfully complained that I wasn't doing what I was supposed to be doing. Her brittle, businesslike demeanor cracked and behind that façade a hurt confused, adorable, crying little girl emerged. I said I was sorry that I had confused her. After I comforted her, she was able to tell me about the agony she experienced when she went on auditions because she never knew which one of the persons in her personality would emerge. I only made an acquaintance with three of them. There was her businesslike person and her dear confused child, and later in our work another person in her personality would confront me. Every once in a while, an older woman would gruffly speak to me in a language that neither Naomi nor I understood.

This kind of engagement runs contrary to traditional thinking about the posture of a therapist that goes back to Freud's difficulty with emotionalities in his relationships with his patients. They were so difficult for him he took refuge behind the couch and became the arbiter of their realities.

The skill of using one's person as a dynamic part of the therapeutic process is not simple and many current psychotherapy training systems teach their students to remain aloof and *objective*. Therapists who consult with me find learning this skill, depending on their level of emotional skill, difficult but rewarding. This practice helped me to get into the characterological emotional rigidities of my people, which I could not touch before I learned how to do this.

Mine is an upside-down way of thinking about personality disorder. If our personality problems are so difficult to shed, even after we bring them out into awareness and understanding, is it possible that the brain has become habituated to rely upon them for the maintenance of its own equilibrium?

This is the beginning of a paradigmatically different way of understanding human nature. The next chapter describes the theoretical paradigmatic shift that occurs when the mind and the body are integrated.

Notes

1. In an effort to avoid interrupting the flow of the story of my psychotherapeutic adventures, I will omit some bibliographic references in this chapter. They will be cited in the rest of the book. The names of authors to whom I am referring can be found in the bibliography.
2. Breuer was clear these were "auto-hypnotic experiences." In the beginning of his report he states he was unable to hypnotize Anna O.
3. Later in her life Anna O. and Martin Buber were acquainted. He recognized the passionate warmth in her, which resided behind her devoted care for sexually mistreated Jewish women and hostility toward Jewish male chauvinism.
4. Play Mountain Place is a nursery and elementary school in Los Angeles that, in addition to teaching a standard curriculum, is devoted to helping children create emotional skills and vocabularies.

Chapter 2

The Paradigmatic Shift
The Tyranny of Habits of Mind

Humans are champions at simplifying complexity. Solving complex survival problems resulted in the phenomenal growth of our brains. As we learned to make and use tools, as well as make sounds to identify things to communicate with others, we became capable of living in cooperative groups. All these achievements, coupled with physical skills, happened because our brains grew to accommodate, store, and organize increasing amounts of information that accompanied our increased survival skills.

For the most part, we have been devoted to making ourselves safe and luxurious with the resources of our physical world. Until very recently, in evolutionary time, we had so little knowledge about the brain that we were unable to have a way of knowing that it also brings psychological phenomena into awareness. Today, we have clear evidence that personality emerges into awareness from the brain. How it does that is another matter. But there is reason to believe that problem too can be solved.

Eons of thinking about the physical world and thinking that personality is a mystery that has no direct connection with the brain has left us with brains that have become highly trained to deal with sensory information and poorly trained to deal with the nonsensory processes of the brain, such as psychological processes emerging from the prefrontal areas of our brains. Plato found it difficult to explain the differences in the way he experienced sensory information (material) and nonsensory process (immaterial). Ancient Greeks sent both material and immaterial experiencing to Mount Olympus and let the gods manage them. Descartes's error (Damasio, 1994) simplified the Greek solution by declaring that nonsensory experiencing could not be scientifically investigated because it was a God-given consciousness. Even as late as the early twenty-first century, a highly respected research psychologist concluded that research psychology (sensory based) and clinical practice (nonsensory process) are irreconcilable separate worlds (Roediger, 2004). This confusion continues to plague psychotherapy research. It is very difficult to construct operational definitions of nonsensory process without reifying them. The paradigmatic shift I am describing in this chapter presents an alternative to the conventional psychological metatheory which does not integrate sensory (material) and nonsensory (immaterial) phenomena. A paradigmatic shift can create a way of creating a common language enabling an integration of sensory and nonsensory experiencing. Shifting from one way of thinking about the world, out there, to thinking inside about ourselves requires that we change the ways we think about things to thinking about processes. Kuhn's (1970) description of how paradigmatic shifts come about in scientific research predicts that a paradigmatic shift for a theory of personality would likely use cerebral dynamics as its database.

A paradigm is a set of theoretical ideas or assumptions scientists use to solve the puzzles of their science. Scientists build instruments to measure the results of their experiments in order to expand the reach and precision of solutions to questions their theories raise. Most research results in measuring the existing paradigm. Instruments are used to conform to the rules of their paradigm, and when scientists play their game well, the instruments accurately measure what the rules say they should measure. It is an orderly procedure until scientists are presented with information their instruments cannot measure, or a new instrument is invented that enables them to measure things they could not measure before. We are now developing instruments that can do that.

Our new ability to literally see aspects of the brain in homeostatic movement destroys the Cartesian metatheory that the mind and the brain are irreconcilable phenomena. This metatheory has become a major habit of mind that needs to be changed. In addition to creating a new way of thinking about personality, which did not recognize the brain in homeostatic operation, we have habits of mind that interfere with thinking about the brain's dynamics as a part of personality process.

The change from a geocentric view of the world to a heliocentric one is an example of a sensory based paradigm shift. Paradigm shifts are not easy to come by. It took centuries for us to discover that the world is not flat and to adapt to our thinking about the global nature of our world. The creation of a paradigm shift in the "soft" sciences like psychology is much more difficult than it is in the "hard" physical sciences.

The experience of physical things and their interactions in the external environment is the display of information in sensory awareness of physical phenomena. The experience of physiological and psychological phenomena is the nonsensory display in awareness of dynamic cerebral autoregulation (homeostasis).

The alternative metatheory I am presenting integrates sensory and nonsensory information processing by identifying the fact that the anterior (prefrontal) areas of the brain process nonsensory information and the posterior areas of the brain process sensory information. While it is true that there is a general acknowledgment that the Neurological Self (NS) triggers limbic activity, there is no emotion theory that describes how it activates emotional process or what the functional relationship between the self-system and limbic systems is.

The paradigmatic shift of my theory states that personality is the experience and behavior created by the brain to stabilize itself. This being the case, I, now, think of psychological phenomena in terms of homeostatic process rather than thinking of psychological variables as the operations of entities.

Until recently, psychologists had no direct sensory data about the brain as it operates in the moment against which they could validate their psychological theories. Operational definitions of psychological processes—those based on behavior—as the standard upon which to conduct psychological research—have been less than satisfactory in describing personality. Using the conventional metatheory underlying psychological research, it is not easy to simply translate nonsensory processes, like feelings, into sensory information about things. Psychological tests, attitude scales, or paper-pencil personality scales are thought of as measuring instruments, but they are not spectrographs, oscilloscopes, microscopes, or thermometers producing measurements of things we can see. They do not translate psychological information into sensory reality. Brain imaging technology promises to fill this gap.

Today, there is an increasing recognition that psychological phenomena are displayed in awareness and behavior from operations occurring in the brain. With the growth of neurological imaging technologies, we are now able to see the brain engaging in a variety of different tasks. While neurological imaging technology is still in its infancy,[1] the glimpses of the brain we now have give us enough information to call for the paradigm shift. To do this we have to liberate ourselves from habits of mind that blind us to the ways personality emerges into awareness from the brain.

This is a radical break from the philosophic tradition of using observations of experience and behavior to explain the human condition. This way of thinking about what we are and what we do is like looking at ourselves in a distorted mirror. The distortion results from the way our personalities need to stabilize themselves by shaping our perceptions and thoughts for neurological stabilizing purposes. We don't look at ourselves the way we look at simple physical objects. Therefore, such ideas as the Pleasure Principle, "the need to be realistic," morality, rationality, intentionality, Power, and understanding as ways of explaining our "psychological condition" carry little weight in the theory I will be describing. I will be taking the position that the brain and its entropy-resisting systems underlie everything we do and think. It comes first in the way we live our lives. Therefore, we must learn how to cope with our brain. It governs our lives. Before I describe the paradigmatic shift, I will describe some habits of mind that interfere with an easy shift to a new paradigm.

The Tyranny of Habits of Mind

A number of habits of mind nonconsciously contaminate our understanding of human nature and get in the way of making paradigmatic shifts needed to enlarge our understanding of it. They are cultural bias, reification, delusions of knowing, projection, knowing as a remembrance of past experience, the duality/dichotomy confusion, and the hierarchy prejudice. This list may seem to suggest that these habits or tricks of the mind operate as separate processes. I am not suggesting that. I classify them separately only for heuristic purposes.

Cognitively, they are blended into a kind of thinking called common sense, which makes paradigm shifts even more difficult to achieve because it has been the metatheory underlying human thinking for centuries. The very phrase "common sense" implies that effective thinking should be based on sensory perception. For example, the antique, commonsense belief that the earth is the center of the universe was based on the observation of the sun rising in the east and setting in the west and abetted by the desire to have a comforting sense of knowing where we are in relationship to a marvelous star that enables us to exist. Because we "knew" that we were at the center of our world, it was easy for us to believe that the sun rotated around the earth. Over generations, this belief was culturally reinforced to the extent that it was heresy to think otherwise. The Catholic Church recently apologized for what it did to Galileo for proving that the earth rotated around the sun. Today, likewise, we are just beginning to liberate ourselves from the belief that the "I" of intentionality is the control center of doing and knowing.

Cultural Bias

Humans are socialized to standards of conduct, beliefs, mores, values, and emotionalities. Social standards are necessary to establish stable and effective conduct and communication between individuals who reside in the same culture. Internally, cultures speak the same language, have a national character to their emotionality and, by and large, share similar beliefs and religious values. Acculturation ensures that people, when in public, will regularly behave in similar ways enabling them to interact, for the most part, automatically (Wyer, 1997).

The rules of social conduct are so important for the stability of society, they are frequently regarded as having the same truth-value as the meaning of traffic signals. They demand obedience. Each culture has strongly held beliefs about how people should or should not behave. In the United States, the fierce debates about abortion or the nature of marriage are examples of how passionately social mores command our behavior. Socrates was sentenced to death for his challenges to Greek values.

The consistency of cultural biases is similar to the consistency of neurological invariance—biological response systems such as fight/flight, feeding, and mating operate automatically. It is easy to conflate or confuse these three very different phenomena with culturally based beliefs. The psychological counterparts of these genetically structured systems are experienced and have psychological meanings that are different from their genetic imperatives. Psychologically, fighting has many different meanings and purposes. Psychologically, anger is not simply defending oneself from attack or engagement in predatory behavior. Anxiety is different from fear. Overeating has different psychological meanings other than a reaction to nutrient hunger. Psychologically, mating has many different meanings other than procreation. Psychological meanings, unlike their genetic origins, all are influenced by the cultures within which individuals are socialized.

The automaticity of cultural regularity is a product of practice. Practicing the same information over the same neurological structures creates automated skills, preferences, sensibilities, and beliefs. The automation of skills enables them to operate without awareness. Musicians practicing the same piece of music with the same instrument over and over eventually physically perform musical notation automatically. Conflating neurological invariance with cultural bias has led to erroneous beliefs about human nature, cosmology, and the perception of reality. Knowing we must eat to survive is not the same as knowing the earth is flat or that we must pray to a particular god. Psychological reality is very different from physical reality.

Cultural biases contribute to the difficulties encountered in making paradigmatic shifts, including (or even especially) in psychology. One of the cultural misconceptions of the self that has become a foundational belief is that our "I," the first-person singular pronoun, is the doer and knower of the person (James, 1890/1950; Damasio, 2010). The "reasonable person" criterion used in jurisprudence is a hangover from Plato's ardent wish that reason should rule over emotionality. Unfortunately, courts of law ignore the equally common observation that people, especially those who appear before them, do not behave rationally. Or they have the eighteenth-century belief that humans have the ability to suspend emotionality at will to arrive at rational judgments (Gabriel, 2014). The pleasure of love is not a universal experience: love really does not "make the world go 'round." For many, the "pleasure" of love can also be the cause of dreadful anguish. Who can "rationally" decide when and with whom to fall in or out of love?

Reification

Reification, another trick of the mind, gets in the way of thinking creatively about personality. As discussed earlier, it attempts to integrate the experience of immaterial phenomena, like feelings, with the experience of physical things by cognitively classifying a psychological process as a thing. Ordinarily, this occurs within the visual sensory system, which is the primary sensory system human beings use in their relationship to the external environment. Visual information processing occupies more of the cerebral cortex than does any one of the other sensory systems.

Consequently, our cognition has a richer vocabulary in the classification of visual information than of other sensory systems. For example, smell and audition consistently borrow from the visual vocabulary to label and/or describe their phenomena—e.g., a bright sound. The same is true of the nonsensory experience of emotionality, which uses words like blue, red, green, dark, and high and low to describe emotional experiences. Our experience and cognitive construction of physical reality is shaped by the nature of our cerebral equipment. Because of this, sensory information powerfully influences the way we think about psychological matters. Dawkins (2006) eloquently describes the effects of sensory specialization on the creation of our sense of physical "reality":

> the perceptions that we call colours are tools used by our brains to label important distinctions in the outside world. Perceived hues—what philosophers call qualia—have no intrinsic connection with lights of particular wave lengths. They are internal labels that are *available* to the brain, when it constructs its model of external reality, to make distinctions that are especially salient to the animal concerned. In our case, or that of a bird, that means light of different wavelengths. In the bat's case, I have speculated it might be surfaces of different echoic properties or textures, perhaps red for shiny, blue for velvety, green for abrasive. And in the dog's or rhino's case, why should it not be smells?
> (p. 418) (original emphasis)

What Dawkins says about the brain's sensory structures creating different ways of experiencing and labeling physical reality also holds true for its role in experiencing and classifying the nonsensory nature of psychological processes, some of which emerge from the brain as experiences we label as self, feelings, and personal reality.

Reification gets in the way of understanding human nature as a nonsensory process. It is easy to attach such names as "guilt," "the subconscious," or "persona" to mental processes or abstractions as if they were things, but the "understanding" of these names is illusory. Single word labels that presume to explain the motivation of behavior, such as laziness and guilt, and other words denoting feelings, are descriptions of either behavior or experience; they do not explain the complexity of what is happening within a person that causes them to experience a particular feeling, emotion, and/or self-awareness.

Reification is a form of "essentialism," which Barrett et al. (2010) describes in the following quote:

> One consequence of scientific categorization is that we sometimes essentialize our subject matter, then search for evidence of those essences, without considering how context might influence or contribute to

its very nature. The main consequence of essentializing is that people ignore the influence of context.

(p. 1)

The introduction of the idea of context changes cognitive classifications of phenomena from categorizing singular, static "things" to describing process; the relationships existing between different systems. Phrenology is the old belief that personality traits are located on bumps in the head of a person. The bumps are literal things on the top of a head, things. Reification is the linear classification of singular static "things." The classifications of process are nonlinear descriptions of relationships between processes. This is exactly the nature of cerebral process. Homeostasis is the action of different systems interacting with one another to maintain the steady-state condition of the brain.

Duality Versus Dichotomy and Hierarchy Versus Complexity

The cognitive classifications of duality and dichotomy and the notions of hierarchy and complexity are reifications of psychological process by casting the ideas of dichotomy and hierarchy into binary classifications. Duality is a structural condition of human existence. Dichotomy is a cognitive habit of mind. Duality is a ubiquitous human condition. Just as our bodies have two more or less symmetrical sides, so do our brains. While a discussion of the functional origins of human duality is beyond the scope of this book, the "twoness" of our bodies and brains is obvious.

Dichotomy categorizes things and processes in either/or terms. Good and bad, positive and negative, right and wrong are linear ways of categorizing phenomena. Dichotomy describes the psychological "appearance" of things without describing the structural or functional relationship that causes us to classify a thing in either/or terms. Things are good or bad because our values dictate them to be so; feelings are positive or negative because that is the way that we experience them to be. Right or wrong judgments are categories of value. Judgments about something do not describe a thing. They are experiences of our reactions to it—they are not the thing in and of itself. Dichotomizing does not describe what things are. It describes the ways we feel about and/or evaluate things in simplistic either/or categories.

In outdated, old-paradigmatic, dichotomous ways of psychological thinking, the self reacts to psychological phenomena from two generalized categories: good and bad; for example, the Pleasure Principle is one leg of the good or bad dichotomy. The other leg is pain. Even though we now have much research information describing feelings and/or emotions as emerging from the limbic system of the brain, some current theories still dichotomize emotions as "positive" and "negative" (Tomkins, 1962, 1963). Is anger a "bad" emotion? Some people feel invigorated and fueled by it. Is contentment a "good" emotion? Some worry that it makes them complacent and lazy.

Again, right or wrong judgments are categories of value. Judgments about something do not describe a thing. They are experiences of our reactions to it—they are not the things in and of themselves. There is a Kantian ring to this habit of mind. Dichotomizing does not describe what things are. It describes the ways that we feel about and/or evaluate things.

The same logic holds true for the idea of hierarchy. I believe this way of categorizing structures or processes arises because we feel that it is better to be on top, a value judgment. It implies a top to bottom organization of phenomena of the brain, from single nerves to higher organizations of cognition, personality, or emotionality. There is no top supercell or superstructure that provides a complete explanation of cerebral process; there is just the mystery of cerebral complexity. As the brain has become more complex, it has also grown in size.

It's so much easier to find a single thing to explain a psychological or neurological phenomenon. Freud at the beginning of his psychotherapy wanted to believe that sex was the root of human misery. Today there are neuroscientists who want to find a single neurological location for anxiety, the self, or God. Some of the ways the brain is homeostatically organized remain unexplained. We need to think of the neurological underpinnings of personality as complex neurological systems organized to preserve the integrity of their systems.

Theorists believe, as do I, that cognition and consciousness reside at the highest levels of human development, as do I, but my pride in the beauty of human achievement doesn't help me understand the complexity of the brain and its miraculous growth by believing cognition and consciousness are on top of something. Of what I don't know. The unease of not knowing is eased, for some, by assuming that knowing what's on top will help us understand. Shortly, I will be describing the genetic relationship of explanation which reduces the tension of not knowing.

The Delusion of Knowing

Another trick of the mind that makes the creation of a new paradigm difficult occurs when we sincerely believe that we know things we cannot define. In that condition, it is easier to be unaware of our ignorance than suffer the tension of being unable to solve an important problem. The difficulty and dilemma of "knowing" about psychological processes like thinking, feelings, the experience of self, and the "I" without being able to define them is dramatically exemplified by St. Augustine's confusion about the idea of time. Crosby (1997) quotes St. Augustine saying that, "I know well enough what it [time] is, provided that nobody asks me; but if I am asked what it is, and try to explain it, I am baffled" (p. 75). It is fascinating to note that 14 centuries later, William James (1890/1950) said, "personal consciousness is one of the terms in question. Its meaning we know so long as no one asks us to define it, but to give an accurate account of it is the most difficult of philosophical tasks" (Vol. I, p. 225). George Kelly (1955) also recognized the difficulty of articulating abstract nonsensory psychological process when he described a client who, while discussing psychological change, said, "[I] may be able to talk about it, but still be inarticulate as to what it was" (p. 804). Reddy (2001) begins his book by restating the same dilemma:

> What are emotions? To most of us, the question hardly needs asking; emotions are the most immediate, the most self-evident, and the most relevant of our orientations toward life. But from the moment the question is taken seriously, troubling difficulties of definition arise.
>
> (p. 3)

These are examples of illusory knowledge based on frequent cultural usage. Time, consciousness, and psychological processes are all nonsensory phenomena with which we are familiar, but because they are not physical objects, we have difficulty defining them. Classifying the experience of neurological processes as though they were physical things (reification) creates a false but reassuring sense of knowing. We have greater security of knowing what we are looking at when we see a table than we do when we experience a feeling. The idea of time is a classic example of the reification of a psychological process. Aristotle classified time in terms of past, present, and future. Since then, time has been reified as places, a past or a future that time travelers could visit. Time is also reified as the fourth dimension added to the three visual dimensions of space. Actually, time did not become cosmologically relevant until Einstein's theory of general relativity replaced the Aristotelian concept of a stationary universe with the past, the present, and the future running concurrently. Einstein introduced the idea of movement between objects. With that it was necessary to develop measures of the duration of movement in order to be able to describe where and how in space objects are related to one another at any given time.

My service as a celestial navigator sensitized me to this cognitive process. When I took celestial fixes on the stars to locate where my airplane was in its flight path, I had to note the time of the observations I was making through my bubble octant. With the time and measurement of my geometric relationship to the stars, I was able to locate my position on earth.

Unlike the other three dimensions of space, we do not see time. Time is a measurement of the duration of movement. On earth we measure time based on the duration of the earth's rotation in relationship to the sun and its orbit around the sun. Cosmologically, time is based on the speed of light. As such they are cognitive operations. Hawking (1988) reifies time by describing time, like Aristotle, as having three cosmological directions. I must confess while being intrigued with his cosmological descriptions of time, I could not follow his logic out into space. But here on earth, using Occam's razor, defining time as a solar based measurement of duration is conceptually simpler; it helps me to be punctual in my practice.

Behavior, as a source of inference about the nature of psychological process, cannot be looked at through the same lens of consciousness used for the observation of physical objects. Using a visual lens, devoted to the linear/sensory perception of things, to understand psychological processes reifies human nature.

The observation of two students interacting in a psychological laboratory experiment—or even a rat in a maze or a pigeon in cage—is not the same as the observation of a chair. In other words, observations about static familiar objects, which have little or no emotional relevance to the observer, are different from observations about processes for which we do not have well defined visual categories, and which have emotional meaning for us. We have a greater emotional reaction to the perception of another person than we have looking at rocks—unless, of course, we are a geologist or a jeweler looking at rocks which may have specialized meanings for them.

Much of the time when both research-oriented and clinical theorists discuss the person, selves, feelings, and/or emotions, they believe they "know" what they are talking about but are unable to define their terms. Neuroscientists and neuropsychologists who attempt to reduce psychological concepts—such as attention, consciousness, executive functions (forms of thinking and cognition)—directly into neurological operations are premature in believing they know how psychological and neurological phenomena are related. As long as they attempt to classify psychological processes based on the ways they appear in experience, without having a clear idea about underlying neurological purposes being served by the experiences of feelings or selves, they will continue to flounder in the illusion of knowing that which they are unable to define.

We have a sense of knowing when we think we have a meaningful explanation about something. "Meaningful" does not necessarily mean "true." A stabilizing sense of familiarity is frequently construed as being meaningful. Explanation is thought of as making that which is explained meaningful.

The need for explanation is constant and universal in humans (Gazzaniga, 2010). Humans are in an unending pursuit of explanation. Explanation is one of many cognitive processes which have different psychological purposes. In addition to explanation, also subsumed under the cognitive label are language, classification, planning, and knowing. However, neurologically cognition serves as an equilibrating process to modulate limbic process.

We surround unclassified familiarity with explanations. Greek mythology is a sexual and violent, if entertaining, example of this (Graves, 1988). In its beginning, the mythology was a set of explanations about the physical world within which they lived. By projecting what they experienced within themselves, they explained how the sun rose each morning, what made the seas roil with rage, and how authority in relationships between people should be organized. Furthermore, the truth of the explanations is not questioned so long as the repetitiousness of familiarity is not challenged. This is especially true of psychological phenomena.

I like ice cream cones. I have liked them all of my life. Therefore, I "know" I am motivated to do things I enjoy. From Plato to the present, in one form or another, self has been what William James (1890/1950) described as the "knower" or "doer" of the person. Like stating my pleasure with ice cream cones, I constantly use my "I" when I am describing my knowing or doing. Almost invariably, when we describe our intentions, desires, feelings, motivations, and/or behavior, we use the first-person singular pronoun to explain what we are doing. For example, we say, "I want that," "I did that," "I felt this or that," and so on to describe what we are doing or feeling or thinking. If my "I" is always there in my descriptions, I must believe that it is the "thing" that is causing the experience of knowing or initiating or causing behavior. Within this cognitive frame, we have come to believe that "I am motivated to seek pleasure because I like ice cream." The repeated coupling of two separate experiences does not necessarily mean they are, neurologically, causally related.

Knowing as a result of explanation and the experience of familiarity with things are different kinds of knowing. Familiarity is frequently confused with knowing. For example, the psychological literature abounds with descriptions of "self" and "consciousness" with an underlying assumption that we know what they mean. Not true. We don't even seem to know exactly what it means to "know" something. There are no consensual definitions of these terms—not that consensus defines truth. But because we experience and use them every day, we, like William James and Saint Augustine, think we know what they are and how they work. This is a commonsense kind of knowing. Unfortunately, it can be dreadfully misleading when one is trying to create new knowledge about human nature.

Common sense is a habit of mind that can be effective in helping us manage physical objects that can be touched and seen. However, psychology also deals with other sources of information—thoughts, feelings, memories, and the "I"—whose experience is not mediated in the brain by any of the five senses, and so common sense about them is not to be trusted as we are able to do with tactile and visual information.

Projection

Projection is another habit of mind that contributes to our misunderstanding of personality. We anthropomorphize the mysteries that abound in the nonsensory experiences of our brains and bodies. We make up for our lack of experiential and cognitive skills by projecting into these experiences explanations based on how we as people would feel if we were causing them. "My foot has gone to sleep." "That pizza disagrees with my stomach." Such projection, while of no practical use, enables us to have a stabilizing cognition about the experience in our body; it "explains" things. Throughout human history, humans used this trick to escape the unsettling mystery of existence. Ancient Greeks, who had not yet developed a clear sense of self, projected themselves into their gods to explain their motivations (Jaynes, 1976; Snell, 1982). People who love their pets believe they have human motivations and feelings. Those who are cared for by robotic caretakers and/or keep robotic pets project human feelings into them (Turkle, 2011).

In psychological theory, perhaps the most pernicious projective trick of our minds is the homunculus. It creates the illusion of a meaningful explanation by assuming there is a "little person in the head" doing that which provides the illusion of explanation. This assumption is rarely made explicit, which makes it a nonconscious trick because theoreticians who project the homunculus into our heads are not aware of what they are doing. Both Damasio (2010) and Kahneman (2011) recognize that it is a theoretical "sin" to resort to the homunculus as the explanatory root of their theoretical explanations, but after making this acknowledgment they forget about it, and probably nonconsciously, use the homunculus to explain their beliefs.

Another example of projection is Freud's three-part description of the person—the ego, id, and superego. They are three "little people in the head" serving different functions. The ego is a rational person, the id is an irrational pleasure-seeking one, and the superego is a harsh punitive person trying to force both the ego and id to behave in socially appropriate ways. Freud was unaware of the homunculi in his explanations of his tripartite person; to him, they were literal entities. But there are no little men (or women) in our heads; there's a brain in there that is doing it.

Knowing as a Remembrance of Experiencing

Remembrances are cognitively categorized, remembered, and brought into awareness. At the moment of experiencing something, we do not experience the experiencing itself. We experience the immediate circumstance. However, a moment after the focus of our attention has shifted from whatever it was that we were experiencing, we can remember that we had a related previous experience. We are also able to remember what our emotional reaction was to that remembered experience. For example, when I look at my rose garden, I am not experiencing my experience; I am experiencing the sight of my roses. While I am looking at the roses, I can shift the focus of my attention to liquidambar trees in the background. But at that moment, there is no experience of experience itself. Only after my attention is turned to myself am I able to think retrospectively and recall experiencing the roses and/or trees and then remember some of my reactions to or thoughts about them at the time.

Despite the extensive research by Dr. Elizabeth Loftus, who needed bodyguards to protect her from death threats inspired by her research demonstrating that memories are unreliable explanations, there still exists another trick of mind that causes the belief that memories are accurate descriptions of the past. Remembrances are not accurate recountings of what was experienced. A remembrance is shaped by the demands of the situation that instigated the recall.

There is a difference in what will be remembered if a lover asks you a question about what you were experiencing during an evening drive or if an angry policeman questions you about why you were speeding. When I am in the process of remembering, my experiencing is shifted from the sensory processes used when the original event occurred, to the nonsensory process of my "self" as it is being neurologically used in the moment. I have a memory of experiencing and the memory is displayed in awareness from nonsensory sources within my brain. That memory is shaped by the self-system's equilibratory needs that are occurring at the moment of recall. This is a theme that will recur throughout the rest of this book. The homeostatic needs of the brain nonconsciously influence and shape what we experience and what we do.

Nonsensory self-process is not experienced the same way we experience things or behavior. This has always been and still is a difficult distinction to make. In order to make it, one is taken away from that comfortable familiarity of common sense. The ease of looking at one's car and knowing how to start it and drive to the grocery store is the kind of knowing that provides one with a sense of security and safety. This kind of knowing is very different from the kind of knowing with which one is confronted during a loving fight with a partner who has misinterpreted you. It is frustrating when you cannot find words to express and explain your emotional pain.

Recognizing the sensory/nonsensory duality of the mind is so difficult that a significant sector of research psychology does not differentiate between these kinds of knowing. Their difficulty raises questions in my mind about the meaningfulness for psychotherapists of much of their research on personality issues such as the self and its emotionality. Without being aware of it, they do not differentiate between knowing based on sensory-based common sense and knowing about the emotionality of the person, a nonsensory phenomenon.

Roediger (2004) in a Presidential Column in the *Observer*, a journal of the American Psychological Society, quotes Endel Tulving in an email communication to him:

> It is quite clear in 2004 that the term "psychology" now designates at least two rather different sciences, one of behavior and the other of the

mind. They both deal with living creatures, like other members of the behavioral sciences, but their overlap is slim, probably no greater than psychology or sociology used to be when the world was young. No one will ever put the two psychologies together again, because their subject matter is different, interests are different, and their understanding of the kind of science they deal with is different. Most telling is the fact that the two species have moved to occupy different territories, they do not talk to each other (anymore), and the members do not interbreed. This is exactly as it should be.

(p. 48)

Talk about Descartes's error! Tulving adheres to it well. His is an unfortunate classification. The two psychologies to which Tulving refers are psychologies based on sensory and nonsensory kinds of knowing. The science of behavior is sensory based—e.g., how many times the pigeon pecked the lever, how many seconds it took the rat to run the maze. Investigations of the mind, of course, study nonsensory process. It is regrettable that many on the clinical side of psychology feel similarly about not talking to their research colleagues (Stricker, 1992; Gross, 2001). This has been a long-standing complaint about the different cultures of science and art (Snow, 1964). It is sad and wasteful that two rich bodies of knowledge about the person are unable to communicate with one another. I do not agree with Tulving's conclusion that "This is exactly as it should be." The paradigmatic shift contained in my theory integrates the science of behavior with that of the mind.

The Abandonment of Common Sense About Psychological Matters

Like most habits, habits of mind, therefore of personality, are resistant to change. Despite this, we do change. As my psychotherapeutic practice progressed, I found that most of the commonsense beliefs about what persons are and what causes them to think, feel, and behave in the ways they do led me into psychotherapeutic blind alleys. For example, over the centuries, beliefs that rational persons are pleasure-oriented and pain-avoidant have become the commonsense, foundational beliefs on which most personality theories are anchored (see Averill, 1994; Mahrer, 2000). William James and Freud agreed with the almost universal belief that the self is the source of rational intention which directs behavior to seek pleasure and avoid pain. Yet from the beginning of my practice, I was confronted with the fact that people are not primarily motivated to seek pleasure or happiness, and that stated intentions are poor predictors of what shapes behavior. People do not do things because they like to do them. There are those who will more readily endure the pain of a fight than suffer the "pleasures" of love. Rational decision-making is irrelevant when a person is in the throes of emotional turmoil. Despite this knowledge, many still believe intentions can and should control behavior.

Much of present-day explanations about the self and its relationship to intentionality dates back to Plato's brilliantly hopeful but necessarily limited observations about human nature. He said,

> it is proper for the reasoning part [of the individual] to rule, because it is wise and has to use forethought for the whole soul; and proper for the high spirited part to be its ally and subject.
>
> (Plato, 1984)

He recognized the difference between the rational (the "wise") and the emotional (the "high spirited") as the duality of human nature. This recognition was the beginning of a tradition of unfortunate beliefs that emotionality should be subservient to logical thought. It should be noted that Plato, with the use of the phrase "the reasoning part," implies a self but does not directly refer to it. He did not have a word for self (Snell, 1982). He knew that intentionality was unreliable, when he stated that rational thought should control behavior and that emotionality should be subservient to the dictates of sweet reason. This ancient form of wishful thinking continues today and drives many people to seek psychotherapeutic help when they are confronted with the fact that their rationality is impotent in the face of the commands of their emotional imperatives. The failure of intentional control is a continuing cause of anxiety and self-hatred.

Plato's long-standing distrust of emotionality continues into the present. Many still cling to the widely held "mind over matter" fallacy, as witnessed in the birth of eighteenth-century philosophical empiricism (Becker, 1932), modern day jurisprudence, and economic game theory. They were and are hung up on the crucifix of this unfortunate belief or hope.

Because the factual underpinnings of my theory are different from those classically used, the conventional beliefs about pleasure, pain, and intention are irrelevant to my way of thinking about personal motivation. These conclusions have led me to abandon common sense as a way of understanding people or as a guide to the conduct of my practice. Instead, I turned to some factual observations about brain structures and functions. Gazzaniga (2010) provides numerous examples of the unintentional explanatory behavior of his neurological patients to fill in the gaps of perception and/or experience caused by their neurological injuries.

Commonsensically, and within conventional theoretical frames, we think of feelings as psychological "things" (Barrett, 2006), separate from the self, to which the self reacts. This is another example of reification, projection, and cultural bias, which also contains a hidden homunculus. It is a major reason why "the self" has not been successfully defined.

Conventional explanations in psychology are classifications of the ways we experience ourselves in social situations. They are the experiences of visual observations of behavior. For example, most of the time people in simple, relatively unemotional situations experience themselves wanting to do things that are pleasant and avoiding things that are unpleasant. From this vantage point, it is reasonable to assume that the experience of pleasure motivates us to move toward pleasurable things or engagements and away from unpleasant things or engagements (cf. Carver, 2001 for a review of this way of thinking). This is a misleading conventional explanation based on simplistic visual observation.

Explanations based on immediate experience, the "appearance" (the reification) of anything, usually do not reveal the underlying processes that determine the nature of whatever is being explored. The appearance of psychological process has very different characteristics from those we experience when we look at physical objects, like tables or green apples. If a psychological process looks like a duck, walks like a duck, and quacks like a duck, it does not necessarily mean that it is a duck.

Outside→In or Inside→Out?

The casual observation of the sun rising and setting can be misleading because it does not enable us to see our planetary relationship to it. The familiar observation that I will invariably pick up a glass of water when I feel thirsty does not mean that my intention to drink caused me to pick up the glass. The work of John Bargh and his colleagues illustrates how easily we confuse the automaticity of everyday behavior with intentionality (see Wyer, 1997).

Classically, theories of personality are based on observations of behavior; reports of introspections have also been classified as behavior. They are outside→in ways of thinking about what personality is and its role in the life of the person. They classify what a person does and says and then project reified and anthropomorphized explanations for that into a theory of mind. While we assume the explanation somehow relates to brain function, none of these theories uses the brain as the explanatory cause of personality. This is a bit like coming up with a theory of breathing without taking into account the organism's need for a steady supply of oxygen or how the lungs fulfill this need.

In the early 1600s, the telescope liberated astronomers from simplistic observations and their projective, culturally biased explanations about the heavens. In the twenty-first century, instead of speculating about what goes on in the brain with similarly simplistic observations of behavior, we are now able to solve the material/immaterial dilemma that misled us about human nature. It is now possible to scientifically explain the nonsensory/nonlinear operations of the brain that emerge into awareness as psychology.

We know now that instead of hovering mysteriously over the brain, personality emerges from the brain. The epistemological difficulties discussed above can be resolved with our present-day recognition that psychological process is an emergent function of the brain. That being the case, it is logical to build a theory of personality based on brain operations. In other words, as science did centuries ago with breathing, we can take an inside→out approach to psychology: what vital physiological function does the brain fulfill that then results in the inward and outward manifestations of behavior and the brain's mind?

Homeostasis is the regulatory function of the brain (Granit, 1977). Like the rest of the body, it is an entropy-resistant organ. It keeps itself and its body alive. One of the things that distinguish humans from other mammals is the tremendous evolutionary growth of our brains. Part of this growth is the prefrontal cortex of the brain, sometimes known as the "executive brain." It has a homeostatic relationship to the rest of the brain. It emerged from our brain's ability to solve the problems of physical existence.

It is so complex that when it is destabilized it, like any other part of the brain, seeks regulation from the mind, which will be described in the next chapter. This is where the mysteries of personality emerge into awareness. With the recognition of duality of sensory and nonsensory process, we no longer have to be theoretically weighed down by "Descartes's error" nor do we have to remain confused as Plato was by the different experiences of the material and immaterial phenomena. This line of reasoning calls for a paradigmatic shift in the ways we think about personality.

The Paradigmatic Shift

The shift occurs with a truly brain-based description of personality. It is an inside→out way of thinking about personality. This shift occurs in the recognition of the relationship between information-processing functions of the brain as they emerge into awareness as the self, emotion, cognition, and consciousness. Personality is the experience of the brain engaged in the process of keeping itself in its optimal operating condition—in its homeostatic condition. My paradigm shift does away with the tyrannical habits of mind that generate and perpetuate psychological fallacies. It not only accounts for the psychological phenomena of self, emotion, feelings, and so on, but it also sheds new light on the function of the therapeutic dyad and opens the door to more effective modes of psychotherapy.

All of the habits of mind that I have described partially resemble genetically structured neurological systems in that they are regularly repeated over long periods of time. Like genetically organized systems, they are functionally autonomous and change resistant. They reflect the cognitive integration of the dynamics of personality development and the structural dynamics of the brain. The difference between genetically and developmentally structured systems is that developmentally structured ones can, with effort, be changed.

Before that door can be opened, a theory of personality must have a theory of the mind that is able to integrate the dynamics of functional personality development with the structural dynamics of homeostasis. The next chapter will present a brain-based theory of the mind.

Note

1. President Barack Obama committed $45 billion over a span of 20 years for research on the brain. The first year focused on expanding brain imaging technology.

Chapter 3

A Theory of the Mind

A Paradoxically Unreliable Stabilizer

The mind is a homeostatic process that enables us to create miraculous engines and breathtaking beauty. It is both the loving sustainer of life and a heartless destroyer of it. The complexity and mystery of the mind has been the cause of our endless search for its functional definition. Our increasing understanding of its neurological nature will enable us to more effectively find ways to reduce the pain of existence: a major cause of our self-destructiveness.

"Mind" is a word with a long history and a list of different definitions as long as its history (Hampden-Turner, 1981). The word "mind," like most psychological terms, is experienced with a familiarity that leads some of us to believe we know what it is without being able to define it. Because current definitions of the mind have become culturally habituated, I will begin my description of the mind by differentiating it from traditional ways of thinking about it.

Current Definitions of the Mind

Current theories of the mind have three characteristics which make them different from mine. First, they do not recognize the role of brain processes in the creation of the mind. Second, conventional concepts of the mind are, for the most part, shaped within sensory cognitive formats. Therefore, it is categorized as a singular physical-like "thing" causing it to be reified. The mind is not a thing. The mind is a process arising from the interaction of neurological systems. Third, many concepts of the mind anthropomorphize it by nonconsciously sneaking a homunculus into its definition. There is the belief that the mind is governed or initiated by the person's "I" or self. This inserts a homunculus into the mind.

Hampden-Turner (1981), at the beginning of his book, raises the antique question over which many psychologists and philosophers have stumbled. "How can that, which knows, know itself?" Notice! In the last sentence, a homunculus is snuck in by assuming there is a "knower" hidden in the brain. There is no "little person" hidden in the brain.

However, it is important to know that this is exactly what the mind does! It does "think" about itself. The Gordian knot of Hampden-Turner's question is cut by exorcising the homunculus. The mind is not a "thinker" nor is it James's (1890/1950) "knower." These are erroneous explanatory devices that project a homunculus into the experience of the mind or to reify it.

A Biological Definition of the Mind

Mine is not a complete definition of the mind. I think about the mind as one of three systems enabling a description of personality dynamics. Ideas about information storage, distribution, and transformation that are needed to describe repression, suppression, memory, emotional transformation, assimilation or accommodation, while important for a more complete description of the mind, are beyond the purpose of this book.

The word "think," in my theory, denotes complex cerebral processes, which are activated when the brain is disequilibrated by information it is unable to automatically process. When that happens, an orientational process in the brain initiates a displaying process (consciousness), giving the brain time to allow cognition to classify the information and return the brain to its stable-state condition.

In other words, when a person is confronted with any kind of information that she cannot automatically (nonconsciously react to) process, her brain turns her head in the direction (orientation) from which the stimulus is coming and she becomes aware (conscious) of it and then tries to figure out what the stimulus is and what to do about it (cognition). I used the word "she" for heuristic purposes only. There is no "she" in the brain that thinks. This example describes the mind's reactions to sensory information. However, as the brain grew, it was increasingly able to respond to the nonsensory complexity of the brain itself, including its own operations.

The mind operates in the brain when, orientation (self-process), the display of information (consciousness), and simplification processes (cognition) interact with one another. The idea of simplification is another way of identifying what Gestalt psychologists have recognized as creating a gestalt, a way of organizing information within a holistic format. I prefer using the term "simplification" rather than "gestalt" because it carries with it a biological function. This is the new paradigmatic way of defining psychological processes, in this case the mind, as homeostatic ones.

The brain has its own dynamics in the ways it manages information. These dynamics influence both perception and personality. This book is dedicated to the need of incorporating cerebral dynamics in a personality theory to more fully explain it. They anchor personality definitions to cerebral processes. The conventional words for these three processes are orientation, cognition, and consciousness. The relationship between them will be described in greater detail in the rest of this book.

The mind operates most effectively when three survival conditions exist. They are "practice makes permanent," "use it or lose it," and "grow or die." Together they describe the conditions that are needed for the maintenance of stable, effective nervous systems. This also will be a continuing theme throughout the rest of this book. Their normative operations make for a stable personality.

In neurological terms, the mind is an autoregulatory system that stabilizes systems within the brain which for a variety of reasons are thrown out of their steady state conditions. Also, because of its own internal complexity, the mind becomes a major destabilizer of the brain and of itself.

Before humans had much of a prefrontal cortex, cognition simplified sensory information about the environment. The prefrontal cortex, after it grew with the rest of the brain (Jerison, 1997), had the ability to classify information arising in the frontal (anterior) areas of the brain. Cognition became able to classify information about orientation's relationships to the external environment and its relationship to itself. These became experienced as the person's self-system, its "I" and the selves. In different relationships and contexts, we have different selves as in business, at home with the family, on a golf course with high school friends. At the same time, the constant presence of the orientation reflex is experienced as a singular self, which is displayed in consciousness as the "I" of personal experience.

The orientation reflex reacts in the same way to any kind of information the brain is unable to automatically process. When this happens, the information is routed to the display function. In everyday language, I call the display function "consciousness." Orientation is the survival function of "The Self." I will be calling the anterior cingulate cortex and other associated limbic structures the "Neurological Self." I regard simplification as the biological function of cognition. And I see the display of information (consciousness) as a way of giving cognition time to simplify complexity.

This is the point where the power of the paradigmatic shift can be most clearly demonstrated. This definition of the mind cuts the Gordian knot of the confounding dilemma of the erroneous mind/body dichotomy. With homeostatic definitions of cerebral information-processing systems, I was able to not only eliminate the pernicious homunculus; I was also able to describe, what we have termed, the mind as a homeostatic function of the brain.

One of the major characteristics of my theory is that it describes relationships between processes rather than describing the essences of "things" (cf. Barrett et al., 2010). When psychological processes, like thinking, are reified they are presumed to have essential characteristics that enable them to have moving relationships with other reified psychological processes. It is a way of trying to explain psychological movement without recognizing its underlying neurological structure. This is an awkward and incorrect form of psychological explanation.

My theory is similar to Kurzban and Aktipis's (2007), where they propose that "the mind is modular, consisting of a large number of specialized information-processing devices, each of which processes only a narrow, delimited set of inputs. Modular architectures result in systems that are potentially computationally isolated from one another" (p. 131).

The idea of "systems that are potentially computationally isolated from one another" requires clarification. It makes sense that information-processing modules manage information in ways that are different from one another; however, they also must be functionally related to one another. What I mean by neurological systems being "functionally related" is that they interact with one another to fulfill a homeostatic purpose: they work together to stabilize the brain. Unless information processing modules are functionally related, it is impossible to construct a theory of the mind.

Many current studies of brain/psychological relationships are caught in the trap of classifying psychological phenomena as singular things. As a result, they resemble the phrenological speculation of the nineteenth century where complex psychological processes were thought to be located in various bumps on an individual's skull. This is, also, an example of the "simplifying" talent of the mind. Sometimes it doesn't simplify accurately. These days, there are studies that attempt to "locate" a psychological process like "spirituality," or a "God Spot" (Biello, 2007) or anger or some other singular psychological term to a particular location within the brain (Uttal, 2001).

Locating a psychological concept to a specific location in the brain does not explain its relationship to personality in general nor does it describe its role in the symphony of the mind. This pointillist description of the relationship between a psychological "thing" and a brain location neither describes the movement of the mind nor does it explain its unique role in mental information-processing.

The brain has 100 billion cells which are connected to one another in numbers that range from a few to 1,000. This complexity is maintained in working order by homeostasis. The body has very narrow requirements for survival. These include body temperature, chemical balances, oxygen and carbon dioxide levels, nutritional requirements, and mating needs among other requirements for survival. Homeostasis manages these requirements.

The brain itself has requirements for its own effective functioning. It has a need for exercising its own neurological systems on familiar information, much like muscles need repetitious exercise like weights and running. This is an example of the use it or lose it aphorism. I call this need "affect hunger."

The brain's primary purpose (Granit, 1977) is to keep all these needs in optimal condition for the organism's survival. And therefore, its most important client is itself. The mind is an evolutionary development that emerges from the growing complexity of the brain to maintain its own equilibrium. This is an example of the aphorism "grow or die," which describes brain growth. It grows because of its increased use trying to reduce complexity. This growth enabled humans to build a safer and more productive environment that enables humans to live longer and to increase their population.

With this knowledge, we can no longer accept the "mind over matter" aphorism as a meaningful truth. It perpetuates the Platonic/Cartesian belief that the mind is a different phenomenon from the body. The mind does not communicate with the body/brain in a mysterious quasi-religious way. It is the biological "servant" of the body. Being a homeostatic process, the mind conforms to the structural needs of the brain and, therefore, brings these needs into neurological systems underlying personality systems.

This book is devoted to calling attention to how important the structural needs of the brain are in developing a more complete personality theory. Hypothetical personality systems such as self, feelings, emotion, motivation, "etc." are insufficient in this theoretical task. Commonly used psychological terms have little or no functional relationships to the cerebral structures that presumably emerge from them.

The Evolutionary Development of the Mind

Learning about the evolution of the mind helped me understand more about the functional nature of the mind as it exists today. As the human brain grew, we have grown in our ability to cope with the nonlinear/nonsensory complexity of our brains. But we are, still, more skilled with seeing a physical something than feeling an emotion. Nonetheless, our minds are better able today to think about and experience a broader range of psychological phenomena than we were in earlier evolutionary times. These realizations aided my understanding of how the increased skills of the mind have expanded our understanding of nonlinear psychological phenomena.

Knowing that the internal movement of the brain's homeostatic operations is not processed by its sensory information-processing systems opens our understanding to long-standing mysteries of human nature. Because most of these systems interact automatically, we do not experience them. When there is a disruption of automatic operations, we experience movement in our bodies. This movement occurs when the nerves of the brain interact with other nerves or other parts of the body. The nature and location of these experiences depends on which systems of the brain are disrupted. If the disruption occurs in the prefrontal cortex, we are likely to experience an emotion. If the disruption happens in the thalamus, we might experience a stomachache. None of these experiences is processed by the sensory systems of the brain.

We will see the powerful role that cerebral evolutionary growth plays in the changing nature of human nature. Edelman (2004) describes the role that evolution plays in my theory of the mind, when he says,

> There is one principle that governs how the brain works: it evolved; it was not designed. As stated, this principle sounds almost simple minded, doesn't it? But we must not forget that, although evolution is not intelligent, it is enormously powerful. The power comes from natural selection acting in complex environments over eons of time.
>
> (p. 32)

Since the later part of the twentieth century, the mind has been seen as an emergent experience of the brain keeping itself alive. This is a dramatic change from the way it was viewed in past centuries. Dennett (2006) describes this change in the following quote.

> For many centuries, most philosophers and theologians contended that the human mind (or soul) was a rescogitans (thinking thing). It was in some sense infinite, immortal, and utterly inexplicable by material means. Now we understand that the mind is not as Descartes confusedly supposed, *in communication* with the brain in some miraculous way; it is the brain that has evolved in much the way our immune system or respiratory system or digestive system has evolved. Like many other natural wonders, the human mind is something of a bag of tricks, cobbled together by the foresightless process of evolution by natural selection. Driven by the demands of a dangerous world, it is deeply biased in favor of noticing the things that mattered most to the reproductive success of our ancestors.
>
> (p. 107) (original emphasis)

The hundreds of thousands of years cobbling together the tricks of the brain have enabled it to cope more complexly not only with the external environment but also with the growing size and complexity of its own physical structure. The cortex's cognitive homeostatic relationship to limbic structures grew in its ability to classify them. With that equipment, a mind was created to manage nonsensory psychological process. It displays some of it in awareness and classifies self, feelings, and other psychological functions with varying degrees of skill.

The growth of the physical size of the brain provides humans with awesome cognitive abilities. In human evolution, brain volume and the encephalization quotient (EQ) have increased dramatically over the past several 100,000 years. The encephalization quotient provides an estimate of human brain size relative to that of any other mammal or primate of the same body size. Geary (2005) describes this growth in the following quote:

> An EQ of 2.0 indicates that [human] brain volume is double that of the average species of the same body weight. Since the emergence of australopithecines about four million years ago, brain volume has roughly tripled, and EQ estimates have increased two- to threefold. . . . We are now at a point in our evolutionary history in which there has been a very rapid (over a relatively few 100,000 years) increase in brain volume and EQ.
>
> (p. 6)

There are estimates that speech originated in humans 500,000 years ago (Geary, 2005). This talent was enabled by the increasing cognitive capacities of the prefrontal cortex to classify single physical things; we were then able to symbolize things, we experienced with our senses, with the use of our voices. We could then identify the different things we saw and heard with our voices. This is the beginning of a rudimentary mind.

The nonsensory perception of processes within the prefrontal cortex is a relatively recent human development probably emerging within the last 10,000 to 15,000 years. When this happened, we were confronted with experiences of nonsensory process in our brains for which we were experientially and cognitively unskilled. It is here that the mysteries of human existence confronted humanity.

As the prefrontal cortex gained the ability to process nonsensory information of the limbic system, it eventually began to have the ability to display into awareness the neurological systems related to orientation. The ability to perceive and classify the nonsensory information of the anterior cingulate cortex (ACC), which houses much of the orientation process, confronted humans with the mystery of being. The proximity of the ACC to the prefrontal cortex led Allman et al. (2001) to see this as an evolutionary development enabling the brain to cognize emotion.

The cognitive classification of the ACC results in the creation of three major psychological phenomena. First, the classification is displayed in awareness with the label "I." Second, there are numerous other cognitions about the ACC in different kinds of relationships. These are the selves which are used to help us navigate the complexities of social living. Conventionally, "The Self" is thought about as a single stationary thing. In my theory, the activity of the ACC is a homeostatic process. Therefore, I refer to self-phenomena as processes. Third, it shows the close anatomical relationship between self-process and emotion. I have come to think of orientation (as a biological function of self-process) as the Neurological Self (NS). The NS is a physical structure and, therefore, it earns the "the."

In the beginning of this ability, there were no words with which to label nonsensory ACC experience. Self, at that time, was not clearly experienced as it is today. Nor was there an explanation of how that experience came to be. Snell's description of Homer's understanding of the psyche illustrates the early beginnings of how mentality and personality were conceptualized in ancient Greece. He says,

> Concerning the psyche Homer says that it forsakes man at the moment of death, and that it flutters about in Hades; but it is impossible to find out from his words what he considers to be the function of the psyche during man's lifetime. One would do well to remember how little Homer says about the psyche of the living and dying man; for one thing, it [like a "breath"] leaves its owner when he is dying, or when he loses consciousness; secondly, he says that the psyche is risked in battle [it leaves the body through a wound in the skin], a battle is fought for it, one wishes to save his psyche, and so forth.
>
> (p. 8)

Plato called the experience of the nonsensory process of feelings interacting with other structures in the limbic system and the rest of the brain as the immaterial (nonphysical). And he called the sensory experience of physical things the material. He was puzzled by their experiential difference, as we are today. The experiential result of this new nonsensory ability was the experience of internal processes in the brain which eventually have become experiences of the selves, feelings, and emotions.

We are genetically attached to trying to find a commonsense relationship between "things." When confronted with a mysterious psychological phenomenon which we don't understand, we reify it,—that is we attempt to classify self and other psychological processes in the same ways we classify sensory process. Unfortunately, we have tried to classify immaterial (psychological) phenomena using information processing systems developed to manage material (physical) phenomena. This is a clumsy way of describing human nature. Describing the antiquity of this human characteristic, Murphy (1949) says,

> Plato introduces us to a clarification and full defense of the already ancient belief that soul and body are fundamentally different things. . . . While with primitive man and with early Greeks, the immaterial soul had been confusedly regarded as possessing some qualities of a more or less physical nature.
>
> (p. 7)

In another description of the sensory orientation of the ancient Greeks, Snell (1982) states that "Never does Homer, in his description of ideas or emotions, go beyond a purely spatial or quantitative definition: never does he attempt to sound their special, nonphysical nature" (p. 18).

Becker (1932) also elegantly describes the birth of eighteenth-century philosophical empiricism as a negative reaction to the disruption of rational thought by emotionality (a nonsensory process) and a positive reaction to the emotional security of the perception and experience of sensory information, as exemplified in the phrase "seeing is believing."

Even our present-day language reflects this sensory prejudice. The word "nonsense" (something that is not sensed) is used to denote the ridiculous or absurd. If something is not sensorially experienced, then it can or should be dismissed. On the other side of this prejudice, if we understand something, we say that it "makes sense." Freud (1927/1957) weighs in on this issue in his declaration that "all knowledge has its origin in external perception" (p. 26). The American Psychological Association has declared the first decade of the twenty-first century the Decade of Behavior, that which is visually observed.

Plato got it right. We do not see the reality of physical objects or human nature directly. We see "shadows" of reality on the walls of the "caves" of our minds. Observation of phenomena, physical or psychological, is influenced by the homeostatic requirements of the brain (the structural dynamic of the brain) as it processes information (Shepard, 1990). Observed sensory information is cognitively shaped by brain process. Gestalt psychologists recognized this with their observations of pragnanz and the figure-ground illusion.

The brain affects psychological (nonsensory) process in similar ways. The observation of behavior and personality is not like looking at physical objects. Behavior and personality arise from the brain processes that are not displayed in awareness via the sensory systems. The behavioral observation of people does not have the skill or reliability of sensory observation of physical objects. The experience of other people is also influenced by the genetically organized systems of the brain; it is also shaped by the habituated organized systems of the brain shaped by the personal development of the individual.

The experiential quality of nonsensory process is very different from that of sensory experience. The sight of a tropical sunset and the "rush" of infatuation have very different experiential qualities. Different parts of the body are aroused when the orienting process is thrown off center. We have different bodily experiences when we are confronted with scenic or sexual beauty. It took many centuries for the brain to grow large enough to generate a mind with the ability to cognize these different kinds of experience. Five or six thousand years ago, humans were not able to classify, or label, or experience an "I" or "me" orienting itself to disequilibrating information.

Self-Experience Was a Human Mystery

It was only after the brain developed autoregulatory neurological structures related to consciousness and cognition that self-awareness became possible

(Viamontes et al., 2004). When humans had a way of identifying and classifying a self, they could then dialogue about social process. It took centuries of tribal living before humans were able to develop a coherent set of rules to which they tried to conform. Buddha, Confucius, and the Ten Commandments occurred in different parts of the world at roughly, in evolutionary terms, about the same time. Each of these traditions provided humans with explanations and instructions of how to behave with one another at a time when they only had rudimentary experiences of themselves. Throughout the world in different cultures, the brains of Homo Sapiens grew at about the same rate.

There are many examples illustrating the evolutionary growth of intelligence, perception, and understanding. The ability to draw buildings in perspective occurred during the thirteenth century (Schlain, 1991). It took several centuries for Medieval European mathematicians to become comfortable with the notion that zero was a number (Crosby, 1997). The development of psychological skills progresses from concrete, sensory familiarity to abstract nonsensory relational process. Experiencing ideas or words about the self, which is a nonsensory/nonlinear (relational) process, is a relatively late development in human evolution.

It was not until about 900 B.C. that the ancient Greeks created a word for their selves; "I" or "me." They explained their behaviors as being motivated by their gods. Historians (Snell, 1982), sociologists (Gouldner, 1965), and psychologists (Jaynes, 1976) studying the literature of the early Greeks, particularly the *Odyssey*, have made fascinating observations about Greek self-consciousness in the century before Jesus changed the world by calling our attention to interpersonal love (Pagels, 1988). According to Jaynes, ancient Greeks were unaware of a self-process that had intentional control of their behavior. He describes the Greeks as believing their behaviors were caused by one or another of their gods. Zeus, Athena, Apollo, or some other god made them "do it."

It is interesting to note that in the mystical traditions of Eastern philosophy and religion human consciousness arose at about the same time it did in the West. It is no coincidence that Confucius also described a code of conduct between 500 and 600 B.C. And Deikman (1982) quotes Ellenberger (1974) as saying that the Upanishads were composed around 900 B.C. Deikman goes on to say that

> The Upanishads teach that the way to relieve the suffering of life is to go beyond the categories of thought to experience reality that underlies everything, the Real Self of each person. . . . The basic mystical experience is that of an undifferentiated unity, interpreted by the Upanishads as (1) the Real Self of the individual, and (2) the Real Self is the Ultimate that lies beyond and within all reality, mental and physical.
>
> (p. 34)

Armstrong (1994) also suggests that the mystery of early forms of self-experience, 5,000 to 6,000 years ago, played an important role in the creation of the monotheistic religions. Christians who believe the bible literally believe the earth began at that time.

It is not surprising that the vocabularies of sensory information are much richer than are the vocabularies of nonsensory information, that is, vocabularies of psychological process. Unfortunately, as we saw in the last chapter, this is a distinction that is overlooked in psychological research and theory (Gross, 2001). When it is overlooked sensory process is conflated with nonsensory information (Pinker, 2007) or it causes many influential psychologists to deny the existence of nonsensory experience as a meaningful enterprise for scientific investigation.

There are other psychological differences between sensory and nonsensory experience. Visual experiencing has a constancy in experience, a breadth of vocabulary and a diversity of categories that does not exist in the cognitive repertoire of feelings. For example, ghosts are likened to souls, which, in turn, are thought to be aspects of our selves or our "I," which many hope will continue to exist after their body dies. Visualizations of these ideas, like Casper the Friendly Ghost, are represented as fluid, amorphous shapes with vague boundaries—for instance, Casper is a visual metaphor of nonsensory process.

Summarizing the structural definition of the mind, I have described orientation as a genetically structured survival system, consciousness as a display system holding information in place permitting cognition to classify what it is and how it is related to the self-systems, and cognition as a homeostatic process classifying information and stabilizing midbrain structures. A more detailed description of orientation, cognition, and consciousness follows.

The Three Processes of Mentality

Orientation

Identifying what is hurtful, novel, or unfamiliar and how it is related to us is the ever-important survival question answered by the mindless interactions of orientation, cognition, and consciousness. When the brain is confronted with information it is unable to automatically process, an orienting process is triggered which sets cognition and consciousness (awareness) in motion to create an experience of an explanation (cognition) about the relationship of the individual to the destabilizing information.[1] There is no general theory of how this miracle happens, but we do know that it happens automatically and because of this (the miracle) it is not displayed in awareness. When the brain processes information automatically, the information is not displayed in awareness.

Orientation is the first step in the solution of any problem confronting a person; be it an internal psychological conflict or an external circumstance demanding our attention. There is research evidence, which is presented in the next chapter, that led me to believe that a major neurological contributor to orientation is the anterior cingulate cortex (ACC). We genetically need to know where we are in relation to any situation before we can think about defining the problem and before we can act on its definition. Cognition categorizes various operations of this system, including the experience of self in its various forms, such as the "I" of self-process.

When we enter a room filled with the odor of perfume, we become aware of the smell and look for its source. Did our mother get extravagant with a new perfume purchase? Did our wife or girlfriend want to entrance us with it? If we are able to explain its source or discover that it is unimportant to us in the moment, we stop smelling it. Technically this is called adaptation.

Orientation is a term used to denote a biological function, just as nutrient hunger is a phrase denoting the biological need for food. Orientation is a word denoting the experience of one of the brain's most important survival systems. Thinking this way exorcizes the homunculus about which I have been complaining. If a genetically structured behavioral program is homeostatically activated there is no need to invoke a homunculus to explain its occurrence.

It is imperative that we have an orientation system. Without it humans would never have been able to survive long enough to achieve the remarkable miracles and pains of the human mind. The orientation system is the central recipient of error signals about disequilibrating information whether it arises from the external world, the body, or the internal environments of our brains. Neurological systems devoted to serving the needs of hunger, mating, and protection from danger are among the survival systems that activate orientation which, in turn, genetically turns on relevant hard-wired behavioral systems that mindlessly trigger survival behavior. Without an orientation system, creatures do not live long.

Human orientation has a relatively rare talent. More than in any other mammal, orientation is able to respond to the nonsensory processes of the brain. When this talent becomes interactive with cognition and consciousness, personality processes become operative. Orientation is a homeostatic process, when it interacts with cognition, and consciousness is displayed in awareness with labels we use interchangeably as self, person, and ego. But because we experience it with great familiarity, we have conventionally thought of it as a single thing like a self-concept. We do this without knowing that it does many other homeostatic processes of which we are not aware. Only when it is interacting with cognition and consciousness do we become aware of the center of our being.

Cognition

The ability to cope with environmental complexity is another major survival ability. Humans, with our enormous brains and their massively grown cerebral cortices, are able to simplify the complexities in the external environment and those existing inside the body, including the brain itself, by identifying the similarities of "things" and classifying them into single categories. Being coupled with the motor systems of the brain, the cortex is able to cope with the destabilizing complexity of living in the world and to some extent with itself.

When humans had relatively small prefrontal cortices, they dealt, for the most part, with the complexity of the external environment. A rudimentary mind occurred when humans could vocalize the visual similarities they experienced in the external environment. As the brain grew, its ability to manage complexity grew. Then humans began experiencing nonsensory processes in the prefrontal cortex. This was the beginnings of self-awareness.

The information-processing function of the cortex (Krasnegor et al., 1997; Estes, 1994) is classification. The cortex is a thin layer of cells covering the bulk of the brain. The classic work of Cannon, Luria, and others demonstrates that when the midbrain is stimulated without the regulatory controls of the cortex, it reacts with wild and unrestrained behaviors. Ergo, the biological function of the cognitive function of the cortex is homeostasis. It modulates midbrain processes.

When the cortex repeatedly processes the same kind of information, it develops stable cell assemblies (neurological systems) that become self-perpetuating and functionally autonomous systems. A system becomes functionally autonomous when it is no longer dependent upon the conditions which gave rise to its formation to reinforce and stabilize its operations. The similarity talent of cognition enables the brain to exercise these systems on conditions, both sensory and nonsensory, that are similar to the original habit-forming situation that created them. Exercising these structures makes them self-perpetuating. With repetitive use of similar kinds of information, the brain develops stable systems of neurological structures to manage the information automatically. Pianists who practice a song or concerto over time are able to play the piece without a thought to how their fingers are pressing the keyboard of the piano. The same is true of any human endeavor: if you do it enough times, you learn to do it automatically.

This example shows us two things. First, it illuminates the relationship between nerves and muscles. They react to exercise in the same way. Second, the relationships between the subsystems that are exercised together become strengthened. They, then, become change-resistant structures. They are homeostatically more effective when they can process information automatically.

Unfortunately, there is a cost to this efficiency. As the brain matures, some of the efficiencies that are created when it was immature become outdated, outmoded and, at times, destructive. Developmentally ingrained behaviors occur automatically and, therefore, outside of awareness. As such they are the change-resistant structures with which intensive psychotherapy copes.

This is also the beginnings of human confusion and pain. A disequilibrated prefrontal cortex, like every other system in the brain or the body, seeks equilibratory relief from genetically organized homeostasis of the rest of the brain. Being a late evolutionary development, the prefrontal cortex does not have the equilibratory skills to regulate itself. The rest of this book will describe how the mind of which the prefrontal cortex is a part becomes the paradoxical destabilizer causing psychological pain and confusion and on the other side the source of self-experiencing, joy and creativity.

Cognitive Formatting

Different areas of the brain process information differently. The left hemisphere of the brain processes information in linear formats. The right hemisphere casts information into nonlinear formats. The anterior areas of the brain process nonsensory information of cerebral functions. By nonsensory, I mean that information arising within this area of the brain is not processed by the sensory systems residing in the posterior areas of the brain. And finally, the posterior areas manage sensory information, largely visual information. Throughout the rest of this book, I will be making references to different kinds of cognitive formatting that occur in everyday life. This enables me to escape the static reification of psychological process and gives me the ability to describe the movement of cognitive process as the mind travels on the high wire of its homeostatic existence.

Dialogue can be left-brained (logical) or right-brained (emotional) (Schore, 1994). Commonsense conversation is an example of linear/sensory (left-brained) formatting of sensory information.

Pinker (2007) tells a hilarious story that illustrates linearity and nonlinearity in human relations. During the final days at Denver's Stapleton Airport, a crowded United Airlines flight was canceled. A single agent was rebooking a long line of inconvenienced travelers. Suddenly an angry passenger pushed his way to the desk and slapped his ticket down on the counter, saying, "I HAVE to be on this flight, and it HAS to be first class." The agent replied, "I'm sorry, sir. I'll be happy to try to help you, but I have to help these folks first, I'm sure we'll be able to work something out." The passenger was unimpressed. He asked loudly, so that the passengers behind him could hear, "Do you have any idea who I am?" Without hesitation, the gate agent smiled and grabbed her public address microphone. "May I have your attention, please?" she began, her voice bellowing through the terminal. "We have a passenger here at the gate WHO DOES NOT KNOW WHO HE IS. If anyone can help him find his identity, please come to the gate." With the folks behind him laughing hysterically, the man glared at the agent, gritted his teeth, and swore, "[Expletive] you!" Without flinching, she smiled and said. "I'm sorry, sir, but you'll have to stand in line for that too" (p. 21).

This story illustrates both the linearity and nonlinearity of dialogue, the left and right-brained way of organizing information. The agent, when confronted with the angry passenger's unfair demand, ignored the nonlinear relationship, she had with him. Instead she treated him as an unfortunate object. She took him literally, a linear way of seeing him. When he swore at her, she immediately switched to a nonlinear (a relational) way of dealing with him by reminding him that he had to stand in line "for that too." This example illustrates the applicability of my way of thinking about the mind to Pinker's elegant analysis of language. The agent did not get pulled into a fight with the angry passenger; instead, she rejected both his demand and his disrespectful way of relating to her by ridiculing them: a nonlinear/nonsensory way of thinking and relating.

A Fourfold Classification of Cognition

The external and internal worlds of the person are experienced with the use of different sensory and nonsensory information processing systems in the brain, the posterior and anterior cortices of the brain. The posterior areas of the brain process visual information. The anterior portions of the brain process nonsensory information such as executive functions and personality. This difference creates the different material and immaterial experiences that troubled Plato.

Cognition, eventually, became formatted to classify sensory information residing in the posterior areas of the brain and nonsensory information residing largely in the prefrontal cortex, midbrain, and brain stem. Cognition, also, classifies linear and nonlinear information. This finding from the split-brain surgeries has been so widely published that left-brain linearity and right-brain nonlinearity are now part of everyday language.

Upon becoming aware of the double duality of the brain's information processing systems, I came up with the following description of a fourfold classification of the cognitive systems that makes it easier for me to describe the cognitive dynamics of my theory than when I thought of cognition only as rational thought.

Pairing linear and nonlinear ways of classifying information with sensory and nonsensory kinds of classification has a satisfying simplicity. Moreover, thinking of cognition as formatting information in these combinations enabled me to distinguish between logic, poetry, nightmares, and feelings as cognitive functions. Satisfying though this classification of cognitive process was, it confronted me with the realization I was making the phrenological mistake about which I complained about above. To rescue myself from making this mistake, I want to make it clear that I am describing cognition psychologically not neurologically.

The duality of linear/nonlinear and sensory/nonsensory information processing systems of the brain leads to a fourfold classification of cognition. It is a "pointillistic" way of trying to integrate brain functions with psychological process. Just because the brain appears to break down into left/right and front/back quadrants, this classification does not inform me about how the brain really operates to produce logical thought or poetry. This is another area where knowledge of the homeostatic organization of the brain is lacking. Like the "hard problem" of consciousness, my fourfold classification of cognition looks reasonable, but I do not know what "happens" in the brain to produce experiences of the fourfold classification I am about to describe.

Despite this limitation, I have found classifying cognition in this way to be heuristically useful. It provided me with the theoretical "language" I introduced in Chapter 2. It enables me to explain the dynamics of my theory, which I was unable to do with commonsense language.

The difference between linear and nonlinear thinking can be readily experienced in a thought experiment. Try describing a red apple. Now try describing the arrangement of a red apple, two cups of coffee, a bud vase with a rose in it, and three forks on a tabletop. In both cases you will be trying to describe a singular thing, a single red apple and an array of things. There is a cognitive difference between describing a singular still physical object and a relationship between objects or processes.

The cognitive difference between linear and nonlinear information-processing becomes even greater when organic structures are interacting in fluid movement. The following are brief examples of how information is cognized in these different formats.

Linear/sensory formatting classifies sensory information within straight line, sequential formats. These are left hemisphere/posterior brain functions. Common sense and logical thinking emerge from this classification. They are the most frequently used forms of cognition and one of the most difficult forms of thinking with which therapists, who are interested in personality change, must cope. Help-seekers very frequently want therapists to explain in commonsense terms: nonlinear/nonsensory processes (anterior/right hemisphere) like feelings and emotions.

Personality is organized within cognitive formats arising in the anterior/right hemisphere (nonsensory/nonlinear) areas of the brain. They are poorly influenced to change by posterior/left hemisphere (commonsense) structures. People devoted to commonsense will frequently want the therapist to tell them how to "dance," while remaining comfortably seated in their chairs in the consultation room. They ask for logical explanations of how to rid themselves of their pain and confusions. For many, opening the right hemisphere to awareness causes them to lose the comfort of logic and to experience the pains of childhood. People never learn how to experience their feelings if they refuse to be emotional. They also have difficulty experiencing the nature of their emotional difficulties. All they can do is think about the difficulty without emotionally experiencing it.

60 A Theory of the Mind

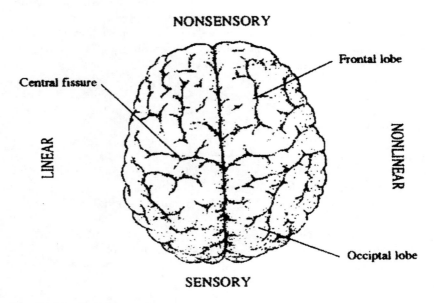

Figure 3.1 The Doubly Dualistic Brain

Linear/nonsensory (left hemisphere/prefrontal cortex) formatting classifies nonsensory information in the linear sequential formats which results in cognitive constructs about processes as though they were static things. Logical constructs about nonsensory phenomena lead to this kind of cognitive formatting. Most conventional psychological constructs exemplify this kind of cognitive formatting. Classifying the mind as a singular thing, thinking of emotions as elementary things upon which to build a theory of emotion, and describing the self as the source of action are examples of cognitive constructions of linear/nonsensory formatting. The ancient Greeks provide us with many examples of linear/nonsensory formatting in their mythologies about the nature of the world. Their gods were nonsensory projections about family life in the logical terms of the kinds of the nonsensory practices of their families with which they were familiar. Zeus, the father, of course, is the head of the family of gods.

Nonlinear/sensory (right hemisphere/posterior areas of the brain) cognition casts the experience of sensory phenomena into relational constructs. Nonlinear/sensory formatting is a poetic process using sensory information to describe psychological movement. It is used to describe processes existing in moving relationships, relationships between people or relationships between neurological systems. The ekphrastic principle in poetry, where Keats used illustrations of runners chasing one another around a "Grecian

Urn" to depict psychological movement, is an example of nonlinear/sensory formatting. Another example of nonlinear/sensory formatting is when I describe myself as "taking flight on wings of joy." Dreaming, poetry, Sufi tales, Buddhist koans, novels, and movies are other examples of this cognitive enterprise.

Ivins (1953) presents an interesting hypothesis that the Industrial Revolution was made possible by the invention of graphic printing. Information about relationships between parts of a machine was much more readily conveyed by pictures than words. The aphorism "A picture is worth a thousand words" exemplifies an understanding of nonlinear/sensory cognitive formatting.

Nonlinear/nonsensory formatting of movement of cognition is a right hemisphere, prefrontal brain process. Intuition, dreams, insight, feelings, the person, and experiences of other personality dynamics are examples of this cognitive process. These formatting structures exist in different kinds of explanation.

The Equilibratory Nature of Explanation

The neurological structures within cognition are reinforced in many areas of human mentation. Religions and science are explanatory systems essential to human existence. The repetitiousness of their explanatory systems strengthens the synaptic relationships of the neurological systems from which cognitive constructs emerge. The pervasiveness of both religion and science as explanatory systems testifies to their meaningfulness in sustaining the emotional stability of the person. Having an idea or explanation containing behavioral instructions within which to cast distressing information alleviates stress, pain, and anxiety.

Explanation is the cognitive label of the experience of cognition stabilizing the brain to whatever it is attempting to genetically manage. This being the case, explanation can also be considered a genetically structured reflex. The reflexive automaticity of explanatory process is vividly seen in neurological patients who easily provide the most absurd explanations of their neurological impairments (cf. Gazzaniga, 2010).

Explanation, thinking, planning, executive functions, and knowing are different forms of cognition. They stabilize the brain in different circumstances. Explanation is the most loved form of human mentation. Planning is the organization of information about what to do in some future circumstance. It provides the brain with constructs enabling it to activate behavioral systems to restore it to its steady-state condition (Miller et al., 1960).

"Thinking" is a word used to describe the experience of cognitive searching for commonalities to reduce the confusions of complexity. Executive function is another term for planning programs and their execution. Knowing is the end-product of explanation. If we have an explanation, we also have an experience of knowing. In other words, under most, but not all circumstances, knowing is the experience of having been cognitively stabilized. Sometimes knowing can destabilize a person when that which is known invalidates existing cognitive structures within him or her. As a matter of fact, one of the purposes of this book is to destabilize some traditional ways of thinking about personality. Socrates and Galileo had a very difficult time when they invalidated dearly held knowledge in their societies. With repeated practice, people come to love belief systems, regardless of their truth, because they stabilize their personalities.

The Dynamics of the Mind

The orienting system automatically engages cognition, consciousness, and behavior to restore itself to its steady-state condition. The first restorative step is the experience of the "I" in focal awareness and a bodily response. It orients the individual to information she is not able to automatically process. Explanation is the second step. It classifies the destabilizing information and classifies its relationship to the disequilibrated person.[2] Third, if action is cognitively integrated with cognitively organized information, stabilizing behavior is activated. Evolutionarily, explanation and behavior are increasingly able to relieve stress, tension, and anxiety. Restoring the orienting system to its steady-state condition causes a person to feel relieved.

"Explanation" describes the relationship of the disequilibrating information to the disequilibrated brain; specifically, the anterior cingulate cortex. If the disequilibrating information automatically activates knowing or action to equilibrate a dysfunctional system operating outside the orienting system, it remains within its steady-state condition and a person does not experience much discomfort. A traffic light turning red activates orientation, cognition, consciousness, and braking behavior.

Cognition either accommodates or assimilates disequilibrating information by casting it into a preexisting cognitive structure or by creating a new one enabling orientation to activate other limbic and behavioral programs to cope with it (Piaget, 1985). The word "cognition" denotes the psychological process underlying other nonsensory psychological processes such as constructs, personality, ideas, feelings, beliefs, and values, as well as sensory information.

Consciousness

Consciousness is the great unsolved problem in philosophy, psychology, and neuroscience. There is no consensus about its biological purpose, its definition, or how the brain creates awareness. While there is a growing body of knowledge about the neurological geography of consciousness (Damasio, 1999, 2010) (Koch, 2004), no one has a good explanation of the "hard question" of how information is displayed in awareness in the brain (cf. Chalmers, 1996). I do not intend to present a solution to this challenging mystery.

There are many different states of consciousness (cf. Fischer, 1971 for a description of varieties of altered states of consciousness). I will only discuss the state of consciousness the person uses in everyday healthy life. Other states of consciousness, as in dreaming during sleep, zazen in deep meditation, or panic when a person is in great immediate danger, will be mentioned in passing with no attempt to fathom the mysteries creating these changes in consciousness. Consciousness has seven characteristics that are useful in my description of the mind and in the practice of psychotherapy.

First, consciousness is the display of information. It is like a biological television screen, or like a hologram (the three-dimensional illusion that Disneyland uses so effectively). The essence of the "hard question" is how does the brain do that? How does it display a hologram in our awareness? When a television set is turned on, information is displayed on the tube. This definition is composed of visual analogies. But, obviously, other kinds of information are also displayed in awareness. Smell is displayed when olfactory bulbs are stimulated. Sound is heard when the semicircular canals in the middle ear are disturbed. Emotion is experienced when different systems of the limbic system are triggered.

Second, in all of these examples different kinds of information are displayed in awareness when they cannot be processed automatically (cf. Baars, 1997 for a description of this way of thinking about consciousness). Consciousness is turned on when our brain is unable to process information automatically. When we are very skilled with, familiar with, or habituated to anything, we do not experience it. When we drive a car over a familiar route, we do not experience much of the ride. We automatically stop, avoid other cars or obstacles, and turn corners without awareness of doing these things. A few moments after entering a perfumed room, we stop smelling the fragrance. Skilled tennis players react brilliantly without experiencing any conscious thoughts about how to move.

The Ditchburn-Riggs (1960–1970) experiments on visual perception also verify the fact that adaptation to visual information is accompanied by the loss of awareness of the adapted visual information. In these experiments, a tiny beam of light is cast on a single spot on the retina of the eye. The light is adjusted so that it is coordinated with the saccadic (small involuntary) movements of the eye. In this way the light stimulates only a single spot on the retina. After a relatively short time, the subjects of the experiment report that they no longer see the light.

This experiential shut-off mechanism plays tricks with our personalities. We all have characteristic ways of presenting ourselves. There are the "jovial glad-handers," the "dour melancholics," the "darling good guys," the "sexy sweethearts," and on and on. These presentations are formed in early childhood and are practiced the rest of our lives. They become so skilled and automatic we use them without awareness and are embarrassed when they are brought to our attention.

Third, consciousness holds information unmoving in awareness. This idea is similar to Koch's formulation which he and Francis Crick developed. The following quote is from an article they wrote in 1995.[3] This quote is taken from Koch (2004).

> Our . . . assumption is based on the broad idea of the biological usefulness of visual awareness (or strictly, of its neural correlate). This is to produce the best interpretation of the visual scene, in the light of past experience either of ourselves or of our ancestors (embodied in our genes), and to make it available for a sufficient time, to the parts of the brain that contemplate, plan, and execute voluntary motor outputs (of one sort or other).
>
> (p. 233)

We use different words, reflecting our different professional backgrounds and theoretical paradigms. I use the word "cognition." They use the words "interpretation," "contemplate," and "plan" which are cognitive operations of a homunculus. The vocabulary differences are differences that do not make a difference in our theoretical understanding of this aspect of consciousness. Consciousness holds both sensory and nonsensory information in the display of awareness. Koch focuses only on the display of visual information.

Fourth, I have found it important to recognize the homeostatic function of consciousness. It is a system within the mind that manages information that is not being automatically processed. When information is being automatically processed the person is not conscious of its interaction with cognition and orientation.

Fifth, like Koch, the holding nature of consciousness gives cognition time to assimilate or accommodate information. When information is reacted to automatically, reaction times are much shorter than when a person has to think (being aware of classifying information) (Gazzaniga, 2010; Kahneman, 2011).

Sixth, consciousness displays information dualistically. Information is displayed in both the fore- and backgrounds of awareness. The figure/ground illusion of Gestalt psychology is a visual example of the duality of consciousness. The figural nature of consciousness displays information in the center of attention.

Whatever exists in focal awareness as a singular "thing" is relatively meaningless unless there is a context to which it is related. The relational context is displayed in the background of awareness. This is the homeostatic function of the figure ground illusion. It enables the person to be focally aware of something and experience it within a context.

Figure 3.2 Figure Ground Illusion

Source: File:MooneyFace.png. (2016, March 19). *Wikimedia Commons, the free media repository.* Retrieved 08:01, March 26, 2020 from https://commons.wikimedia.org/w/index.php?title=File:MooneyFace.png&oldid=190634213, licensed under (CC BY-SA 3.0)

Before I leave the definition of consciousness, I want to differentiate between the unconscious, consciousness, and nonconsciousness. Consciousness is the display of information that orientation is unable to automatically process. Nonconsciousness is the processing of information that is being automatically processed.

Within this definition, the Freudian "unconscious" is the product of habituated personality structures processing information automatically. The automaticity of habits creates the nonconscious nature of habits. Throughout the rest of this book, I will be using the term nonconscious rather than unconscious because I wish to avoid contaminating my ideas about automatic information processing with the excess meanings of violence, pain, or other emotionalities contained in the Freudian "unconscious." Currently, some (Ginot, 2016), within the psychoanalytic tradition use consciousness and unconsciousness dichotomously, as though they were two sides of the same thing. I use these terms to distinguish between two very different ways the brain processes information.

Seventh, consciousness in the forms of focal awareness, suppression of consciousness, and the repression of memories are intimately related, in everyday conversation, with self-process, when it is regarded as a homunculus. Focal awareness is frequently associated with a person intending to figurally attend to something. The same is true of suppression, which is defined as a person intentionally putting something out of awareness. And repression is presumed to occur when information is so severely self-dystonic a person cannot bear the experience of it.

These phenomena are commonplace in human experience and are explained as being related to self-process in different ways. These explanations do not explain how the neurological systems underlying orientation interact with the neurological process of consciousness, or for what homeostatic purpose. This is another area of future research that will explain the nature of personality more richly. It is beyond my purpose to address these issues and their relationship to memory in this book.

The following vignette about my work with a man who suffered with the experience of anxiety daily from childhood into his adult life exemplifies the structural and habituated nature of emotional processes. In one session, he told me that he was puzzled because when he awakened in the morning, he felt good and was without anxiety. But the moment he became aware of where he was, anxiety returned with full force. At first, I, too, was puzzled. But some time later, I realized that the experience of self during sleep was different than its experience in waking consciousness. I, then, became aware that waking consciousness and sleep and dreaming during sleep were different states of consciousness, as I mentioned above. When he awakened, he was calm and rested. He, then, shifted from the nonsensory awareness of sleep, as in dreaming, to the sensory experience of his psychological self in his bedroom.

The wakeful awareness of this self was habituated to the experience of anxiety that had been his lifelong companion. He, then, had to explain why he was anxious. That was easy to do; over the years he had created an elaborate repertoire of explanations to modulate his anxiety; not get rid of them. Almost immediately, he would recall some misadventure or mistake he had made. He then took a shot of vodka and became normatively (familiarly) anxious. In this vignette, we can see the brain responding to two different conditions of consciousness and of explanatory cognition.

To this point, I have identified orientation (ACC), cognition (prefrontal cortex), and consciousness (brain stem and midbrain structures) as homeostatic functions contributing to the stable-state condition of the brain. I am now at the edge of my ignorance. How these neurological systems homeostatically interact with each other awaits further research. The theory of personality in this book is a psychological theory that depends on the creation of more neurological information on which a more descriptive personality theory can grow. Despite this limitation, a psychological theory of personality based on well-known facts about the brain is useful for therapists interested in personality change because it introduces knowledge about brain dynamics that significantly influences personality dynamics.

From Neurology to Psychology

Early psychoanalytic thought described emotional difficulties as disturbing memories of events or relationships submerged in "The Unconscious" that could be changed with insight or understanding. A brain-based psychological theory is useful for research because it can enrich neuroscientists' understanding of the complexities of emotional process. Almost from the beginning of psychoanalysis, analysts recognized that something more was needed (Reich, 1933/1945) than "returning the repressed to awareness."

Neurological research has demonstrated that the repeated interactions of different nervous systems cause them to be "cemented" together (Eliot, 1999). Practice makes permanent. Neurological systems become habituated. When this happens, personality structures are subject to the homeostatic imperatives of the brain, which are not influenced by understanding or insight. When I recognized this, I was able to integrate my dynamic (psychoanalytic) therapeutic practice with cognitive behavioral psychotherapy.

The Mind as the "Homeostat" of the Brain

As long as we live, equilibration (homeostasis) is constantly in motion. Autoregulation and homeostasis are terms denoting the processes of internal stabilization that are genetically designed to keep neurological systems in their optimal life supporting condition. When the brain is operating in its steady state or homeostatic condition, the personalities that emerge from it have experiences of familiarity and stability about their selves.

The stability and change-resistant nature of a neurological system may be experienced as miserable or joyous for a person, but as long as it is being automatically processed its operational integrity remains intact. Old curmudgeons are created in childhood where pain became a habituated part of their personalities. Much of their structural grouchiness is used to stabilize their elderly brains.

We are so used to thinking that our feelings are reactions to something that has happened in the moment, we do not recognize the internally initiated operations of habituated brain structures. For example, many people think that their reasons for being angry are explained as something or someone has hurt them in some way or other within the recent past. Yet upon more detailed examination, I have found that there are those who use anger in different ways to stabilize themselves in their emotional relationships with others.

It is productive to think of repetitious emotional reactions as being structural parts of the person's character. When a person has a consistent and repeated emotional reaction, it is helpful to look beyond the immediate interpersonal situation to make sense of the emotional expression. Doing that has enabled me to see a person attempting to stabilize themselves by using a particular emotionality with which they have the greatest familiarity and skill. The transformational dynamics of emotionality will be described more fully in the second half of this book.

We are so complex that awake or asleep our internal process and our relationship with the external environment constantly require stabilization in some parts of our body. The "stream of consciousness" (James, 1890/1950), dreaming, and the kaleidoscope of feelings happening in emotional engagements are examples of the perpetual motion of our mind.

The mind being an experienced part of the homeostatic function of the brain displays this "flow of being" in awareness. The movement of the mind is the experience of homeostatic movement and, therefore, accounts for the movement of personality and other forms of mentation. It is not uncommon for an individual who is deeply puzzled about work or love to "sleep on" the confusion and awaken the next morning with a solution to the problem or with a greater understanding of his or her feelings. The brain continued to work on the puzzlement or emotional upset during sleep. Many great problems are solved during sleep (Bronowski, 1956; Polanyi, 1958).

The stable-state condition of neurological systems can be likened to a river flowing within its beds. The water level may vary, depending on weather conditions, but as long as it stays within the boundaries of its banks, it remains in its steady-state condition. So it is with neural systems: as long as they are able to process information within the normative bounds of their biological structures, then they remain within their steady state conditions.

In some respects, the way the orienting system stabilizes the brain is similar to the way we ride a bike. When we ride a bike, we make constant balancing adjustments to keep from falling down. Unlike riding a bike, the brain adjusts, not only to the external environment, but it also adjusts to the movement of the body and to its own structures, especially its prefrontal cortex. Everyday adjustments to the prefrontal cortex result in brief flashes of self-awareness and/or emotionality. Using the brain as the database upon which to build a theory of personality has the advantage of describing internal psychological movement as well as describing the way it reacts to the external environment. This enables my theory to escape the limitations of stimulus/response theories of personality. We are more than machines who move only when our buttons are being pushed.

My theory, like Piaget's (1970), proposes that open system homeostatic regulation is the neurological underpinning of the movement of personality and mental stability. Granit (1977) describes homeostasis as the brain's purpose. Cannon's (1932) definition of homeostasis has been criticized for being a static, closed-system, balancing process. This is a common misinterpretation. Actually, he described it as a dynamic, "open," autoregulatory system. Open systems permit limitless changes and permutations, while closed systems are limited by the range of change that is defined by the nature of the system. Closed systems are bounded by the walls that define where the system functions and where it ends. Open systems are just that. Their unlimited capacity to grow enables the brain to become increasingly complex, which enables it to enjoy a boundless creativity. Grow or die. This is exactly what occurs in cerebral development. It has unlimited growth and the capacity to explore unlimited ways of classifying the information with which humans are confronted both in the external environment and within the mystery of their brains.

Homeostasis is the motivational center of my theory. There are a number of terms that are roughly synonymous with homeostasis such as equilibration, heterostasis, homeorhesis, restoring the steady-state condition, autoregulation, and autopoiesis (cf. Mahoney, 1991 for a more detailed discussion of these terms), all of which means bringing a neurological, and hence a psychological system, back to its normative range of operations. This condition is experienced as being "centered" or "balanced." This does not necessarily mean that the person is happy or has a sense of well-being. What a person experiences as stabilizing depends upon the kind of personal system into which its steady-state condition has become habituated (cf. Chapter 8).

In Piaget's (1970) terms, homeostasis "equilibrates" neurological systems by either accommodating or assimilating the disequilibrating information. Accommodation creates new structures to allow information to flow within a normative information-processing system. The shift from seeing the earth as the center of the world to recognizing that the earth rotates around the sun is an example creating a new cognitive structure. The heliocentric concept of our relationship to the sun accommodates new information about the gravitational rotation of the earth.

"Assimilation" modifies information to fit into a compatible information-processing bed to permit its uninterrupted flow (see Edelman, 1989 for a neurological description of this process). When Freud retreated behind the couch, he was probably influenced by his experience with hypnosis to accommodate this retreat. He believed that a patient lying on the couch could follow the "golden rule" of free association more readily. The use of the hypnosis model enabled him to explain his retreat as being clinically more useful, without modifying his psychoanalytic theory. None of these systems could function effectively without an orienting system being activated by information the brain is unable to automatically process. In other words, the brain's primary biological task is to keep itself in its steady-state condition. It is genetically structured to keep itself alive. When this is not possible for the person, suicide becomes a personally acceptable solution. If this is the case, then it is reasonable to think of psychological phenomena as the display in behavior and experience of cerebral homeostasis.

This is an upside-down way of thinking about human nature, which reverses the "mind over matter" aphorism. If the mind is the experiential display of a nervous system keeping itself and the rest of its body alive, then homeostasis is the beginning of an explanation about the dynamics of personality. Personality is the behavior and experience of homeostatic operations of the brain.

The mind, as an autoregulatory process, is the servant of the body. When any part of the body, including the brain, is unable to process any kind of information automatically, the orienting system is turned on. It homeostatically attempts to restore itself to its steady-state condition. To do this, it, in turn, activates consciousness and cognition. Consciousness displays the unsettling information in awareness, holding it steady, giving cognition time to classify it. Cognition attempts to classify the nature of that information's relationship to orientation to stabilize it.

This interaction also triggers an experience of a self which is a classification (a form of cognition) of neurological processes devoted to orientation. Sometimes the adjustments are minor; like the flashes of self-awareness that occur when riding a bike. At other times, the person can fall into enduring suicidal despair or enjoy the beauty that surrounds and exists within him/her.

Mindstorms

In my practice, I have worked with people who suffered from inescapable intense anxiety, pain, and self-hatred. I call this condition a "mindstorm" because it denotes the intense panic and pain of a nightmare. I also think of it as a "storm." I call it a mindstorm because there are no other familiar terms with which to describe it. Panic or terrors do not fit for me because they imply an external danger; the mindstorm is an internally generated anguish.

Mindstorms are born in the nonsensory chaos of cerebral systems. They are both physical and mental torments. Heart-pounding sensations, nausea, an inability to control movements frequently are simultaneous experiences. Impulses to run are defeated; one's legs are unable to move. A single theme runs throughout the experience. They are experiences of internal disequilibria. The mind is in chaos.

The experience of a mindstorm is extremely intense, pierced with inescapable self-hatred. It is depression at its worst. It also occurs in paralyzed stroke patients and the agony of the destabilized orientation system can be found in Gawande's (2009) description of the "Hellhole" of solitary confinement in prisons and prisoners of the terror wars. Many prisoners, when deprived of human contact and sensory stimuli, cannot escape the self-hatred that rampages through their minds. When the orientation system is deprived of validating feedback, many socially isolated persons are driven mad. It suffers from affect hunger. The brain, specifically the Neurological Self, is not getting enough validational exercise to maintain the integrity of the neurological systems. Use it or lose it.

As I was writing this chapter, I started reading Eckhart Tolle's (1997) book *The Power of Now*, which begins with the following quote:

> Until my thirtieth year, I lived in a state of almost continuous anxiety interspersed with periods of suicidal depression. It feels now as if I am talking about some past life time or somebody else's life. One night not long after my twenty-ninth birthday, I woke up in the early hours with a feeling of absolute dread. I had woken up with such a feeling many times before, but this time it was more intense than it had ever been before this. The silence of the night, the vague outlines of the furniture in the dark room, the distant noise of a passing train—everything felt so alien, so hostile, and so utterly meaningless that it created in me a deep loathing of the world. The most loathsome thing of all, however, was my own existence. What was the point in continuing to live with this burden of misery? Why carry on with this continuous struggle? I could feel that a deep longing for annihilation, for nonexistence, was now becoming much stronger than the instinctive desire to live.
>
> (p. 1)

Tolle's description of his mindstorm is not unusual. His language and the feeling tone of his experience of mental horror are essentially the same as those written by others who have suffered the same human misery (Styron, 1951, 1992; Kronkite, 1994; Solomon, 2001). They all describe the dread of being incapable of escaping the horror of suicidal self-loathing.

His mindstorm was triggered by his inability to escape from his habituated self-hatred, but the anguish emerged from his inability to still the experience of the intensity of the chaotic, painful psychological selves arising into awareness within him. His orienting system was unable to activate validating behavior from within his creative abilities or loving relationships with others. This helplessness triggered genetically structured anxiety systems. He experienced an anxiety from which he could not escape.

None of these are reactions to external events. Earthquakes, storms, car crashes, for example, do not initiate these internally generated forms of anguish. Panics are associated with helplessness when confronted with physical violence approaching from the outside. Underlying mindstorms are self-perpetuating brain structures. They are the reverberating interactions between orientation process and disequilibrated cognitions about them, that seek autoregulation from one another that I described earlier. They rampage through a person's consciousness causing suicidal pain. It is a condition arising in a brain that cannot homeostatically regulate itself.

Alcoholism, all of the addictions, and the whole array of other maladaptive behaviors associated with the incessant extremes of anxiety and depression are ways the individual uses to escape from the discomfort of a mind plagued by habituated pain or dreadfully uncomfortable experiences in the body which do not have culturally familiar names.

For the most part emotionality is thought of as a reaction to something happening outside of the person. The emotional reaction is explained as "They are insulted," they are "ripped off," misunderstood, treated badly, and so on. In short, the conventional explanation for hurt or angry feeling states is that the feeling is a reaction to something happening "out there."

I have come to see emotionality differently. Most of the distress and pain a person experiences arises from discrepant and invalidating cognitive personality structures upon which our experience of our person is constructed. In fact, as I described earlier, they arise from the disequilibrated person seeking stabilizing help from his or her mind. These structures are all formed in childhood and become habituated, automated validation-seeking systems.

The strength of the mind affects the ways it responds to invalidating information. By "strength of mind, I mean what is ordinarily called "ego strength." Ego strength refers to the ease or difficulty the mind has in its ability to restore itself to its steady-state condition when it is confronted with destabilizing information. When confronted with great amounts of destabilizing information, a strong mind is able to keep equilibrating functions intact,—that is, keep disturbing information in focal awareness and maintain the ability to categorize and/or classify the information. I will not use the phrase "ego strength."

A strong mind in a steady-state condition is variously called "balance," "Chi," and "being cool." On the other hand, a weak mind becomes chaotic when confronted with invalidating information that a "cool" mind would shrug off as a minor annoyance. In this case, the mind activates stabilizing constructs that were formed earlier in childhood as a means of coping with disequilibrium.

There are genetic factors that contribute to the stability and volatility of the mind. The work of Kagan (1989) and recent brain scan studies of learning patterns of young children and observations of infants at moments of birth clearly indicate that there are genetic factors that determine the strength and stability of the mind. However, they are malleable. Much more study, observation, and research are needed before we will be able to understand the structural dynamics of genetic factors and how they contribute to the formation of the strength of the mind.

Nurture factors also contribute to the strength of the mind. These are the well-known practices of familial and cultural socialization that either strengthen or weaken the operational integrity of the mind. Early childhood experiences affect the strength of the mind. Childhood experiences which nourish growth, autonomy, and emotional skills enhance mind strength. Childhood abuse and emotional deprivation contribute to weakness in the mind. Furthermore, physical and emotional abuse cause parts of the person's character structure to become fixated or habituated in a functionally impaired mind. The person's character structure is comprised of stable, primarily nonlinear, cognitive systems, which define the person's self, emotional (character) structure, and personal reality (Gross, 1992). They operate automatically and provide the mind with stability in the forms of habituated response systems and/or explanations.

To this point, I have described the mind as a complex system of brain structures related to one another. This required a different way of thinking about it. This difference is based on the paradigmatic shift I described in the last chapter.

The Paradigmatic Shift

The shift began with my distrust of conventional explanations of why we are the way we are. Conventional explanations arise from simplistic, mostly visual, experiences of frequently occurring psychological processes. The Pleasure/Pain dichotomy is an erroneous, ubiquitous explanation for why we do or want things and avoid others. For example, I have a sweet tooth and enjoy ice cream and candy. Therefore, it is logical that I do things that please me and it is my pleasure that guides my behavior. On the other hand, when I burn my hand on a hot stove or hurt myself in other ways, I avoid things or relationships that are painful. These repeated experiences have led us to generalize our reactions to a belief that they represent universal human motivational structures.

Before I entered my practice as a psychotherapist, I mindlessly (automatically) explained myself to myself or others with these explanations. However, at the very beginning of my practice, I found people avoiding the pleasures of love and sex and repetitively engaging in painful, self-destructive behaviors and relationships. Obviously, conventional behavioral explanations touched only simple, highly overlearned ways of thinking and behaving. Being influenced by Hellmuth Kaiser, I began thinking of character structure and the brain.

There, I found that the experience of familiarity could be related to existing structures in the brain. Duality in large structures of the brain could be related to the dualities of emotionality and personality. Finding these relationships between brain structures and psychological variables led to the development of my theory of personality. Having described the homeostatic role of the Neurological Self in the center of the mind, in the next chapter I will present the neurological evidence that it is the "ghost in the machine" that makes us human.

Notes

1. Gazzaniga (2010) provides numerous examples of the unintentional explanatory behavior of his neurological patients to fill in the gaps of perception and/or experience caused by their neurological injuries.
2. I will describe the person in Chapter 8.
3. For the record, I described this point in 1992 in my book *A Portrait of the Person*.

Chapter 4

The Ghost in the Machine

The Neurological Self

The mystery of what the self is has occupied our minds from the beginnings of self-consciousness (Seigel, 2005). This chapter will solve this mystery by describing the neurological underpinnings of self-experiencing. In my theory, "Self" is the experience of cognitions about the orientation process of the brain as it is engaged in different kinds of relationships. The last chapter proposed that the anterior cingulate cortex (ACC) plays a major role in the orienting process. It is, with other yet undetermined limbic structures, the underlying experience of self-phenomena. However, the experience of self is not as simple as the first three sentences make it sound. It took centuries of evolutionary growth before the brain was able to achieve the miracle of self-consciousness.

As the ACC increased its functional intimacy with the prefrontal cortex, humans sensed a "ghost in the machine." In ancient times, the experience of self-process was so unfamiliar, we were not certain what it was or where it came from. Ancient theologians labeled it as the jinn or the numina. They were nonsensory psychological experiences (experiences of cognitions about the ACC) that were projected into the external environment as malevolent or beneficent forces. Currently, as I mentioned in Chapter 2, some hard-bitten empiricists have declared nonsensory experience either meaningless or impossible to scientifically investigate (Roediger, 2004). Self-experiencing has been difficult to understand because it is not processed by any of the sensory systems that have guided humanity from the beginning of its existence on earth.

I have come to think the metaphor of the "ghost in the machine" is the nonsensory description of the experience of orientation. The Neurological Self (NS) is the homeostatic process about which the mind cognizes and experiences (displays in awareness) the psychological selves, feelings, and the person. In its orienting function, the NS is the monitor of cerebral disequilibrium. It receives messages from any of the destabilized systems in the brain and responds to them by automatically activating other cerebral systems to restore the disequilibrated ones back to their steady state conditions.

The NS, experienced as the "I" or a self, is like a mindless traffic cop in the midst of the brain's enormous communicative systems, with cars and trucks (other neuronal systems) coming at her from all directions. It is not a psychological system. It does not think. It is not intentional. It is not rational. The maintenance of its own integrity and stability is genetically structured to come first. It is genetically built to stabilize itself before homeostatically responding to the disequilibrium of other cerebral systems. When the NS is disoriented, the biological imperative for neurological integrity sweeps aside intentions, knowledge, or values as irrelevant.

The cop's primary task is to keep itself from being run over. She either automatically uses her genetically endowed relationship with the rest of the limbic system to get the traffic to flow in orderly patterns or she activates genetically organized homeostatic survival systems for that purpose. For example, if you're hungry, you will experience yourself, you might even talk to yourself, telling yourself that you are hungry, that you need to think about a course of action, and then you'll act in compliance with your plan. The "you" in the earlier sentences is a cognition about the NS. It is not a homunculus. Frequently, this routine is completed automatically, without intentional instructions.

In doing so, the NS nonconsciously (genetically) uses those systems with which it is most familiar or skilled. This is another way of saying that the cortex (cognition) uses a "similarity" process. If two things or processes have similar characteristics, they are categorized into a single classification. This is a way the brain simplifies information, enabling it to process information rapidly.

An understanding of this imperative enabled me to replace Freud's idea of the "death instinct" with a recognition that under the duress of mindstorms, death is a frequently desired and acted upon alternative to the continuation of agony. Certainly, in these days when we are in the midst of the chaos of the Shiite/Sunni religious wars, we can see that death is not a universal dread.

The idea that orientation is a function of the NS gave me a way of looking at human nature that enriched my psychotherapy practice. It enabled me to explain the movement, the dynamics, which is evident in all aspects of personality growth and change. It liberated my thinking from cultural misconceptions of why people do what they do and helped me to use the lens of homeostatic efficiency in my search for an understanding of their experience and behavior.

Furthermore, when I understood the biological purpose of the NS, I was able to replace the Freudian concept of the unconscious with a description of the relationship between automaticity and consciousness, about which I wrote in the last chapter. If information is automatically processed in the brain, it is not displayed in awareness.

Freud's recognition of unconscious motivation was a major contribution in helping psychotherapists escape from a total reliance on the erroneous belief in the curative power of intentional control. Moreover, instead of seeing the unconscious as the psychoanalytic warehouse of repressed desires, unresolved conflicts, and traumatic memories, I have come to see that nonconsciousness is the condition of the brain when it is processing information automatically. With that, there is no need to call upon the more complex structures and processes of self and consciousness to explain why we do what we do. The NS is a theoretical cousin of the old psychoanalytic explanation of drives or biological needs, like libido or aggression, to describe and explain the movement of the mind and personality. The idea of drives gave psychoanalysis the ability to describe the movement of personality. Using a neurological process provides my theory with the same ability.

The NS as the material basis of psychological process also integrates the body with its mind. Personality paradoxically provides the brain with homeostatic stability. In other words, psychological process is the experience of homeostatic operations of the brain. The complexity of its development is also a major source of the brain's destabilization.

The idea of the NS also expanded my thinking about the Freudian triumvirate of id, ego, and superego in a more complex and theoretically more acceptable (nonhomuncular) way. There is a strong similarity between the NS and the Id. They are both described as mindless, powerful, biologically based, and self-preserving systems. Commonsense cognition (rationality) has a marked resemblance to the Ego, which is another word for self. Personal reality—cognitions about the NS in relationship to the world around the person—can easily be cast into the role of the superego. I will put these together in Chapter 8, when I describe the person.

The idea of an NS enabled me to explain the paradox of the self: how it can be both the experientially singular and the bafflingly, kaleidoscopically multiple entity over which theorists have quarreled and puzzled (Allport, 1955). The NS is experienced and classified in so many different contexts that some (Gergen, 1991; Gross, 1992) believe there are many different selves accommodating different circumstances and conditions in which the NS is engaged and therefore they are experienced differently. Yet while the many psychological selves play their parts on the stage of our awareness, there is a continual experience of a singularity behind the action of the selves. Hidden within the diversity of its multitudinous cognitive expressions is the homeostatic constancy of a singular orienting NS: the ghost in the machine.

Because we have been unaware of the importance of the psychological (nonsensory) aspects of orientation, we have not recognized or given much attention to the ubiquitous role it plays in our lives. Instead, we have been preoccupied with commonsense experiences and explanations of what the guiding principles of our lives should be. We have looked to the heavens for guidance or to the wisdom of old men (e.g., Confucius, Moses, Buddha, and Freud). Foremost among the dilemmas of human existence has been the experience of emotionality, which, I will be describing as the experience of the NS in homeostatic movement.

The Neurological Self and Emotion

When the NS genetically re-equilibrates itself, the accompanying bodily movement is experienced as emotion. The disequilibrated NS mindlessly activates genetically structured survival systems to restore equilibrium. This is the neurological situation I mentioned in the last chapter, where the NS seeks stabilization for itself from the limbic system. In doing this, the NS activates body (survival) systems which are usually called emotion. Cortical equilibration of emotion is cognized and experienced as feelings. When one is anxious, he experiences adrenaline rushes in his body. When he is lonely, he experiences a prefrontal cortical reaction (i.e., a nonsensory psychological experience).

Affect Hunger and Homeostasis

Affect hunger is a physiological need (an emotion) which, when cognitively classified, is experienced as a feeling of loneliness. The emotion of affect hunger is a profoundly important survival system. It is one of the essential physiological needs of the NS. The loneliness of affect hunger is one of the most frequent feelings, and one of the mildest reactions to it, with which a therapist is confronted. Severe affect hunger deprivations lead to psychosis and/or suicide. Ferenczi (1931), in the early stages of psychoanalysis, recognized its existence in the emotional neediness of his patients. Spitz (1946), in his tragic study, wrote about the literally deadly effects of emotional deprivation on infants.

Many people, who over long periods are deprived of the personal validational feedback needed to feed their affect hungers, are driven to insanity (Gawande, 2009; Haney, 2008). Solitary confinement in prisons has a long history in the United States, beginning in 1843 with a Quaker experiment to help prisoners with their religious meditations. The effects of that social deprivation were so devastating that the experiment was short lived. Traditionally, prisons have used solitary confinement as a form of punishment. Recently, however, it is being used in an attempt to control gang activity in prisons. California, in 1989, built what is generally regarded as one of the first supermax prisons at Pelican Bay. In it prisoners are housed singly in eight-by-ten-foot concrete cells with concrete beds, desks, and stools. The cell also contains a sink and toilet. They are confined to these cells for 22.5 hours a day and permitted into a small concrete outdoor pen for one and a half hours. They have contact with no one. Some prisoners are held in these cells for five or more years. At this writing, prisoners at Pelican Bay are on a hunger strike protesting the dreadful punishment of solitary confinement. In 2005, the number of states using supermax prisons increased to 40 holding an estimated 25,000 prisoners. Anecdotal accounts of men coming out of these prisons describe them as being socially crippled and/or totally psychotic. Sensory and social deprivation is also used as a form of inquisitional torture by secret service agencies. Stories of the madness of shipwrecked sailors induced by being stranded alone on uninhabited islands are commonplace.

Solitary confinement profoundly affects the psychological condition of prisoners. Gawande (2009) reports that:

> And what happened to them was physical. EEG studies going back to the nineteen-sixties have shown diffuse slowing of brain waves in prisoners after a week or more of solitary confinement. In 1992, fifty-seven prisoners of war, released after an average of six months in detention camps in Yugoslavia, were examined using EEG-like tests. The recordings revealed brain abnormalities months afterward; the most severe were found in prisoners who had endured either head trauma to render them unconscious or, yes, solitary confinement. Without sustained social interaction, the human brain may become as impaired as one that has incurred a traumatic injury.
>
> (p. 39)

This report dramatically illustrates the brain/personality nexus I described in the previous chapter. Social and emotional contact provides the person with validational feedback. Validation does not mean only pleasure or support. Validation is simply based on the repetition of familiar exercise of an existing system. If an existing system was formed on a kind of pain then the repetition of that pain validates that system. If a person's childhood love is formed within a painful relationship, in adulthood that person will experience pain in loving relationships.

The affect hunger of the NS of most adults is fed by work, love, and play. Most people are nourished by whatever meaningfulness exists in their work. It is beyond the task of this book to do more than briefly comment on the complexities of the adult loving experience. The nourishment of a kind of love can occur in the sexuality of a loving couple if the immature aspects of the person, which exist in all of us, is validated. Play and work nourish the person in the exercise of an experience of her excellence. There are fortunate people who have integrated work and play so well they are well fed by both. When this happens, they don't experience a great difference between them.

The pain of social isolation is caused by the inability of the NS to receive emotional validational feedback. We are at the "use it or lose it" condition. The feeding of the affect hunger of the NS is important to its emotional health and integrity. And therefore, it is as vitally important to the person as food is to the physical well-being of the person's body. The absence of sensory and emotional feedback can cause the mindstorms I describe in Chapter 3.

The need to stabilize the NS is a constant exercise in interpersonal relations. When I came across Ferenczi's (1931) description of affect hunger, I saw the dynamics of the psychotherapeutic relationship in a more meaningful way. The needs generated by affect hunger guide the here-and-now dynamics of all interpersonal relationships including (and especially) the psychotherapeutic relationship. We will see that feeding the affect hunger of the NS and the neurological underpinnings of the person are necessary for the creation and continuance of the therapeutic alliance.

Affect Hunger: The Heart of Loneliness and Love

Living systems require exercise. In everyday terms, exercise is the repetitive use of muscles. If they are not used, they suffer the atrophy of disuse. The same holds true of neurological systems. They need repetitive invariant use to sustain the integrity of their operations; use it or lose it.

Affect hunger of both the NS and the neurological systems underlying the person is a major contributor to the internal conditions which motivate people. The loneliness caused by affect hunger is an example of internal motivational dynamics. If a loved one is absent for a long period of time, personal structures suffer from affect hunger—the affect-hungry person experiences a longing for the loved one

One of the major biological functions of love is to provide validational feedback to the persons of the loving couple. Saying "I love you" to a lover, almost invariably elicits an "I love you, too" reaction. The validation of personal structures is essential for the homeostatic regulation of the NS. When the psychological selves are chronically outside their steady state conditions or if they do not receive sufficient validational feedback, they deteriorate and disequilibrate the NS. Depression, pain, and/or anxiety ensue.

Deprivation of validational feedback in early childhood prevents the establishment of a stable, strong system of relations between the NS and its stabilizing cortical structures in the prefrontal cortex, causing the person to have continuing and confusing experiences and behavior in his adult life. Without a stable NS, a person has great difficulty being alone. The stability of the NS, its structural strength, shapes the nature of the person's attachments. It affects the ways a person experiences a loving relationship and relates to work.

Sandor Ferenczi's description of affect hunger as his patient's need for affection is congruent with Hellmuth Kaiser's (Fierman, 1965) concept of the "fusion delusion" where a person nonconsciously strives to make the other person conform to her reality. Ferenczi's definition of affect hunger connoted infantile dependency. However, when looked at from a neuropsychological perspective, affect hunger has a somewhat different meaning. On the biological level, affect hunger denotes a crucial, continuing need of all living creatures with brains for some form of consistent invariant validational feedback (Platt, 1970; Eliot, 1999).

Evidence from anthropological, neurological, and psychological studies demonstrate the need of humans and other creatures for invariant validational feedback. The devastating effects of solitary confinement attest to the significance of validational feedback for a person's emotional well-being. The lack of adequate loving stimulation results in weight loss and depression in infants (Spitz, 1946). Sensory and social isolation studies richly demonstrate the "general deterioration and lability of mental processes" during periods of social isolation (Zubek, 1969). Lynch (1977), in his book *The Broken Heart*, about heart disease, documents "the medical consequences of loneliness." Karl Menninger (1958) wrote this couplet: "Sticks and stones may break your bones, but silence will break your heart." More recently, Hawkley and Cacioppo (2007) describe the medical consequences of loneliness in the following quote.

> The accrual of loneliness effects with age is well illustrated in a recent longitudinal study (Caspi et al., 2006). In this study, social isolation in childhood and feelings of loneliness in adolescence and young adulthood predicted how many cardiovascular risk factors (e.g., body mass index, waist circumference, blood pressure, cholesterol) were elevated in young adulthood (mean age = 26 years). Moreover, a number of developmental occasions (i.e., childhood, adolescence, young adulthood) at which participants were lonely predicted the number of elevated risks in young adulthood. These data suggest that the effects of loneliness accrue in dose-response fashion to accelerate the rate of physiological decline.
>
> (p. 187)

There is also neurological evidence describing affect hunger. Eliot (1999) discusses the establishment of strong neurological systems in her description of the growth of nerve cells, their synapses, and their formation into interrelated systems during infancy. After her description of the genetic structure of "brain wiring," she describes the role of "nurture" in the establishment of these neural systems. She says:

> There are perhaps 80,000 genes scattered among the miles of DNA in our chromosomes, and even if a generous half of these were allotted to the delicate job of brain wiring (after all, the body does have some other important functions to perform with its genes), we would still be far short of having enough cues to specify an accurate wiring diagram for the entire brain.
>
> This is where "nurture" steps in and finishes the job. By overproducing synapses, the brain forces them to compete, and just as in evolution

or the free market, competition allows for the selection of the "fittest" or most useful synapses. In neural development, usefulness is defined in terms of electrical activity. Synapses that are highly active—that receive more electrical impulses and release greater amounts of neurotransmitter—more effectively stimulate their postsynaptic targets. This heightened electrical activity triggers molecular changes that stabilize the synapse, essentially cementing it in place. Less active synapses, by contrast, do not evoke enough electrical activity to stabilize themselves and so eventually regress. It's "use it or lose it" right from the start; like other forms of Darwinian selection, this synaptic pruning is an extremely efficient way of adapting each organism's neural circuits to the exact demands imposed by its environment.

(p. 30)

Never the Twain Shall Meet

The recognition that affect hunger is an emotion, the neurological evidence that "practice makes permanent," and the "use it or lose it" description of "synaptic pruning" helped me come up with a description of personality structures that become change resistant and functionally autonomous. Neurological systems whose affect hunger are repeatedly used (exercised) are change resistant. Moreover, they need not be nourished (reinforced) by the same conditions that brought them into existence. When children are repeatedly mistreated, unseen, abused, they grow into adolescence and/or adulthood with change-resistant, functionally autonomous personality systems.

This realization brought to mind Rudyard Kipling's announcement, in 1892, that "East is east and west is west and never the twain shall meet," which is strikingly similar to Roediger's (2004) belief that sensory-based psychological research and nonsensory clinical practice occupied different theoretical worlds whose twain couldn't meet. Here in the twenty-first century we are able to see a meeting of both the east and west. The technological revolution crosses all continents and educates all cultures about the management of information. The current technological revolution discoveries about the brain can now unite sensory and nonsensory phenomena within the same theoretical system.

Psychological structures are not only emotional or personality systems, they are also psychological operational systems such as those that exist between the NS, cognition, and consciousness: our minds. Eliot's description of neural "cementing" supports the idea that enriched nurture in early childhood affects the stability and strength of neurological structures.

Seeing the ways that neurological systems emerge into awareness as psychological phenomena integrates the body with the mind. Furthermore, finding ways of thinking about the nature of psychological emergence as part of the homeostatic process of the brain provided me with a way of theoretically integrating psychological with cerebral process.

I hasten to say what I am presenting here is a beginning. As our technology provides us with more information about the nature of homeostasis our thinking about the relationship between sensory and nonsensory processes in the brain will grow and become more complex.

A Few Current Examples of Brain/Mind Integration

"Affect hunger" is a succinct description of the psychological idea of reinforcement. Reinforcement is a common explanation for both the establishment and continuation of psychological structures in learning theory. In neurological terms, it is what is useful in the establishment of psychological structures enabling rats to run mazes. It is also useful in establishing personality structures. Like maze-learning structures, personality structures that are continually reinforced become overlearned, highly stable, automated, and change-resistant. This way of looking at reinforcement liberates it from the limitations of nutrient hunger as an explanation of learning and from Pleasure Principle explanations. Instead, the aphorism "Practice makes permanent" covers a greater variety of explanations about personality dynamics. When they become permanent, they are change resistant.

Change-resistant personality structures reside at the center of psychotherapies with personality change goals. Like muscle systems, they are habits of the mind, self, emotionality, and consciousness. While insight is helpful, it is not enough to change habits that have been exercised over long periods of time. One of the most effective ways of changing both physical and mental habits is to interrupt the automaticity of their occurrence. This reduces habit strength, which, in turn, facilitates homeostatic changes in the brain.

Affect hunger is ubiquitously acknowledged, even in our fairy tales. Like Snow White's stepmother, we look into the eyes of others wanting them to tell us that we are, indeed, "the fairest one of all." The definition of "fairest" in day-to-day living is a paradoxical one. It is not based on some culturally accepted standard, but by our character structures. Fairest can mean the kindest, wisest, the most understanding, the ugliest, the meanest, and so on. The meaning of what is validating is determined in childhood by whatever has been established as the stable-state condition of the neurological systems underlying the NS and its stabilizing cortical structures, which appear in awareness as the person.

The feeding of affect hunger is frequently accompanied with experiences of pleasure, but not always. When a person develops functionally autonomous self-hating structures, these too need validating exercise. In this condition, they nonconsciously, automatically solicit invariant feedback by engaging in behavior that is designed to alienate and antagonize others.

The underlying validational needs of the cortico–limbic systems that have become habituated to self-destructive behaviors explain why the ancient belief in the pleasure principle is mistaken.

A fine theory, you may say. But where's the evidence?

Over the years, many experiments have supported my theory of a Neurological Self. They show the anterior cingulate cortex (ACC) in the limbic system as a major structure within an orienting system. Other related limbic structures such as the caudate nucleus and the insula (Damasio, 2010) also interact in the production of self-process. The neurological underpinnings of consciousness and cognition are found by other research to be in the limbic region. It is not my purpose or ability to present a detailed map of the neurological geography of the NS and the structures that enable it to experience and know itself, but so far, the data at hand suggests we're on the right track.

The Neurology of the Neurological Self

The association of orientation with the ACC does not suggest a solution to the mind-body mystery. Like other findings of a psychological operation related to a particular brain structure, the NS interacts in many as yet unknown ways with other neurological systems creating the orientation, classification, and experiencing processes that enable us to know where and how we are related to the outside world.

More detailed neurological maps of what I call the NS can be found in Damasio (1999, 2010), Koch (2004), and Beitman and Nair (2004). They call it the "proto-self," which I believe is theoretically similar to my NS. The difference between us resides in my description of this neurological system as one devoted to orientation and homeostasis and how its relationship to the prefrontal neocortex creates the experience of self.

Scientists, using neurological imaging and scanning technology, are beginning to visually see the brain in operation. This is just the beginning. Newer technological advances will help us to see more than blood flow in working parts of the brain used by the present fMRI machines. These technologies will enable us to acquire "harder" new knowledge about personality. In the consultation room, this knowledge can potentially help us more clearly "see" the structural dynamics of why a person acts, feels, or thinks the way she does.

Orientation has had a long and honorable history in neurologic investigation. Sokolov (1963) describes its early theoretical formulation in the following quote:

> The concept of the orienting . . . reflex was introduced by Pavlov in 1910. Its feature is that, developing on any change of stimulus, it takes

exactly the same form irrespective of whether the stimulus used is stronger, weaker or of different quality.

(p. 283)

When there is a "change of stimulus," the change itself is new information that cannot be automatically processed. Then the orienting reflex is activated. Damasio's (1999) proto-self resembles Pavlov's description of the orienting reflex as a response to changing stimuli. Damasio describes this system in the following quote:

The proto-self is a coherent collection of neural patterns which map moment by moment, the state of the physical structure of the organism in its many dimensions . . . . It is a reference point.

(p. 154) (original emphasis)

In addition to "orientation" and "referencing," other neuroscientists use words like "localizing" and "monitoring." They denote essentially the same functional meanings except they do not differentiate between the experience of genetic (reflexive) process and cognitions about reflexive process. Recent research has identified some aspects of nonsensory orientation, as opposed to orientation to sensory information, residing in the ACC. This has been repeatedly confirmed by investigators using neuroimaging techniques (Posner et al., 1997; Damasio, 1999, 2010; Goldberg, 2001; Beitman and Nair, 2004) and those studying the effects of cingulotomy (Cohen et al., 2001), a form of psychosurgery for patients suffering intractable pain that cannot be alleviated by conventional medical treatment.

In the area of neuropsychological investigation, the idea of orientation is also related to self-process. Posner et al. (1997) say that

We view attention as involving three major functions: orienting to sensory stimuli; executive control . . . and maintaining the alert state. . . . [The NS is associated with these functions.] Although knowledge of the precise neural mechanisms responsible for these operations is not conclusive; many of the brain areas and networks have been identified. Thus, the orienting network for visual attention [sensory] is believed to involve posterior structures such as the parietal lobe, pulvinar, and superior colliculus. The executive network [nonsensory—self process] is located more anteriorly and includes midline frontal areas and the basal ganglia. The alert state is maintained by a network involving the norepinephrine system arising in the locus coeruleus and including widespread frontal and parietal activation, most strongly of the right hemisphere.

(p. 278)

Posner and his colleagues in this study describe neural systems related to visual orientation. However, they do recognize that "executive functions" (self) are located more "anteriorly." They also refer to the locus coeruleus which has relations with the rest of the cerebrum, and which could provide the communication system that connects the ACC with the rest of the brain. Other recent research describes the ACC as playing a significant role in psychological operations that I believe are the behavioral and experiential underpinning of self-process (Beitman and Nair, 2004).

The following studies cite the ACC as being consistently associated with orientation, pain, attention, and monitoring. It is not my contention to declare that it is the only site of orientation; future research will describe what specific role it plays in that function. It is highly probable that it will play a part in what I call self-process.

The Cohen study found that among patients treated with cingulotomy for chronic pain (a) bilateral lesions involving the anterior cingulate cortex produced changes in emotional experience and (b) these changes were associated with alterations in certain aspects of attentional functioning (p. 44).

Later, this article reports that performance on measures of intention and focused attention together enabled optimal discrimination of patients who reported benefit. This finding provides additional evidence that attentional and emotional functions under the influence of ACC may share common processes (p. 47).

Emotion, pain, intention, and attention are processes generally associated with self-process. In addition to these findings, a review of the functions of the ACC (Davidson et al., 2002) describes many research findings which when put together create a picture of the neurological underpinnings of the self. The ACC has the capacity to monitor and regulate information arising from both the internal and external environments of a person. It also has connections to emotion, cognition, and consciousness. They cite Thayer and Lane (2000) describing the ACC "as a point of integration, for visceral, attentional, and affective information that is critical for self-regulation and adaptability" (p. 211). They also say the "cognitive subdivision of the ACC monitors conflicts or crosstalk between brain regions." This is precisely what I have been saying the NS does when it is responding to nonsensory information.

Wager (2006) identifies the anterior cingulate in relation to activity in other parts of the brain. With regard to the usefulness of making psychological inferences from neuroimaging data, he says:

> My colleagues and I have asked: Is pain different from negative emotions such as sadness and anger, or are they variants on a common theme? In meta-analyses we have found that pain and negative emotions activate distinct brain networks but share features such as anterior cingulate and

prefrontal cortex activity with a broader class of processes, including attention.

(p. 26)

This description matches my hypothesis that these structures serve an orienting function and are activated when other parts of the brain are destabilized. Pain as an emotion is an intimate feature of the emotionality of self-process.

Recent archeological research also supports the idea that the ACC and prefrontal cortex in *Homo sapiens* played a significant role in our survival in contrast to the Neanderthals who existed with them in Europe. Writing about the Neanderthals, Wynn and Coolidge (2008) say that "Their lack of inventiveness and lack of long-range planning suggest that they did not have a second kind of modern problem-solving ability, one known to psychologists as 'executive functions'" (p. 45).

They go on to discuss ideas of A. Baddeley (2007) about "working memory" and its role in executive functions, stating that his ideas have "received much empirical support."

Investigators have found "that the attention and decision making aspects of working memory depend both on the prefrontal cortex . . . and the cingulate cortex" (p. 46).

Beitman and Nair (2004) also describe the evolutionary development of the cingulate cortex in a way that is congruent with my description of the increasing ability of the human brain to experience and classify information.

> A possible neurobiological correlate of the cingulate's ability to integrate information of diverse origins is the finding of large, spindle-shaped neurons in layer Vb of the cingulate cortex. The density of these cells correlates remarkably with phylogeny: the highest density is found in human brains, next highest in chimpanzees, then in orangutans and gorillas. They are not present at all in nonprimate species. It has been hypothesized that these cells connect spatially distant regions in large brains, and that they participate in the integration of motivational, sensory, and cognitive information that characterizes cingulate function.
>
> (p. 52)

The ACC assesses and responds to the significance of external stimuli. In other words, this neurological system monitors internally and externally generated information—that is, sensory and nonsensory information. Supporting the findings of the research of Allman and colleagues (2001), the abstract for Beitman and Nair's article summarizes their research by saying:

> We propose that the anterior cingulate cortex is a specialization of neocortex rather than a more primitive stage of cortical evolution. Functions

> central to intelligent behavior, that is, emotional self-control, focused problem solving, error recognition, and adaptive response to changing conditions, are juxtaposed with emotions in this structure. Evidence of an important role for the anterior cingulate cortex in these functions has accumulated through single-neuron recording, electrical stimulation, EEG, PET, fMRI, and lesion studies. The anterior cingulate cortex contains a class of spindle-shaped neurons probably related to these functions. The spindle cells appear to be widely connected with diverse parts of the brain and may have a role in the coordination that would be essential in developing the capacity to focus on difficult problems. Furthermore, they emerge postnatally, and their survival may be enhanced or reduced by environmental conditions of enrichment or stress, thus potentially influencing adult competence or dysfunction in emotional self-control and problem-solving capacity.
>
> (p. 107)

In short, the anterior cingulate cortex has all of the neurological equipment needed to enable a psychological self to emerge into awareness and to function interpersonally. It monitors and orients itself toward information arising from the internal and external environments using consciousness and cognition (the mind) to restore itself to its steady-state condition. All intensive psychotherapies are theoretically invested in ideas about psychological development.

Allman et al.'s (2001) proposal that the ACC is a "specialization" of the neocortex is congruent with other research findings of the intimate relationship between the prefrontal cortex, especially its orbital surface (Krasnegor et al., 1997), and the NS. These findings support my description of the intimate relationship between orientation, cognition and consciousness, that is, the mind.

Finally, Geary (2005) supports the hypothesis of an NS in the following quote:

> The increase in overall brain size during human evolution almost certainly resulted in an enhanced ability to integrate information within and across modalities, including enhanced executive control. The latter would be associated with gradual evolutionary expansion and potential reorganization of the dorsolateral areas of left and right prefrontal cortices and the anterior cingulate cortex.... The absolute and potential EQ-based enlargements of the right prefrontal cortex and the frontal pole, as well as the potential reorganization of area 11 and the anterior cingulate cortex, are all consistent with important and substantive evolutionary changes in a host of social competencies including self-awareness, social problem solving, the ability to cope with social novelty, and the ability to project oneself through time.
>
> (p. 233)

Clinical observations also support this hypothesis. Damasio (1994) as a clinician describes the internal nonsensory orienting function of his "neural self" in the following terms:

> I must first clarify what I mean by self, and to do so I offer an observation that I have repeatedly made in many patients struck by neurological disease. When a patient develops an inability to recognize familiar faces, or see color, or read, or when patients cease to recognize melodies, or understand speech, or produce speech, the description they offer of the phenomenon, with rare exceptions, is that something is happening to them, something new and unusual which they observe, puzzle over, and often describe, in insightful concrete ways. Curiously, the theory of mind implicit in those descriptions suggests that they "locate" the problem to a part of their persons which they are surveying from the vantage point of their selfhood.
>
> (p. 236)

Finally, Pribram and Bradley (1998), in their study of two brain-injured patients, come to the conclusion that

> These two case histories illuminate two very important dimensions of self. One dimension, portrayed by Ms. C., *locates* us in the world and also with respect to our body's configural integrity. The other dimension, highlighted by TJ, *monitors* our experience. Without such monitoring the events comprising the experience fail to become evaluated and encoded into memory.
>
> (p. 279) (original emphasis)

Ms. C.'s comment about her condition is eloquent and so meaningfully related to orientation's survival function that I will quote it here. She wrote, "How do I live with an illness I am unaware of having? How do I function when I am not aware that I have deficits? How do I stay safe when I'm not aware of being in danger?" (p. 277). Note the referencing and relational use of her "I."

The Neurological Underpinnings of Psychological Structures

The recognition of orientation as the functional underpinning of self-phenomena creates a powerful theoretical linkage between neurological structures and psychological phenomena. Piaget's (1970) definition of psychological structures as "self-perpetuating wholenesses" has a biological ring to it which is consistent with that linkage. Gordon Allport's (1955) idea that psychological structures can become "functionally autonomous" allows for the description of the change-resistant nature of self-perpetuating structures. Living systems require use in the form of validating information that reinforces the stability of neuronal structures that underlie them. All this provides a basis for thinking about psychological systems as psychological habits with characteristics similar to physical habits.

Paradigmatic Implications of a Brain-Based Psychology

Reading the growing literature of the neurology of the self (Damasio, 2010), I thought of myself as one of the participants in the timeworn Zen story of six blind men examining different parts of an elephant to discover its nature. Two added complications compound the blind men's difficulties in communicating with one another about the strange body they are trying to understand. First, not only are we blind in our exploration of the "elephant" of the self, but we also speak to one another in different languages—the paradigms which we are trained to use in our various specialties are different. Second, the difficulty of transcending the different languages is complicated by the fact that despite the differences that exist in the underlying theoretical structures of the way we experience the self, we all use the same words, even though they have different meanings in our theoretical systems (Gross, 2001).

If one accepts the idea that the self has an orienting function, then the interactions of the ACC with other brain systems are logical nominees for the neurological substrate of the self. Within this paradigmatic frame, self-process emerges into awareness from the ACC. This conviction brings me back to ideas about homeostasis or autoregulation as the source of psychological movement.

Homeostasis and Personality Systems

Conceptually linking the neurological underpinnings of my theory to personality processes is the beginning of a description of human nature as a relationship of the multidimensional movement that exists between motivation and personality. I found the explanation of homeostasis clinically useful because it helped me understand why some of the people with whom I work avoided pleasure and/or engaged in self-destructive behaviors, and why so many of them found the loving experience to be difficult and painful. If personality structures formed in childhood are organized by experiences of pain or deprivation in the presence of pleasure or love, then the stable-state (change-resistant) condition of the person is pleasure and love-avoidant. As I pursued my search for a better understanding of personality, I came to the conclusion that the person is a massive, loosely integrated, and frequently conflicted cognitive system (psychological structures) comprised of self-concepts, feelings, and a "personal reality," this is the person whom I describe in Chapter 8.

Then it was easy to see the structures of the person as being shaped by early childhood relationships, many of which are emotionally deprived, abusive, and insulting. Over time, they become habituated—functionally autonomous and self-perpetuating. They are the character structures of the person. As such they seek validation to stabilize their structures and increase their habit strengths. This is the reason why personality structures, even painful ones, are change-resistant.

In adulthood, personality structures seek the same kind of validating information upon which they were built during childhood. Affection may be validating for some, but it can be vastly disturbing for others. Personal systems, as cognitive structures, emerge into awareness from neurological interactions between cortical and limbic systems. The primary biological purpose of personal systems is the regulation of the Neurological Self. The idea and belief in the pleasure principle grew from superficial observations of simple pleasures. At the time this belief was born, people had no idea about the habituation of childhood personality structures that endured throughout the life of the person.

I worked with a woman who exemplified this condition beautifully. She had been raised from early childhood on conflict. She, her mother, and her father were in a constant fight. After a few months in group therapy, where she battled with group members, things settled down. As she became more comfortable with the group, her sweetness began to show itself. This drew a complimentary response from one of the group members who had previously detested her. After the group session, she sent me the following email.

> Dear Zoltan, I tolerated what [Herman] said to me at the end of the group. YET, it is hard for me to take a compliment. It's hard for me to say "thank you." I have always had a hard time taking compliments. I believe in my entire life whenever I have been given a compliment, I have always felt it was wrong to feel good. Instead I feel it is shameful that someone thinks highly of me.

In combat, she is clear and articulate; in affection, she is embarrassed and confused. As it is with many people, it is much easier for her to give love than to receive it. With these realizations, it was easy for me to see how her habituated emotional structures prevented her from engaging with others in ways that would bring her the love and regard she said she needed. Her relations with her mother and others improved. But the realizations contained in her email did not dramatically change her overnight. The young woman's idea that "it was wrong to feel good" is an emotional cognition created in childhood yet persists in creating the pain and loneliness of her life. While her loving experience in childhood may have been painful and confusing, the same rules of engagement she used then are not operative in her adult loving relationships. Nonetheless, they are triggered and become operative when loving feelings are experienced. If in childhood these systems are designed to cope with pain, they reinstate painful processes in adult loving relationships, which in and of themselves may not be painful. As Eliot said earlier, such structures become "cemented" in. If the steady-state condition of the person is wretchedness, then whether he likes it or not, wretchedness is the emotional state to which he will most likely go.

This is what makes psychotherapy so difficult. Even if the person wants to change, the NS works mindlessly and busily to maintain character structures in their steady-state conditions—including right there in the therapy session. Homeostasis trumps happiness. Further on, I will explore ways to work around this therapeutic Catch-22.

This chapter concludes the first part of this book, which described a brain-based theory of personality. The rest of this book will describe the psychology that emerges from the theory.

Chapter 5

The "I" and Its Psychological Selves

Without Our Navigator We Can't Be Sure of Where We Are Going

> The Caterpillar and Alice looked at each other for some time in silence: at last, the Caterpillar took the hookah out of its mouth and addressed her in a languid, sleepy voice.
> "Who are you?" said the Caterpillar.
> This was not an encouraging opening for a conversation. Alice replied, rather shyly, "I—I hardly know, sir, just at present—at least I know who I was when I got up this morning, but I think I must have changed several times since then."
>
> (Carroll, 1965, p. 60)

"Who are you?" is a daunting question. Like Alice's selves, our selves change several times in the course of our daily lives. Which self will we hold up as an answer to that question? Humans, from the time they became conscious of having a "something" within them, have been mystified by its presence. Self-process as a part of the brain's autoregulatory process has been overlooked for centuries (Hood, 2012).

Until recently, it was believed to be an immaterial phenomenon which was disconnected from the body and was, therefore, impossible to study scientifically. This prevented philosophers and neuroscientists from thinking that "the self" could be the servant of the brain. They believed that the mind, where self-process partners with consciousness and cognition, controlled the brain: "mind over matter."

Today we know that all psychological process emerges from the brain. This enables us to ask a brain-based question. "Where in my brain is my 'self'?" This is an extraordinarily difficult question to answer. There has been no generally accepted definition of what self is. Classifying experiences of nonsensory cognitions emerging from the brain without anchoring them to brain functions contributes to the definitional muddle that plagues psychology.

Conflation, anthropomorphizing, and reification are three tricks of the mind that confound our thinking about personality. When I began looking at personality through the lens of neurological equilibration, I found myself empathizing with Alice's astonishments in her encounters with the "realities" with which she was confronted in Wonderland. The recognition of the homeostatic function of self-process as orientation reminded me of Alice's conversation with the Duchess who inquired about the temper of the flamingo Alice was carrying under her arm.

> "He might bite," Alice cautiously replied. . . . "Very true," said the Duchess: "Flamingoes and mustard both bite. And the moral of that is—'Birds of a feather flock together.'" "Only mustard isn't a bird," Alice remarked. "Right as usual," said the Duchess. . . . "It's a mineral, I think," said Alice. "Of course, it is," said the Duchess . . . "there's a large mustard-mine near here and the moral of that is—'The more there is of mine, the less there is of yours.'"

Without clear definitions of what we are talking about when we discuss self-phenomena, we are likely to be caught in a bewilderment similar to Alice's. In everyday conversation, terms that have similar or the same meanings, like "self," "I," and "person," erroneously flock together in commonsense misunderstanding.

Habits of Mind About the "I" and Self-Process

Current habits of mind about the "I" and self-process are misleading. The following discussion of the "I" and self-process recaps and expands some of the epistemological issues I discussed in Chapter 2. I am presenting them here, in a different form, to clarify how my understanding of the nature of self-phenomena differs from cultural misunderstandings of it.

Freud's tripartite description of the self as the interaction of Ego, Id, and Superego was a brave attempt to functionally define self-process. Unfortunately, psychoanalytic self-theory anthropomorphizes these three processes. Ego is a rational homunculus. The "reflective" self or ego, when stripped of the homunculus, is the commonsense mind. The Superego is a righteous homunculus demanding that the id conform to the rules of society. The corporeal or the id aspect of self-process is easily recognized as the NS in disequilibrium, the bodily movement of emotion. It truly is corporeal. It is not a psychological system. It is a neurophysiological one. Therefore, it does not theoretically flock together with the Ego, which is a psychological (cognitive nonsensory) construction. Try mixing thoughts of lemons with water. You will never get lemonade.

A Brain-Based Definition of Self-Process

Like Freud's theory, mine is also a tripartite theory of self-process. However, unlike Freud, who defined the self as the interaction of the Id, Ego, and

Superego as three different conflicted persons, the three parts of my theory are the NS, cognition, and consciousness. As I described in Chapter 3, they are labels of neurological systems, which interact to create the experience (consciousness) of the mind.

A destabilized NS activates homeostatic systems within the body to restore itself to its own steady-state condition. In the last chapter, we saw cognition is more than common sense about the stuff of the outer world. Neurologically, cognition stabilizes the NS. It classifies and labels the NS as the "I" and selves. They encompass much of the Freudian definitions of the ego and superego.

Cognition in its classificatory function labels phenomena that have common characteristics and describes the nature of its functions. Labeling is a straightforward linguistic process. It attaches a word to the experience of a classification. The description of a function is a different matter. Cultural biases and limitations of knowledge shape the ways the NS cognitively appears in consciousness and behavior.

The selves are cognitive classifications of the NS in the variety of different circumstances in which they are homeostatically used. To put it in non-technical terms, our selves (e.g., the work self, the husband self, the father self, and on and on in different social and emotional contexts) are how we experience the NS as it acts to stabilize itself in various situations.

The relational or superego system appears in my theory as "personal reality." Instead of being an oppressive, righteous homunculus, personal reality is a cognitive system comprised of NS's habituated relationships to the social environment. The social environment refers to culturally and familiarly defined behavioral conventions to meet the requirements of the culture within which the individual lives.

At times, we project what we think we know about ourselves to fill the gaps in our knowledge about anything we do not understand. Projection, here, is a form of explanation: a cognitive function. The ancient Greeks put humanlike gods in charge of the sea, sun, and families in order to explain their functions and hopefully to control them. These days we insert homunculi into the gaps of our knowledge about psychological phenomena.

Self-Process

Self-process is the label of the ways we use ourselves in our interactions with others and in their autoregulatory relationship with the NS. The selves we use with our loved ones are different from those we use in the marketplace or public institutions. Externally, selves in the form of self-presentations, a behavioral aspect of self-process, facilitate interpersonal operations. Internally, selves seek validation to feed the affect hunger of the NS.

The NS's relationships to the external environment are enormously complex. Cognition classifies this complexity by creating the variety of different selves we use in our life. For example, in a courtroom, we interact with the judge and attorneys differently than we do with our sister as we prepare for a Thanksgiving dinner. Creative work validates our self-system, and the constructively unique way we do it feeds the affect hunger of the neurological underpinnings of the self we use and our NS. My sister's affection more directly feeds the affect hunger of my NS because she loves me.

In the normative flow of homeostasis, we experience self-process as the "self-concepts" of conventional psychological theory. In whatever way they are experienced, selves are cortico/behavioral systems. Thinking that cortical regulation (cognition) is the same kind of bird as limbic regulation (id process) is as misleading as believing that mustard and flamingoes are birds of a feather.

Conventional Explanations About the "I" and the Selves

"I" and its grammatical twin "me" are two of the most used words in the English, or any other language, and the least understood. True to the paradigmatic nature of my theory, my description of the "I" is unusual. It is not the active agent guiding thought and behavior that it has long been touted to be. "I" and "me" are ubiquitous in self-experiencing. They are not just pronouns denoting the self or a person. Without a theory of its function, it is difficult to describe psychological process.

Over a century ago, William James (1890) asked:

> *What is this self of all the other selves?*
>
> vol. I, (p. 297) (original emphasis)

His answers, which are similar to Freud's, remain the commonly accepted but theoretically unacceptable descriptions. James describes self-process in the following quote:

> Probably all men would describe it much the same way up to a certain point. They would call it the *active* element in all consciousness; saying that whatever qualities a man's feelings may possess, or whatever content his thought may include, there is a spiritual something in him, which seems to *go out* to meet these qualities and contents, whilst they seem to *come in* to be received by it. It is what welcomes and rejects. It presides over the perception of sensations, and by giving or withholding its assent it influences the movements they tend to arouse. It is the home of interest.... It is the source of effort and attention and the place from which appear the fiats of the will.
>
> vol. I, (pp. 297-298) (original emphasis)

The major difficulty with his description of his Self of Selves is the homunculus who hides within it operating as the "active element" that presumably lies at the heart of human motivation. The exorcism of the homunculus leaves his description of the "Self of Selves," the "I," with no explanation of its function or its relationship to other psychological processes.

As humans became increasingly skilled with self-awareness, they came to believe the self or the "I" was in charge of conduct and experience. Intentionality arises from this belief. At the same time, it has always been suspect because humans are constantly confused by the inconsistency that exists between their behavior and/or experience and their intentionality. St. Augustine's anguish over the disobedience of his penis to the exercise of his will (Pagels, 1988) and Freud's (1927/1957) metaphor of the Ego as a gallant and reasonable equestrian riding the horse of emotionality unpredictably trying to maintain a balance between the impulses of the id and the restrictions of the Superego are examples of this puzzling awareness. One could even argue that the belief in original sin had its roots in this confusion. Failure to "ride" Freud's "horse" (the Id) effectively is frequently an explanation of devastating self-recrimination.

James's description of the "Self of Selves" is the conventional phenomenal description of the "I" in relationship to the variety of psychological processes it accompanies. Because consciousness, perception, cognition, feelings, remembering, and intention are so frequently associated with the experience of an "I," they are presumed to emerge from or be controlled by it as in Descartes's assertion "I think, therefore, I am," or in our everyday phrases "I know," "I see," "I will," "I can," and so forth. They all contain the presumption that it is the "I" (as in James's "active element") that is doing all these wonderful psychological things.

Besides being the homuncular source or controller of psychological processes, the "I" is also thought to be the control center of behavior—as Alice's Duchess could say, "The moral of this is that 'I am the master of MY fate and the commander of MY ship.'" The dilemma of describing the "I" dissolved when I was able to recognize orientation as its consistent, biological function. I no longer conflate "I" with the self or the person. Since it is the label of an automatic biological function, I stopped hassling myself about the inconsistency of my behavior's obedience to the "instructions" coming from what I believed was my control center, my "I." The "I" has no sensory or bodily experiential properties. It is a non-sensory experience of the label of the NS's orienting process. We human males easily distinguish the rush of adrenaline in our body when we are frightened from the rush of testosterone when we are sexually aroused. The "I" has no such anchor in experiences of the body. This hypothesis is congruent with James's (1890/1950) description of the experiential qualities of the "spiritual self":

> the *"Self of the selves," when carefully examined, is found to consist mainly of the collection of these peculiar motions in the head or between the head and the throat.* . . . I feel quite sure that these cephalic motions are the portions

of my innermost activity of which I am *most distinctly aware* . . . . *it would follow that our entire feeling spiritual activity, or what commonly passes by that name, is really a feeling of bodily activities whose nature is by most men overlooked.* (pp. 301–302) (original emphasis)

Heinsen (1982) quotes Edmund Husserl's description of the experiential quality of the "pure (polar) ego," which has characteristics strikingly similar to James's "spiritual self." Husserl says that

> the experiencing Ego is still nothing that might be taken *for itself* and made into an object of inquiry on its *own* account. Apart from its "ways of being related [to objects]" or "ways of behaving" . . . it is completely empty of essential components, it has no content that could be unraveled, it in and for itself is indescribable: pure Ego and nothing further.
> (p. 150) (original emphasis)

Note, that both James and Husserl describe the "I" as being intimately associated with experiencing. However, the absence of clear sensory or somatic experiential markers within the "I" makes it difficult for them to describe or explain. Describing the antiquity of the sensory bias in human mentation, Murphy (1949) says,

> Plato introduces us to a clarification and full defense of the already ancient belief that the soul [self] and body are fundamentally different things. . . . While with primitive man and with early Greeks, the immaterial soul has been confusedly regarded as possessing some qualities of a more or less physical nature.
> (p. 7)

There is a growing recognition that, instead of thinking of the self as a singular "thing," we can know it as a moving, highly interactive equilibratory process. There are many psychological selves (Gergen, 1991) each serving different interpersonal purposes while, at the same time, there is a single neurological homeostatic self: the NS. One might then suddenly wonder, which one is the real self? The good news is that they are all real. The bad news, for some, is that there is no core self any more than there is one "real" bodily stance among the many we assume in a day. Selves change to fit the emotional and social circumstances with which they are confronted.

Despite the fact that the experience of the "I" is without sensory content, some of us still think in terms of a "Real Self" (cf. Masterson, 1985). The idea of a "Real" Self contains the same difficulty we have in experiencing and classifying all other forms of nonsensory phenomena. The thenness and realness associated with the idea of self create the illusion that the self is a real "thing" out there like other things we see with our eyes, a form of reification.

The Constant Presence of the "I"

From the beginning of modern psychotherapy, the self has been at the center of psychotherapeutic attention. Freud wrote about "Das Ich" in German, which in English is "the I." Unfortunately, it traditionally has been translated into English as the Ego. This is another example of the conflation of the "I" with "self," "knowing," and "rationality." By calling the "I" of our experience the Ego, psychoanalysts avoided the difficulty of trying to describe and define the "I" experience by hiding it in the homuncular Ego.

In the beginning of psychoanalysis, Sandor Ferenczi controversially espoused an active role for the therapist. However, until recently, mainstream psychoanalysis mandated an isolated and interpretive role for the therapist (Wallerstein, 1995). In this therapeutic mode, the therapist could with greater ease overlook his own experience of self—except, of course, when he is in the throes of countertransference.

There is a renewed interest in the meaningfulness of the therapeutic relationship as an instrument of psychotherapeutic and/or characterological change (Mitchell and Black, 1995; Constantino and Castonguay, 2003; Wachtel, 2008). Ferenczi has been rehabilitated as a meaningful contributor to psychoanalytic theory, and with this change comes an increased recognition of the significance of the "I," emotionality, and the self as important parts of the psychotherapeutic process. The following description of the experience of the "I" has been helpful in my relationships with the people I serve in my practice.

In relational psychotherapy, where the therapist engages the person with whom he is working in a direct, immediate, you-and-me encounter, a kind of interpersonal dialogue rarely used in secondary relationships occurs. The person is caught off guard and is unable to automatically process the emotionality generated by that unexpected and unfamiliar engagement. "I" emerges into awareness when the automaticity of interpersonal process is interrupted. One or more of the selves of the person becomes operative in the therapeutic relationship when this happens. This is especially true when a therapist works with someone who relies upon multiple personalities in his or her social relationships.

Recognizing the difficulty of experiencing and cognizing nonlinear/nonsensory process helps explain why, until the late 1980s, there was an almost total absence of any mention of the self in the research literature of emotionality. The self is barely mentioned in Ekman and Davidson's (1994) volume, *The Nature of Emotion: Fundamental Questions*. In one of the rare comments about the self in this volume, Lazarus (1994) remarks:

> I am forced to conclude that there must be an elemental self or ego for emotion to occur, one that specifies and distinguishes one's own

individual interests in the world from others. . . . At present there is little agreement about how to think about and study the problem.

(pp. 363–4)

Scientists, who investigate either emotionality or personality, regard emotions as systems of ideas responding to the context, which triggers their appearance in awareness. However, these scientists have no psychological explanation of how ideas, cognitions, or appraisals arise in our minds or why they are sometimes displayed in awareness and sometimes not. In the 1990s, there was an increased interest in the self in all areas of thinking and research about personality. Some social psychologists have investigated "self-conscious emotions" such as embarrassment, shame, and guilt (Nathanson, 1992; Gilbert and Andrews, 1998). Other psychologists, like Lazarus, a social psychologist/psychotherapist, sense there must be some kind of a self lurking around in emotionality. Damasio (1999) describes a "proto-self." Panksepp (1998) writes about "the SELF" in the following quote:

> The critical issue that I have avoided until now [at the end of his book] is the nature of consciousness and the self. Emotional feelings cannot be fully understood without understanding these matters.
>
> (p. 300)

Pribram and Bradley (1998) see localization and monitoring as a self-function, as do I; however, they, like Panksepp, do not relate them to emotionality or other personality processes. Damasio (1994, 2010) does discuss the self and emotionality, but his understanding of emotionality remains within the conventional cultural frame, and he does not explain its relationship to the brain. Brothers (2001) describes Damasio's confused understanding of the relationship between the brain and the mind in the following quote.

> What Damasio accomplishes in Descartes' Error is to suggest an innovation in the way we normally relate feelings to cognition. He does not show that the grammar of feeling can be replaced with language appropriate to brains: although in some respects he inconspicuously suggests it, he reverts elsewhere to using "feeling" in its normal way. He quietly undoes what would have been a radical act—reducing the language of the mental to the language of the physical—by retaining the everyday mental term and simply suggesting a modification to the grammar of its everyday use.
>
> (p. 18)

This is precisely what I am doing in this book. I am suggesting "modifications to the grammar" of everyday use of emotionality. While it is true some social scientists and neuroscientists recognized there must be a self or its "I" around somewhere, they discussed it largely within the conventional, homuncular frame or described it so abstractly that it had no relationship to the psychological selves with which we grapple in everyday life. This paradoxical condition of the position of the "I" in psychological theory reminds me of the jingle where:

> Yesterday, upon the stair
> I met a man who wasn't there
> He wasn't there again today
> I wish, I wish he'd go away.
> ("Antigonish," William Hughes Mearns, 1899)[1]

The "I" as a Cursor

The biological function of the NS is orientation and the experience of the "I" is its label. It is similar to a cursor on a computer; it locates the person where her NS is on the screen of her awareness. It locates her in relationship to something her brain is unable to automatically process and prompts her awareness of this inability. If a person experiences pain in her stomach, she knows it resides in midsection of her body. If her boyfriend rejects her, she knows the pain is emotional and it resides in her person.

When humans had much smaller prefrontal cortices, the NS genetically responded to information automatically. The NS triggered complex survival information such as feeding, fighting, fleeing or mating reflexively, without thought or self-consciousness.

With the growth of the autoregulatory functions of the prefrontal cortex, humans became self-conscious. With that a referencing function of the "I" emerged. When spoken or written, it lets others know where a person is in relationship to whatever she is discussing. This is a cognitive function. Referencing classifies a relationship between the NS and whatever it is dealing with. Referencing my "I" as the location where this writing is coming from does not mean that "I" is doing the writing. In this case, the "I" is used to denote the mind of the person as the writer.

The "I" as a referencing device has no desires or thoughts. The experience of "I want" is a cognitive construction displayed in awareness as personal disequilibrium. The "I" simply shows that the disequilibrium is within the individual, a person with a feeling (a cognition) of wanting something. This is the experience of an internally generated disequilibrium. Here, the NS is triggered by either its own affect hunger or other affect hungers within the person. Rather than being the operator of perception, an active agent of thinking and feeling, or the activator of behavior, the "I" associated with these processes simply shows that information is disturbing neurological systems, which produce the equilibratory experience of a person.[2] The experience of loneliness exemplifies internally generated feelings. A man, whose wife is visiting her sick mother, experiences loneliness because he is missing her validating loving affection, which he needs to feed his affect hunger. Different feelings arise from different of parts of his personality that have been neglected.

The presence of the "I" in relation to a particular psychological information-processing system shows that cognition, perception, remembering, feeling, and more are going on within the brain of an individual for the purposes of identifying the sources of disequilibrium, and the mind is thinking about them (attempting to classify them) to restore the NS to its steady-state condition.

Since the "I" is either an orienting (a neurological) or a referencing (cognitive/psychological) device, it resides in the center of one's experience. The constant orienting and/or referencing ourselves in relationship to disequilibrium, whatever it may be, creates the sense of centrality existing about the self or the "I." Sherif and Cantril (1947) describe this function in the following quote.

> The personal world of every individual thus becomes centered around himself, as William Stern (1938) has pointed out. . . . In making judgments of "space" and "time" the individual inevitably uses himself as a central point of reference. This holds for what we regard as "inside" and "outside" ourselves, what we regard as "above" and "below" and "before" and "behind" as "left" or "right" as "future" or "past."
>
> (p. 92)

This ubiquitous sense of centrality contributes to the impression that "I" is the control center of the person. If "I" am at the center of my doing or thinking, then it is logical to think that it is the cause of these processes. This is the logic of believing that we are at the center of the universe because we "know" that the sun rotates around the earth because it always rises in the east and sets in the west.

Centrality, Intentionality, and Control

Within the neurological perspective of my theory, homeostasis (equilibration) is the goal of a person's automated motivational systems. The NS in the process of stabilizing itself produces emotion. Control, then, is defined as the ability of the NS to restore itself to its steady-state condition as quickly as possible.

The centrality of the "I"/self-complex also holds true with respect to judgments about internal nonsensory sources of disequilibrium. It is not a great leap of intuition to have the mistaken belief that the "I" is also the activator of behavior and experience. If "I" am the center of action and experience, then it is easy to think that "I" is the active agent who wanted to instigate it. With that belief, the "I" becomes a theoretically unacceptable homunculus. Believing that I am in control of all of the difficulties of my life, both physical and emotional, is reassuring—that is, stabilizing. Unfortunately, that erroneous belief causes painful and misleading conclusions about human nature and who my "I" should be. If my "I" is only a referencer or cursor, locating my person in relationship to information my brain is unable to automatically process, if "I" am not the control center of my experience and conduct, then I can forgive my "self" for any experience or conduct that does not fit the structure of my person. This permits my mind to seek other more productive explanations about why my homuncular "I" does things, which my mind classifies as an error or a shortcoming.

There are three other reasons why we have believed that the "I" is our control center. It is a constant presence during any unusual action or novel experience. The experience of "I" is displayed in either the foreground or background of awareness. With it, there is an automatic cognitive classification of what that presence means, which is accompanied with a set of explanations and instructions about what to do in that given situation.

First, the experience of "I" and programmed behavior follow so closely upon one another, we think that one causes the other. I experience myself as wanting to do something and "by golly, I do it." Therefore, my mind classifies my "I" as causing my behavior to do what I said I wanted to do.[3] Underlying this delusion is a classical error: just because one thing immediately follows another does not necessarily mean there is a causal relationship between them. The cases, where I say I want to do something and my behavior does not obediently follow my intention, are dismissed and do not invalidate the nourishing sense of self-control contained in Plato's belief that intentional control should rule over emotionality.

Second, it is comforting (validating to the NS) to have an explanation that "I" am in charge of my conduct and the cause of actions, thoughts, ideas, or feelings. This way of explaining myself gives my personal systems the pleasant assurance that my person is in control, which is a nourishing, validating feedback stabilizing the NS's affect hunger. Being out of control anywhere in life is a cause for anxiety. The mere thought that we ride the bus of life not as the driver but as a passenger staring out a back window can induce a panicky feeling. Thinking our "I" is in charge of events or behavior reduces anxiety. However, an explanation that makes me feel better is not necessarily an accurate one.[4]

Patients suffering from anosognosia have a total lack of awareness about a neurological impairment for which they are being treated. Eagleman's (2011) sad description of Supreme Court Justice William O. Douglas exemplifies a common description in the neurological and psychological literatures exhibiting la belle indifférence while denying and explaining away severe neurological impairment. He says the Justice

> was debilitated by a stroke that paralyzed his left side and confined him to a wheelchair. But Justice Douglas demanded to be checked out of the

hospital on the ground that he was fine. He declared that reports of his paralysis were "a myth." When reporters expressed skepticism, he publicly invited them to join him for a hike, a move interpreted as absurd. He even claimed to be kicking football goals with his paralyzed side.

(p. 135)

The delusional explanatory behavior of these patients is a part of their neurological disorder. This is one of the places where neurological process is expressed and experienced psychologically.

The interaction between nonsensory stabilization and sensory information from the outside world creates the remarkable evolutionary growth of the human brain and its creativity. Throughout the rest of this book, I will be describing explanation as a homeostatic process. Much of the time, the truth-value of explanation is incidental to its primary psychological purpose, the equilibration of the NS.

The third reason why we believe the "I" is (or should be) the control center of our conduct arises from the seeming automaticity of obedience to intention. It is true that most of the time, we do act in accordance with what we call our intentions. If I want to get a glass of water, I get it. If I want to turn the lights on in my house, there is no conflict about doing it. It gets done. When a person is in his steady-state condition and his intention involves well-rehearsed behaviors, his behavior and intention are congruent.

Disobedience to intention occurs when it orders behavior that violates habituated emotional structures. If an unmarried woman needs sex to assuage her tormenting affect hunger, but she has been taught over many years that having recreational sex is sinful, it is extremely difficult, if not impossible for her, to go out on the town and satisfy her hunger. Augustine's confusion about the behavior of his penis is another example of where emotionality overrides intentionality. Habituated dietary rules override intentions to eat forbidden food. People become confused when they are unable to recognize emotional barriers to their intentions.

This idea of the "I" as an orienting/referencing system was reinforced when I worked with people with multiple personalities. In these relationships, I observed that while personalities changed, the use of their "I" remained the same regardless of which person was operating.

I recall walking down Market Street on a brilliant San Francisco afternoon with a young woman who lived with multiple personalities in her body. When we thought it would be fun to jump on a cable car and have lunch at Fisherman's Wharf, she transformed into a very happy young boy, skipping down the street and rushing joyously back to me begging for permission to ride on the running board of the cable car. When we decided we could not go that far because of a previous commitment, she returned to her pleasant young womanly self. Her persons changed to accommodate her different emotionalities, but her "I" as an orienting process functioned the same way in her different persons. This constancy is the foundation of the mistaken belief in the unity and singularity of the person (Marks, 1981).

Similarly, when I am talking to you, the self I experience is different from the self I experience when I am talking to my wife. However, my "I" is the same when I am talking with you as when I am talking to her. In both circumstances, the "I" is acting as a referencing or orienting device, but my emotional reactivity will be quite different because a different self-process has been activated. Different self-processes occur because different emotionalities are activated in different relationships. Emotionalities and self-process are intimately related.

Self-Observation

When the person experiences the "observing ego," the "I" is referencing itself to its self-systems and that interaction is displayed in awareness as a person talking to herself. This way of describing talking to oneself serves as another example of the multiplicity of self-process. Usually, this dialogue is between a linear/sensory formatted self and a nonsensory/nonlinear self; a commonsense self and an emotional one.

When one becomes conscious of a previously habituated way of being, he has an epiphany. It is another form of self-observation. It is a major interruption of automated self-process. Sometimes this occurs in the course of everyday living. At other times, it happens in psychotherapy when a therapist calls attention to something a person is unaware of doing or when the therapist engages the person emotionally. Repeated emotional interruptions of habituated personal structures change personality.

A man with whom I worked had a deep loving, fighting relationship with his mother. She was quite compulsive and judgmental. Unfortunately, he and his wife did not keep their home in the neat orderly manner with which his mother was comfortable. On entering their house, his mother immediately set about cleaning it. They experienced this as negative criticism. For years, she was critical of his appearance. She is rail thin, and while he was not as rotund as was his father, in his adolescence he weighed in that direction. In one of our sessions, I helped him become aware of how in one of the fights, he was oblivious to her feelings. He realized that if he had focused on how hurt she was, instead of defending himself, he could have been more effective in resolving their dispute.

At our next session, he told me that he no longer could feel as "innocent" in his reactions to his mother as he had previously been. He now had a different sense of himself. He was aware of an unrecognized purpose he had in their fights. Instead of automatically defending himself against her "unwarranted" criticisms, he was newly aware of the store of anger in his character that was released in his fights with her.

Self-Hatred and Intentionality

The conventional belief that the "self" is (or should be) the source and controller of rationally driven intentionality that activates behavior is not only an unfortunate, erroneous, and pain-inducing belief, it also validates self-hatred.

Self-hatred is a universally miserable experience that perpetuates ignorance about what is actually happening within the person. A person who makes what he believes is a dumb mistake also dislikes his self for being stupid. Once this judgment is made, further inquiries about the causes of the mistake are ended. The person making the judgment "knows" why he made the mistake—he was stupid. When this happens, he embarks on a wretched circular journey of self-blame: I am dumb because I made that mistake; I made the mistake because I am dumb. There is not much useful information in this ridiculous syllogism.

I have just used a relatively benign example to illustrate self-hating explanations. In my practice, this way of explaining psychological pain accompanies most suicidal ideation. I know a woman who used a fantasy of tearing her face off with the claws of her unexpressed childhood pain and rage. I know a man, who, when he is lost in the despair of his loneliness, wishes he could beat himself senseless to make himself behave in ways that were prevented by his depression.

During my tenure as an intern in David Shakow's laboratory at the University of Illinois Neuropsychiatric Institute, I was the psychometrician on an intake team when I tested a young Catholic novitiate who came into the hospital in a body-shaking state of anxiety. He said he was terribly distressed because he would awaken in the middle of the night to find himself masturbating. He knew he was committing a mortal sin over which he had no intentional control. Wracked with guilt and anguished by his inability to do anything about his sexual feelings and behavior, he felt helpless. If he had had the ability to escape his self-hatred, he might have recognized his loneliness and the conflicted feelings he had about training for the priesthood. He could have seen that it was his desire to conform to his parents' wishes rather than his devotion to the church that induced him to train for the priesthood.

Too frequently, people hate themselves because they cannot control the experience of their feelings, frequently their sexual ones. Judging themselves negatively compounds their distress and confusion. Intentions are unreliable explanations of why people do things. They are frequently used as explanations that conceal other, usually nonconscious motivations. Too often have I seen parents wreak havoc on the fragile developing selves of their children with the "best" of intentions. This is the case where the path to psychological hell is paved with good intentions.

There is a difference between intentionality and personal responsibility. Even though we know that intentions are ex post facto explanations and that our use of the experience of an "I" is a shorthand way of describing why we do what we have been or are doing, the neurological underpinnings of our person are responsible for our conduct. Most of the psychological ways in which we live our lives are products of the complex interactions that go on within the neurology of our person.

There is a difference between the experience of the "I" and that of the person. In the rest of this book, I will be arguing that ideas about personal complexity and competence enable my theory to escape the rigidity of determinism. While the "I" is not responsible for conduct, the person, a product of the mind, is.

The Interaction of the "I" and the Psychological Selves

The nonconscious transformation of "I" into a psychological self, a part of the person, is an example of mismatched psychological terms flocking together. The experience of a psychological self is an experience of a process. The "I" is an experience of a thing, the NS. The experiential alternation between orienting and referencing is automatic and rapid. Orienting is a neurological operation. Referencing is a psychological one. The nonsensory experience of a stomachache is different from the experience of a cortical (explanatory) process. A psychological self is the experience of cortical process. It is not the same as the experience of the rush of adrenaline (a bodily experience, usually experienced as an emotional one).

The Structural Dynamics of Self-Process

The psychotherapeutic perspective of self-process differs from neurological and sociological points of view, which arrive at different conclusions about what their most significant aspects are. Sociologists (Goffman, 1959; Gergen, 1991) think of self-process in the context of social management and adaptation. When neuroscientists think of the "self," they are reaching out into the theoretical heavens for a way of creating a bridge between the mind and the body. From a psychotherapeutic viewpoint, the most striking feature of the structural dynamics of self-process is its change-resistant nature.

In other theories, consciousness, cognition, self, and emotion are described as separate and distinctly different psychological functions in which self-phenomena are not significant operational parts. For example, in his scholarly discussion of "Psychology and Phenomenology; a Clarification," Kendler (2005) makes no mention of a "self" when discussing the differences in the ways that psychologists and philosophers attempt to describe the nature of consciousness. Yet consciousness could not exist without the orienting function of the NS to activate the display aspect of consciousness.[5]

My theory takes the position that the structural dynamics of self-process can be best understood if the information-processing systems of the brain can be thought of as the interactions between different information-processing functions. As I said in Chapter 3, the display of information (consciousness), and the classification of information (cognition) are operations of the mind and its psychological process. Finally, when this interaction is successfully completed (the person thinks and seeks a solution), he experiences relief from tension, stress, or disequilibrium of a variety of sorts (emotion). In other words, the NS is restored to its steady-state condition.

The kind of psychotherapy in which I engage is long-term, intensive, relational psychotherapy that seeks to help people change their personalities in enduring ways. In the pursuit of this goal, I think of personality structures as stabilizing information-processing systems. When these systems reduce tension, they continue to endure—they take on a life of their own. I am using the term "tension" to denote various bodily experiences generated when the NS is unable to process information automatically.

Personal systems come into being at different periods of the individual's development. Habituated personal systems, which emerge from neurological systems, require exercise to maintain the continuity and integrity of their operations (Eliot, 1999).[6] Previously, I described this neurological need as affect hunger. Feeding this hunger enables cognitive constructs to become self-perpetuating systems, complex experiential and behavioral structures, which are expressed in a person's self-presentation, personal identity, and character. In part, they are designed to elicit responses from others that validate (reinforce) those personality structures.

Structures that repeatedly feed the affect hunger of the NS stabilize it. Feeding affect hunger is conceptually similar to the rewards of the stimulus/response experiments of the early twentieth century. They, in turn, are reinforced and become habituated. Cognitive structures restore the NS to its stable state reducing experiences of anxiety, depression, and/or pain. Like all behavioral habits, habituated cognitive structures are change-resistant.

Reinforcement is a way of describing the creation and perpetuation of psychological structures. The idea of reinforcement is denoted in psychotherapy with concepts like validation, support, and empathy—in other words, the interaction between the NS, consciousness, and cognition enables the automatic processing of information and produces a reduction of emotionality as the NS returns to its steady-state condition.

Under ordinary circumstances, the NS returns to stability with relatively short-lived experiences (Stern, 2004). They pass out of awareness with the equilibration of the NS, much like our adaptation to the smell of perfume: when we can process the information of its scent automatically, we stop experiencing it. When the NS cannot restore itself to its stable-state condition, the person experiences extreme distress, as in mindstorms, pain, depressions, and anxiety.

A habituated psychological/neurological structure is no longer dependent upon the conditions that were necessary to its formation. It becomes functionally autonomous (Allport, 1960). As a neurological system, it only requires information that matches its information-processing structures to feed its affect hunger with validating feedback from the external environment or from internal cognitive processing. Internal cognitive processing is an abstract way of saying that persons validate themselves (their neurological selves and their persons) with repetitive ideation and/or creative thinking and work.

If personality structures are autoregulatory functions designed to stabilize the NS, then it is fair to say that the primary task of living is the stabilization of the NS, and so everything we do, think, or want has psychoneurological stabilization as its psychological and behavioral purpose. This, of course, is an oversimplification because it does not take into account the complexity of our personalities, which by reason of that complexity also become a major source of the NS's disequilibrium—an issue to be discussed more fully in the next chapter.

For now, if personality were a simple, straight-line, autoregulatory structure, then the wishful thinking of Plato, Freud, and others would hold true. Reason and intelligence would unequivocally reign supreme. Empiricists would be content with the guidance of objective observation of visual information, and poetry would cease to exist.

One of Freud's great contributions was to call attention to the fact that many personal structures formed in childhood remain intact and continue to operate outside of conscious awareness. In so doing, they automatically, mindlessly engage their world in ways that create or reactivate the grief and joys of their childhoods. These childhood structures are change-resistant. Helping to change them is the primary task of psychotherapy for people seeking to alter their characters.

Three men with whom I have worked illustrate the ways change-resistant childhood structures painfully endure in adulthood. Each of them struggled to find a relationship with a woman to assuage an excruciating loneliness that plagued his life. These are stories about men with habituated self-systems who, therefore, nonconsciously and repetitiously engage in frustrating emotional relationships with women.

Jim's Anguish

After Jim's parents divorced, his mother was so intent upon finding another relationship that she lost sight of her three-year-old son. He also lost his father, who married a woman who did not welcome him into her home. His mother felt guilty about her inability to care for him and made promises to make up for her dereliction, only to break them. As time passed, he wrapped himself in a fury that expressed the pain that inhabited his feelings of loneliness and rejection. Finally, at the age of ten, when she could no longer bear his outrage, she sent him away to a boarding school with a promise that if he did well, she would bring him home the following year. He did beautifully. Once again, she broke her promise, sending him back to the prison of the school. He promised himself never again to express anger to his mother. It did no good. Expressing it only caused her to banish him. Unfortunately, that promise to himself laid the foundations of an extremely painful depression in his adult life.

In mid-adolescence, he had an affair with an older woman, who ended it abruptly. He again cried out in despair of rejection by a woman he loved. Later in life, he had two very intense love affairs with women, who, like his mother, had personal, emotional agendas of their own which did not include him. The termination of each relationship was accompanied by deep depressive suffering. By his late thirties and early forties, he could not bring himself to enter a meaningful relationship with another woman. Throughout this period, he was very successful in business. At one point in his career, he was about to make a very significant deal but needed a considerable amount of new money to close it. He took on a partner who promised to raise the money. Here again, this promise was broken, as was a series of other promises.

Finally, he realized he had to confront his partner (a man) and change the terms of the partnership. Before he did this, he broke down. He again became incapacitated with depression and grief. He came into his session with me looking bleary-eyed and exhausted. He said that he had been sleeping for the last 18 hours. He told me about his grief and a punishing despair about himself. He complained that he was not attending to his business well. He was drinking too much. He was smoking pot. He berated himself for all of these "delinquencies."

I had no sense of what was going on with his business deal, which I knew meant everything to him at this point and which I suspected contributed to his suffering. I asked him about it. In a flat drone, he recited to me that things were looking up with other investors, but that development confronted him with the need to get rid of his old partner. He was reluctant to do that because the partner had been helpful, and it was very important for him to avoid getting into an angry confrontation with any partner. I suggested that he was suffering his nonconscious rage over the broken promises made by someone who could have fulfilled his childhood dream of being in a family once more. He sat up from the couch upon which he was slouching and reviewed with me his history of disappointments in loving relationships.

This realization gave him a sense of relief. His depression and despair lifted enough for him to return to work. He could see how repetitive his relationships with women had been. That understanding was not enough to liberate him to seek a loving relationship with a woman. It did help him to end the relationship with his partner.

Henry's Frustration

Henry's mother stayed married to his paranoid father and accommodated to the loneliness of the marriage with numerous extramarital affairs. She kept her home in order and fed her four children well but was unable to identify or empathize with Henry. He never recalled playful, happy moments with her. It was clear from his sweet but impoverished descriptions of her that in his very early years, he had a loving relationship with her.

His father, reacting in part to the rejecting alienation of his marriage, brutalized Henry and his brother and finally broke down and was hospitalized, where he received a series of shock treatments. His mother did little to help her sons escape her husband's brutality except by pleading with her husband, "Not in the face!" She was afraid that the bruises would show in public. When he was 16 years old; Henry fled home and was on the road. He was good with his hands and supported himself repairing houses. By the time he began working with me, he had been married and had a few disappointing affairs.

In his therapeutic work, he spent much of his time complaining about a long-term relationship he was having with a very beautiful married woman. He had been waiting for six years for her to leave her marriage and come live with him. He lamented bitterly about being the "other man." He constantly argued, cajoled, and threatened his lover to coerce her to divorce her husband, to no avail. She loved him, but like his mother, she would not leave her husband. As time went by, he began to realize that his lover was like the other women of his life. They were affectionate and had serious sex with him, which he demanded and appreciated. But each had agendas for living that were not congruent with his hopes and dreams for a stable family life.

The realization that his relationships with women were shadows of the emptiness of his childhood did not free him from his frustrated relationship with his lover. It did give him a new perspective on the emotional meaning of his current relationship. He no longer spent all his time plotting how to change her. He became much more curious about his compelling attachment to women who emotionally resembled his mother.

George's Liberation

Unlike Jim and Henry, George never married. His intimate relationships with women were sporadic. In the early stages of infatuation, he enjoyed himself. But when the glow of fantasy faded from the bloom of the relationship, he would lose interest and become unwilling to engage sexually. His feelings about Helen were no different. Three years before the interview I am about to describe, they separated but kept in touch. They were a part of an active social group, which kept them informed about what was going on with the other.

When George heard that Helen had become involved with John, he began to pine for her. He regretted his rejection of her and was guilty about how badly he had treated her. With a bit of embarrassment, he acknowledged that in other loving relationships with women, he had treated them badly and lost sexual interest once they were committed to him. For example, on the night Helen was having an abortion resulting from her sex with him, he was dating another woman. Helen had special meaning to him, and he hoped that he could rekindle her desire for him. At my suggestion, he would on occasion send her a reminiscence gift, a small thing that would remind her of something sweet they had shared.

When Helen's relationship with John ended, she and George started dating as friends again. They agreed that they would be exploring the possibility of getting married and having children. At least, once a week, they would go to a party, see friends, or go out to dinner. Unfortunately, this time their relationship was devoid of ardor on her part. In one way or another, Helen would rebuff George's sexual invitations.

In our interview, George began expressing his frustration and anger about Helen's reluctance to return to the sexuality of their previous relationship. Behind a glaze, he recounted in great detail each date they'd had in the previous two weeks and how at the end of the date, Helen would arrange it so that they could not be sexual with one another.

He looked up at me. "I know I'm boring you."

"Not true," I said.

"Then what were you thinking about?"

"Your mother," I said.

Insight illuminated his face. He saw how much his mother avoided him. He spoke about a time when he had been out of the country for several months. Upon his return, he called his mother a number of times. It took her two months to return his calls. He spoke about her emotional distance when he was a child in contrast to her more than adequate physical care of him and his brother.

George's recognition of how much his attachment to Helen was based on the template of his relationship with his mother did not completely break the bonds of his attachment to her. However, with this insight, he did not feel as injured in his relationship with her and began a gradual separation from her.

The pain that each of these men suffered arose from the same structural dynamic. The emotional attachments they had to their narcissistic mothers continued to operate in their adult lives (Miller, 1981). Also, in each of these vignettes, it was obvious that no dramatic behavioral changes occurred in these men. They experienced themselves differently and shifted the focus of their attention away from wanting to change their women to a curiosity about their own internal process.

Psychotherapeutic Implications of Personality Habituation

The word "character" is used in different ways in the psychological literature. Some use it moralistically to describe the nature of an individual's personality, as in whether he or she has a good or bad character. Eric Fromm (1941) has used it in his discussions of the "social character" of the person. My use of the term here differentiates psychotherapeutic ways of thinking about character structure from cultural or moralistic ways of using this term. I think of it as a collection of habituated self-systems.

Psychoanalytic pioneer Wilhelm Reich (1933/1945) called attention to stable, "hardened," generalized structures in personality as the target of intensive psychotherapeutic effort. He said, "the continuing actual conflicts between instinct and the outer world give it its strength and continued reason for existence" (p. 146). He recognized it as operating defensively against internal and external conflict (Shapiro, 1965). My understanding of character structures differs from Reich's in three ways. These differences have implications for a definition of psychotherapeutic goals, which I will briefly discuss in the next chapters of this book.

The first difference resides in the way that "instinctual drives" are defined and used in the definition of and creation of personality operations. The idea of "instinctual drives" was the recognition of bodily metabolic processes that activate behavior. The most usual example of this is the relationship between nutrient hunger pangs and the activation of feeding behavior.

Starting with Freud, the early analysts were deeply impressed with the importance of sexual behavior as an "instinct," a "libido" or a "psychic energy," that activated behavior and emotional conflict. These experiences were displays of limbic activity about which the early analysts knew very little. It is a tribute to their clinical awareness that they recognized that the body—and in Freud's case, the brain (Sulloway, 1979)—had a profound effect on behavior and experience.

With our present knowledge of limbic activity and its display in awareness, we have a more complex understanding of its operations not only as a metabolic system but also as the locus of our emotionality. My theory proposes that emotionality is the experience of the NS reaching out to the limbic system to stabilize itself. This produces the experience of emotion. When that experience is cognized (as in a feeling), the emotion and its feelings are experienced as the emotionality of the person. With this description of emotionality, I came to see psychotherapy as a treatment where personality change is not dependent upon understanding or insight. Nor is intentionality a major player in character change.

The second difference arises from advances in our modern day understanding of neurological process. Instead of thinking of character structure as a "resistance" to conflicting information occurring between instincts and the "outer world," I see the neurological structures underlying character as requiring invariant validational feedback to maintain their structural integrity. In receiving validation, they become change resistant. In this way, therapists can avoid the difficulties encountered when patients are accused of intentionally resisting treatment or the experience of difficult emotions or memories (cf. Kaiser in Fierman, 1965). Here again, we see the idea of intentionality creating confusion. Intentionality used in this way implies the existence of a homunculus who is "resisting" the work of psychotherapy.

The third difference exists in my definition of "structure." I found Piaget's (1970) definition of psychological structures as "self-perpetuating wholenesses" compelling. This condition contributes to the change-resistant nature of personality that lies at the center of the psychotherapy I practice. In saying this, I want to emphasize that I do not believe this is the only kind of psychotherapy that should be used.

As a matter of fact, I believe most people do not need or want to engage in this kind of therapy. They enter psychotherapy hoping it will help them cope with circumstances that have confronted them in their present-day lives. Broken love relationships, work difficulties, family conflict, and their emotional sequelae or the anxieties and/or depressions are the circumstances that move most people to seek psychotherapy.

I liken the psychotherapy I practice to that of a person embarking upon a trip with a visible destination. Then having arrived at it, she has another view of the terrain of her personality and may decide to continue her journey to a new and different destination. The journey is an ever-changing one. At this late stage of my life, I am still traveling.

Even though few travel long distances on their therapeutic journeys, my characterologically oriented practice enabled me to be helpful to many people who take only short psychotherapeutic trips. I also work with others who are not concerned about a specific end. For example, with those who are interested only in a short trip, I have found making a distinction between anxiety, as an experience of the NS when it is unable to find a cognitive category for its disturbance, and fear, which is a reaction to awareness of a dangerous circumstance, very helpful to people suffering with anxiety.

Character structure is a gigantic neurological system homeostatically perpetuating its own existence and the existence of the subsystems of the person, which are habituated emotionalities, self-concepts and their presentations, and experiential skills in the display of different systems of the person. As these systems become habituated, such as those in adult, loving relationships, they continue to function and autonomously adapt throughout the life of the person.

In adult loving relationships, the intimate relatedness of the couple feeds the affect hunger of both persons without violating their separateness and autonomy. The affectionate play of lovers satisfies the play of childhood while at the same time enabling them to enjoy the novelty of creative play that stimulates adult personal growth. The facilitation of that growth sustains the beauty of the loving relationship in adult persons.

I, of course, have never worked with a perfectly balanced person in my practice or in my own life. If she were perfectly balanced, she would certainly have no need to see me. Saying that, I do not believe anyone lives in nirvana. No one grows into adulthood as a perfectly contented person. Many of the nagging self-doubts or discontents with one's self are residuals of habituated childhood pains or confusions. No one leaves childhood with all the emotional skills needed in the adult world. There is always the tension of stability and growth in all living systems. The next chapter about emotionality will expand upon this theme.

Notes

1. See Allport (1960) for a discussion of the disappearance of the self as an important area of psychological investigation.
2. The person is a complex cognitive system about the NS. It will be discussed more fully in Chapter 8, along with intentionality, free will, and personal responsibility.
3. This sentence illustrates the paradigmatic shift described in Chapter 2. It is an accurate description of the way of describing how the mind erroneously classifies the "I" of orientation causing behavior. Colloquial description assumes the "I" has a homunculus driving behavior. It is easier to read colloquial language than the paradigmatic language. In the rest of this book, I will differentiate the colloquial "I" from the NS's "I" by putting quotation marks around it as I have here.
4. See Gazzaniga (2010) and Eagleman (2011) for descriptions of the ubiquity of explanation as compelling stabilizing process. They present descriptions of patients' explanations of their perceptual deficits that suggest explanation as neurological systems as well as perceptual ones.
5. I have found in the literature struggling to define and describe consciousness that various theorists conflate consciousness with either self-process as in Jaynes (1976) or with cognition (Dennett, 1991). My tripartite classification of orientation, cognition, and consciousness is a contemporary one based on the limitations of my knowledge. I believe that as we understand more about the neurological foundations of these processes, they will likely be classified differently.
6. Stable change-resistant personal systems are also created under condition of high intensity. Trauma, startle, and sexual arousal create personal structures that are rigidly durable and self-perpetuating. This condition will be more fully discussed in the next chapter.

Chapter 6

What Emotions and Feelings Really Are!

How does one persuade others that the earth rotates on its axis as it orbits the sun, when it is important for them to believe that the sun rises in the east and sets in the west?

We are now at the heart of this book, where we will witness the unity of selves, feelings, and personal realities as they are joined together stabilizing and destabilizing the NS. It is this union that brings the soul back into psychology from which it was banished by Wilhelm Wundt's (1973) determination to construct a "soulless" psychology.

The soul to which I am referring is not a wish for a life forever after. "Soul" denotes the humanity and/or spirituality that are expressions of the rich emotional beauty and wisdom of human nature. In my vocabulary, spirituality and humanity have closely related meanings. Mahoney (2003) describes the meaning of "soul" and "spirituality" to which I subscribe; he says,

> The word "spiritual" is one whose meaning is rapidly changing. To be spiritual once meant that one was "religious," that is a member of an organized church with explicit creeds and identified community of members. But the meaning of the term "spirituality" began to change dramatically in the 20th Century, particularly with the spread of Buddhism, Taoism, and the planetary popularization of spiritual practices. . . . [T]he word spiritual is now being used as a synonym for "wise."
>
> (p. 163)

By recognizing the structural relationship of the selves, feelings, and personal realities that together make up the person, we can describe personality with a depth of understanding and complexity found in parts of the nonlinear wisdom of Eastern philosophies and the emotional beauty found in the arts of literature and drama. The emotionality, with which psychotherapies that are interested in personality change, emerges from the brain that constructs the experience of the person. Current theories of emotionality are not capable of describing its nonlinear and nonsensory nature.

I owe the title of this chapter to Griffiths (1997). When I first read the title of his book, my heart was warmed. For some 50 years after I received my doctorate in psychology, I found nothing in conventional emotion theory that helped me in my practice. I thought perhaps Griffiths would help me better understand emotionality, which had become a central focus of my psychotherapeutic work. Instead, I found he was a kindred spirit when he said, "My central conclusion [is] that the general concept of emotion is unlikely to be a useful concept in psychological theory" (p. 14). Like me, others have called for a paradigmatic shift in the ways we think about emotionality (Gross, 1992; Izard, 2010; Barrett, 2006).

As we become more able to have a detailed theory of homeostasis, we will be able to more fully make the paradigmatic shift I called for in Chapter 2. This chapter describes the paradigmatic shift that matches the needs of a clinical practice dedicated to characterological personality change and emotion theory.

Reading Nico Frijda's (2005) about "Emotion Experiencing" confronted me with how differently we "understand" emotionality when it is looked at from different paradigms. I have long admired Dr. Frijda's work and felt a kinship with his interest in the emotionality of interpersonal relationships. In his article, he touches on many issues that I believe are essential to the understanding of interpersonal emotionality. He uses consciousness, cognition, and self as important foundations of emotional experience. Even though we use the same psychological terms, they have different definitions in our different paradigms. Because of this, he arrives at conclusions that are different from mine. Within his frame of reference, intentionality and the pleasure/pain dichotomy are meaningful explanations of why we do or don't do things. I have found that these explanations have led me into clinical blind alleys.

The debate about whether love is a drive or an emotion (Dingfelder, 2007) illustrates both the confusion that plagues emotion theory and the confusion created by the outside-in way of thinking about psychological phenomena. Drives, feelings, and emotions are poorly defined terms with different meanings defined in different paradigms (Gross, 2001).

Consequently, when the experience of love being fulfilled is experienced like thirst being quenched, love is thought to be more like a drive than an emotion—that is, if an experience is appetitive in some way it is thought to be more like a drive that has no clearly defined relationship with self-process. This way of defining love is based on how some people experience loving. It is a phenomenological description based on an appetitive paradigm. I will be describing love more fully in Chapter 9.

I see emotion as the NS homeostatically restoring itself to its steady-state condition. Emotion, thought of within this frame, has a direct structural relationship with self-process. Cognitions about the disequilibrated NS activates the mind to cognize selves to facilitate the equilibratory needs of the brain. This is an example of a structural description of self-phenomena. It exemplifies the paradigmatic shift I will be describing as it applies to personality and emotionality.

Increasingly, we are recognizing that commonsense observations of behavior are inaccurate. They are inaccurate because the metatheory underlying behavioral observations has difficulty explaining nonsensory processes occurring in the prefrontal cortex (cf. Roediger, 2004 and my discussion of the Paradigmatic Shift in Chapter 2).

The paradigmatic shift, I have been proposing, is able to structurally conceptualize what are commonly called "drives," cognitively structural ways of describing the homeostatic movement of emotionality. It, also, states that these cognitive constructions about the NS require validation to "feed" their affect hunger. A young man, who spent a frustrating day in a strange city, "coming on to" a woman he finds attractive at a bar is a structural example of the man "feeding" his affect hunger. This idea enables my theory to explain the dynamics of nonsensory process as it interacts with sensory based cognitions.

In the following discussion, I will try to persuade you that my way of thinking is simpler and explains psychological phenomena more completely. The great lesson in Thomas Kuhn's (1970) understanding of paradigmatic shifts is that there is no end point. Each shift is another step on the path of the continuing enrichment of human knowledge.

Underlying most theories of emotionality is the belief that there exists within a person a set of emotions that are distinctively different from one another, that are universally present in mammals, and that cause behavior. "The emotions" is a centuries old way of believing that behavior is activated by a natural kind of emotion. Barrett (2006) describes this way of thinking in the following quote.

> The term *natural kinds* is a philosophical label for what many people already assume about emotion. Many of the most influential scientific treatments of emotion are founded on the view that certain emotion categories (such as anger, sadness, fear, disgust, and happiness) carve nature at its joints. It is assumed that each kind of emotion can be identified by a more or less unique signature response (within the body) that is triggered or evoked by a distinct causal mechanism (within the brain). As a result, it should be possible to recognize distinct emotions in other people, identify them in one's self, and measure them in the face, physiology, and behavior.
>
> (p. 30) (original emphasis)

Emotions within this traditional frame are static "building blocks" or "elements" that can be measured, analyzed, constructed into an explanatory whole in much the same way European physical science of the eighteenth and nineteenth centuries enriched our knowledge and lives. However, employing that paradigm to psychological phenomena ignores their nonsensory (physiological) nature. They are equilibratory processes where movement and duality are their autochthonous characteristics. Ignoring them reifies psychological process. Reification lies at the heart of the concept of "basic emotions."

Many theorists have looked for the "elemental" nature of feelings in the hope of discovering that the "basic units" of emotion will enable them to construct an emotional periodic table that could give us the same kind of understanding of psychology that it gave us in chemistry and physics. Others have attempted to conceptualize emotions as though they were like light displayed on a color wheel. Physical things are highly predictable. They don't move. They stay put. Casual observations of everyday objects are experienced with familiarity. The visual experience of color has a tempting invariance that invites simplistic theories of emotionality.

The visual experience of regularity is the invariance upon which scientific theories are built. The regularity of physical processes that are perceived by the sensory systems is different from the regularities of the nonsensory process of the prefrontal cortex. These are the regularities of psychological phenomena. But they are not visually seen or processed by any of the sensory systems.

Psychological theories based on visual observation are cast into a commonsense paradigm. Commonsense oriented psychologists, like Heider (1958) and Kimble (2000) are theorists who rely upon the phenomenal (sensory) appearance of behavior as the data base for their theories. Kimble states this position in the following quote.

> Behaviorism is any psychology that sees its mission as the explanation of behavior and accepts stimuli (more generally, situations) and responses as its basic data. If psychology wants to be a science . . . it must adopt some form of that approach. Science aims at understanding publicly [visually] observable happenings in the world, and only such events available to psychology are responses and the situations in which they are likely to occur.
>
> (p. 208)

If one defines "behavior" broadly to mean any reaction, body movement, or neurological movement and "stimuli" as the cause of (a response to) behavior, then it is "reasonable" to believe that this is the way to conduct psychological science. Within this frame of reference, behaviorism makes common sense (Heider, 1958). While it may have the advantage of an easy, familiar way of thinking, it is unable to readily conceptualize the complexity of the nonsensory nature of personality.

Behaviorism cannot operationalize three issues that are vital to an understanding of emotionality and personality.

(1) The terms "behavior" and "stimuli" are so broadly defined they are unable to describe or explain cerebral dynamics.

(2) Behaviorism tells us nothing about the nature of process, the dynamics of emotionality. By "process," I mean the interaction of small systems designed to restore the integrity of a larger system to its stable-state condition. With respect to the brain, process means homeostasis, the restoration of brain systems to their stable-state conditions. These synonymous terms about autoregulation within the brain all refer to its continuous ongoing activities. Within this definition of process, the concept of a "stimulus and response" (S-R) explanation of behavior becomes meaningless. Furthermore, the nonsensory nature of the unending interaction of the prefrontal cortex with the limbic system raises questions about the nature of stimulus and response that S-R behaviorism cannot answer.

Behaviorism can describe the sequential occurrence of two variables. But it tells the scientist nothing about the processes occurring between the variables that cause them to operate sequentially. It can predict that the lights of my study will illuminate if I turn an electrical switch on the wall of my study. There is nothing between the turn of the switch and the lights coming on that illuminates "how" the lights come on. The absence of process in behaviorism is evident in the static theoretical isolation of such variables as self, feelings, emotion, and person.

And (3) behaviorism has hidden within it a homunculus that enables it to create the illusion that it is able to describe movement (process). There is a "foundational" belief in behaviorism that the self initiates behavior without being triggered by an external stimulus. I will quote again from Kimble (2000) because the following quote exemplifies the nonconscious mistaken use of the homunculus: "Every weekday morning, on your way to work or school, you put your car on automatic pilot and devote your thoughts to the problems you will meet when you get there" (p. 210).

The "you" in the quote refers to a self which is uncritically used. As we saw in the last chapter, the self, like the "I," is the experience of orientation. It simply locates where a person is in a situation that is not being automatically processed. It is not the initiator of action. The "self" and the "I" are different words for the same process. Imbedded in the meaning of Kimble's sentence is the assumption that the self is the initiator of action and thought—"you put your car on automatic." Unfortunately, Kimble does not tell you what the stimulus was that got you to put your car on automatic pilot or how the automatic pilot enabled you to devote your thoughts to whatever. He also assumes that you will think "about the problems you will meet when you get there." That happens sometimes, but it assumes an invariance that doesn't exist.

Most middle-class adults have this experience. It is a familiar experience, which gives his description a ring of truth. Speaking this way conveys meaning about motivation. The truth is about everyday experience. But it tells us nothing, theoretically, about motivation. Yes, we do go on automatic on our way to work. But the self he is referring to is a homunculus because it suggests that it is the activator of behavior and thought. But how does the "little person in the head," a fictional projection of our minds, explain how the self activates behavior? This way of speaking does convey a sense of meaning. Unfortunately, the meaning of social conversation does not explain the paradox of believing we are only responsive to stimuli while at the same time we have intentional control over our behavior. The comfort of social meanings creates the impression of invariance that is used as a measure of "truth" in psychological research.

However, there is a difference between the stability of social custom or habituated behavior and the invariance of planetary rotation. The sun does rise in the east and sets in the west, but beyond casual observation the earth has a gravitational relationship with the sun that is not readily seen at sunrise or sunset.

Like our experience of the sun rising and setting, the axiomatic way of speaking about emotionality creates sets of assumptions about it and its role in the management of psychological information. The assumption that the self is the originator of action leads to the aphorism, "I am the captain of the ship and the master of my fate." This comfortable, habituated belief about the self gives it the appearance of being obviously true. Yet when it is closely examined, the variable and unreliable role that the self plays in the control of behavior, it, clearly, is a weak explanation. Think of New Year's resolutions. The self is only reliably associated with intentional control when an unemotional person is engaged in simple highly overlearned behaviors (cf. Wyer, 1997). I agree with Kimble (2000) that "establishing the physical reality of concepts is difficult, that undertaking has an important benefit. It creates a symbiotic relationship between behavioral and biological psychology. Behavioral concepts tell biological psychology what to look for in experiments" (p. 209).

Turning his conclusion upside down, I think that biological (neurological) psychology can tell behavioral psychology what to look for in experiments. The exploding growth of research through neuroimaging technology can provide the bedrock invariant foundation for which psychology has been looking.

It is upon the physical invariance of brain structures that a productive research-based understanding of human behavior and experience can now be anchored. Theories of human nature based on a folk psychology of phenomenal, culturally contaminated, behavioral observation are an unreliable database for psychology. They have not provided much for the growth of knowledge about emotionality.

In her review of 100 years of research based on the belief that there are such things as "the emotions" or as "basic emotions," Barrett (2006) states that

> Given all the scientific activity, and the general importance of emotion in the science of mind, it is surprising that knowledge about emotion has accumulated more slowly than knowledge about other comparable concepts like memory or attention. . . . I suggest that progress in the scientific understanding of emotion is not, as one might assume, hampered by disagreements. Instead, I argue that progress is limited by the wide acceptance of assumptions that are not warranted by the available empirical evidence. . . . [O]ur perceptual processes lead us to aggregate emotional processing into categories that do not necessarily reveal the causal nature of emotional processing. I suggest that, as a result, the natural kind view has outlived its scientific value and now presents a major obstacle to understanding what emotions are and how they work. (p. 28–29)

Clinicians, regardless of theoretical affiliation, in moments of a psychotherapy session, are most interested in the nature of the unique dynamics that are occurring within the person they are serving. For example, a therapist works with an obese man who is struggling to lose weight, talks about falling off the wagon and eating a Big Mac, a weight-gaining hamburger. The therapist knows that the man did not eat the hamburger because he was physically hungry. The therapist also knows that on other occasions the man successfully resisted stuffing himself with a hamburger, one of his favorite foods. It was only afterward that the man told his therapist he went to a party and none of the single women there were interested in him. He left the party and stopped at a fast food restaurant, had a hamburger and, for the moment, assuaged his affect hunger (disappointed loneliness). Conventional psychological research tells the therapist nothing about these emotional dynamics. Research does not describe the momentary unique dynamics of the individual that do initiate action. In the following discussion, homeostatic movement can describe emotionality.

Emotionality

When the equilibratory dynamics of the prefrontal cortex or information from the external environment cannot be automatically processed in any part of the brain or its body, the NS is disequilibrated. The NS, then, homeostatically attempts to restore itself to its steady-state condition. The NS automatically triggers various limbic systems that sustain the life and reproductive capacities of the individual. When they are activated, different parts of the disequilibrated body are brought into awareness. Experiences of these reactions are the nonsensory experience of emotions.

What Emotions and Feelings Really Are!   123

Some experiences of emotion are cognitively labeled; others are not. When emotions are cognitively classified, they are experienced as feelings. This is the difference between emotions and feelings that has unfortunately been ignored in both clinical and research psychology.

Classification is the beginning of explanation. Recall, in Chapter 3, I described explanation as neurologically stabilizing as well as being a psychological function. Feelings are genetically organized to stabilize emotion; restore the brain to its steady-state condition. In Chapter 8, "A Portrait of the Person," I will again describe the condition where feelings can also become a source of destabilization.

In everyday experience, emotions and feelings are experientially blended. Usually the experience of a feeling is displayed in focal awareness with the experience of emotion lying in the background of awareness. Recall, in Chapter 3, I described consciousness as displaying information in both the fore and background of awareness. This blended experience leads one to believe that an individual is experiencing a singular motionless thing. Contrary to that belief, I will be describing emotionality as a moving dualistic process that is shaped by the evolutionary growth of the brain, the culture within which it matures, and the early childhood socialization of the person.

Evolutionary and Cultural Influences Relating to Emotionality

From ancient times to the present, theories of emotionality suffer with commonsense judgments imbedded in them. While this may be an efficient way of engaging in emotionally casual situations, it can be disastrous when an understanding of emotional growth is necessary. In the next chapter, I will describe the importance of embracing emotions and feelings as information that helps a person know what is happening to her and taking that information seriously without judging it, impulsively acting upon it, or denying it before being informed by the message contained within it.

While reading a review of Freud's thinking about emotionality (Stein, 1991), it struck me that he was experiencing emotionality differently from the ways emotion in the United States is experienced and written about today. In large part, the difference between Freud's experience and current United States experiencing and thinking about emotionality is cultural. People, in different cultures, experience and use feelings differently. Also, people in different historical times, within the same culture, are trained differently in the use of their emotionalities.

People of different cultures, within the same time period, experience emotionality differently. For example, Argentinean and Finnish emotionalities in the early twenty-first century are experienced and interpersonally used very differently. Both cultures love to dance the tango. The emotional differences between them are clearly seen in how they dance it. There are cultural and historical differences between Viennese and American emotionality. These differences contribute to the different ways in which emotionality is conceptualized.

Historical cultural change also shapes the ways emotionalities are experienced and used. The cultural emotionality of Vienna a century ago is different from its emotionality today (cf. Freud, 1997). He had the same negative, aversive reaction toward affect and especially its intensity that eighteenth century-philosophical empiricists had. A quote from Stein (1991) describes his point of view:

> Freud considers hysterical conversion to be superior to the obsessional solution, because "the former deals better with affect" . . . in that the affect in hysteria is expelled from the "psychical sphere," i.e., out of consciousness altogether. This illustrates the prevalent conception that affect is a quantity and that the more definitely one gets rid of it, the better.
>
> (p. 6)

Eighteenth-century philosophic empiricists passionately wanted to rid themselves of emotionality that disturbed the order and comfortable (but illusory) precision of their religious explorations (Becker, 1932). Both Freud and Plato wished that they could intentionally rid themselves of the distress of internal emotional intensity and the disruption of cognitive tranquility.

The difference between Freud's and current thinking about emotionality brings to mind a human conundrum. On the one hand, individuals, throughout the span of their lives, are change resistant, and on the other hand, human nature over a very long span of time and throughout the diversity of cultures is a plastic system molded by the genetic growth of the brain and the changing social environment into which it is born.

The conundrum is resolved when the plasticity of brain structures is seen as being cast into cultural "molds" that change over historical and evolutionary time. I am using the term "molds" as a shorthand way of referring to brain growth. Human nature of a given culture and epoch are shaped by brain growth. The change-resistant homeostatic imperative of these molds results from the development of stabilizing, self-perpetuating cognitive structures, which maintain the integrity and stability of the persons of individuals who are living in a given period of time.

Humans in different parts of the world adapt to the conditions of their differing environments and cultures. Once these adaptations have become established, the Neurological Selves, nourished in these environments, work to homeostatically maintain the automaticity of their operations. As humans gathered together in larger communities, they required more complex ways of creating predictable and safer ways of living together. The effort to establish social order led to the creation of mythic authority figures that enunciated rules of social conduct and created power structures to enforce adherence to them. Once beliefs in mythologies became articles of faith, authority became rigidly established. These belief systems were so complex, they not only served as social accommodators, they also explained the relationship of the individual to his or her environment. These belief systems stabilized the Neurological Selves of community members and they instituted and supported the social power structures of their communities. Habituated socio-emotional systems enabled individuals to be less anxious and more comfortable in predictable and secure social environments, even though in most instances they also frequently become oppressive to individual expression. Freud recognized this in his description of the Superego as the oppressor of the Id.

Mythic systems throughout the world have different names but their cognitive structures are remarkably similar. Many mythologies contain an image of a "warrior" having the courage to face into the anxiety-filled mysteries of personal existence. The conflation of anxiety with fear reflects the continuing human confusion about the difference that exists between these emotional experiences. In the warrior myth, there is also a promise that the exercise of that courage is rewarded with wisdom, the wisdom of emotional knowledge that enables one to have greater control over the direction of his life.

The metaphor of the warrior describes a person who is able to confront anxiety existing within his person. In this confrontation, he can experience the feelings that are hidden in the mystifying clouds of his anxiety. Feelings, as explanations, sweep emotional fog away and enable him to more clearly know the nature of the confusion that resides within him and his relationships to others. With this knowledge, he is calmer, more self-assured, and wiser.

As human emotionality becomes more skilled in its ability to maintain the equilibrium of the NS, humans experience it with greater specificity, articulate it more elaborately, and it becomes increasingly independent of the automaticity of autoregulatory imperatives. By "autoregulatory imperatives," I mean emotional habits formed in early childhoods that were designed to stabilize the developing NS. Escaping habituated emotional beliefs and rituals liberates the person from the confusions and conflicts of childhood and increases his ability to creatively engage in the adventure of adult living.

Histories of the development of theories about self (Martin and Barresi, 2006) and emotion (Reddy, 2001) describe the growth and change occurring in both the experience and complexity of these aspects of human experience. The experience of the NS and its emotionality is an evolutionary and culturally changing process.

Dichotomy and Judgment

In Chapter 3, I described dichotomous thinking as being a commonsense judgment in the sense that the dichotomies are based on how they are experienced as positive or negative, good or bad, or right or wrong. These are largely classifications of cultural value judgments about things. They do not describe the process that is being dichotomized in and of itself (Kant's "ding an sich") or how it relates to personality. For example, the description of emotions as being positive or negative is a judgment about that which is culturally or personally[1] desired or avoided.

Dichotomous judgments are simply classifications of cultural/personal evaluations about different kinds of emotionality. While some find this dichotomy to be correlated with the ways people in a particular culture generally behave, it does not describe emotionality in relation to anything about the dynamics of self-process. I have found that when a person becomes intensely emotional, the regularity of the dichotomy breaks down. While dichotomous regularity may hold true almost all of the time when it comes to ice cream, it does not hold true when it comes to intense adult loving experiences.

In individual experience, curiosity-terminating judgment can occur when a feeling arises from a moment in which character structure invalidates the personal identity of the person.[2] I worked with a man who found it difficult to experience or talk about his pain because he did not want to be called a "wimp." Pain, for him, had become an enduring characterological structure. His pain originated in an emotionally deprived and isolated childhood. Yet to show it would violate an aspect of his personal reality, which he developed to protect himself from his father's competitiveness and the rough and tumble aggression that battered the streets of his childhood. His tough machismo shielded him from the ever-present threat of humiliation that plagued his childhood.

This habituated bravura contributed to the creation of a dreadfully painful marriage. He was unable to let his wife know how much she was hurting him when she withdrew from his anger, which was an expression of his pain that saved him from shedding the tears that would humiliate him. His anger caused her to retreat from him even more, a heart-wrenching vicious cycle. His dread of being humiliated deprived him of the love of his wife that he desired more than life itself. He would have died for her. His judgment about the expression of pain created even more pain.

To this point, I have described the difference between my ways of thinking about emotionality and theories of emotionality influenced by judgment and behavioral observation alone. I have also described the changing cultural and historical ways that emotionality is experienced. Next, I will contrast my theory from other current theories.

My Theory and Others'

While the metatheory, underlying my way of thinking about emotionality, is paradigmatically different from conventional academic ways of thinking about emotionality, it touches upon main themes existing in psychology's laboratory. Like theirs, mine encompasses experiences of both the mind and the body. Mine also recognizes cognition, which is conventionally called "appraisals." Coping and/or adaptation, popular concepts describing the function of emotionality, are also included in the way I use equilibration as the motivational center of the person. Despite each of these congruent theoretical alignments, I found no easy way to integrate my theory with theirs to create a coherent clinical description of psychotherapeutic process. My theory does not dichotomize emotionality, nor does it reify it. It recognizes the duality of emotionality and the nonsensory nature of its autoregulatory process.

Intimately related to the idea of basic emotions is the idea that the basicness can be classified as being "positive" or "negative" (Tomkins, 1962, 1963); a form of the Pleasure Principle. The pleasure principle is another one of the conventional beliefs that created confusion for me in my practice. As I said earlier, dichotomous classification is simply a statement of value. It does not accurately describe what feelings really are. It led me into interpersonal blind alleys with people with whom I was traveling on their therapeutic journeys. In moments of high emotional intensity, people rarely subscribe to cultural emotional vocabularies and practices. Rather, they fall back on characterological emotional habits. When emotionality becomes integrated with an individual's person, it becomes habituated. I describe emotional skills as habituated systems created and repeatedly practiced from childhood to adulthood.

My theory of emotionality is a contemporary restatement of the James–Lange theory of emotion (James, 1890/1950). Like most current theories of emotionality, it is a dual theory where the term "emotionality" encompasses both the body and its mind. While some theories recognize a difference between emotions and feelings, they do not functionally describe their differences.

Unlike James's theory, my theory classifies limbic action that results in experiences of internal body movement, like adrenaline rushes, sweaty palms, or changes in blood pressure or distribution, rather than classifying overt physical behavior. Instead of knowing that I am afraid, when I observe my body running away from a bear (an example James used), I know I am afraid/anxious when I experience a rush of adrenaline in my chest. The experience of nonsensory limbic bodily process is different from the sensory experience of my body running away from a bear. This is the difference between James–Lange's description and mine. We both recognize emotionality as a movement of the body with an equilibratory explanation about that movement. Equilibratory (cognitive) "explanations" are not truth oriented. They are mindless homeostatic processes. This leads me into the next chapter, where I will describe emotion and feelings within my paradigmatic frame.

Notes

1. In the next chapter, I will describe feelings as being either social or idiosyncratic.
2. Character structure and personal identity will be discussed more fully in Chapter 8.

Chapter 7
Emotions and Feelings

There Really Is a Difference!

At the end of the first chapter, I suggested that the difficulty research and clinical psychologists have in communicating effectively with one another is because they use the same words to explain different phenomena. For psychotherapists, "emotion" connotes nonsensory movement in relation to self-process, and conventional research regards emotion as a static phenomenon with no relationship to self-process (Gross, 2001). Furthermore, there are differences between feelings and emotions that have not been clearly described. This chapter will describe how they are different cerebrally and psychologically.

Emotion

A brain-based theory of emotions and feelings using homeostasis as an explanation of the movement of emotionality can integrate it with the dynamics of personality. Emotions are experiences of genetically developed homeostatic processes of the NS returning itself to its steady-state condition. With this definition, emotion becomes a self-process. For example, when a woman hasn't eaten for the whole day, she will experience nutritional hunger. Movement in her stomach will trigger midbrain systems, which send error messages to her NS. These, in turn, trigger her mind to think of food; recall the NS is a part of the mind. This is a description of the experience of a genetically activated homeostatic process. If she had a good lunch, but hasn't seen her lover for three weeks, she is likely to experience a longing to see him as soon as possible. This is an example of a personality process; activated by the affect hunger of her prefrontal cortex that also sends an error signal to her NS, which also responds to it as a hunger signal. But this signal is different from a nutritional hunger signal. A major source of human confusion, because it is difficult for some to differentiate, is the experience of a nutritional hunger from the affect hunger of her NS (self-systems).

Feelings, on the other hand, are the explanations and plans she tells herself about what will happen when she sees him. This is the difference between emotions and feelings. Emotions are experiences of the body. Feelings are experiences of cognitions, explanations, and plans of action, about the meaning (an experience of the mind) of emotions and what to do about them.

Before primates developed a large prefrontal cortex, emotion did not exist. There was only limbic activity regulating physiological and survival processes of the body. Brain size grew in its ability to manage more and more of the complexity of the external environment. This resulted in the creation of a mind with the ability to experience and classify both sensory information and the nonsensory processes of the prefrontal cortex and the rest of the brain.

The prefrontal cortex and parts of the limbic system became the specialized regulator of the rest of the brain including the NS. The integrated prefrontal cortex/limbic system is the neurological home of personality. The neurological systems underlying childhood personality structures, like all other neurological systems, with practice become "permanent." In early childhood, deeply emotional family-based personality systems are created. With repeated practice, they become self-perpetuating and, frequently, are in conflict with emerging new neurological systems to cope with increasingly complex emotional environments.

In following chapters, I will be describing them these systems as character structures. Then, as the child engages more and more with the world of friends, school, relatives, and so on, an externally oriented personality system emerges. I will be describing this development as personal identity. There is always the "child" (character structure) in us, who either destabilizes more mature personality structures or who disturbs its older person residing in personal identity. Not all character structures are maladaptive. Childhood character structures contribute to love and play in the mature person, who has integrated character structures and personal identities that work well together—most of the time.

The experiential blending of the selves, feelings, and personal realities of the person creates the uniqueness of individual experiencing. There is a complication in the last sentence. Underlying the experience of the different cognitions about the person are the homeostatic dynamics of the neurological systems that are not directly experienced. Cognitions about neurological systems and nonsensory, automated physical systems are experienced differently. Together, they form the person. I will discuss this complication more fully in the next chapter.

Emotionality is the term I use to denote integrated experiences of emotion and feelings. Most spontaneous emotional experiences display emotions in the background of awareness and feelings in focal awareness. A man being visited by his mother, whom he hasn't seen for several years, will have uncomfortable bodily sensations, when she walks into his living room and criticizes him for past sins. Her criticism touches the pain of his childhood, which destabilizes his NS. His character structure reacts first with emotion and then with feelings. When this happens, the NS mindlessly activates limbic systems to which it is connected to stabilize itself. This is the experience of emotionality.

Error signals from the prefrontal cortex to the NS are not the same as those triggered by the senses or reactions arising in the body from illness or other dysfunctions. Experiences of the body initiated by the prefrontal cortex are "physiologically structured homeostatic processes." They are experienced like, but are not the same as, information coming from the body or the senses. The experience of body reactions activated by the prefrontal cortex's regulatory process triggering the NS is emotion. This is the difference between the nausea of a sick stomach and the nausea of emotional disgust. This elaborate, strangely experienced system of relationships between the NS and the prefrontal cortex underlies much of the beauty and anguish of human nature.

Things and Processes

The following discussion of emotionality requires a description of neurological process that is consistent with the dynamic interactions occurring within the enormous complexity of the brain. Ordinarily, we think of the interaction of two things as creating a process. If I light a match and touch it to kindling, it will start a fire. Unlike lighting a fire, the brain is a complex, fluid, constantly moving living thing activating many different systems simultaneously.

The brain consists of nerves: 100 billion of them. Cerebral nerves, as things, working in their biochemical "soup," engage in multitudinous relationships with one another. They produce processes some of which are experienced as self-consciousness. There are no simple one-on-one relationships in the brain. They interact with one another with different frequencies. And they have more than one relationship with other nerves. As a matter of fact, they are organized into different configurations, about which we know too little. The next great surge in knowledge about human nature will occur when a theory of homeostasis illuminates the nature of the relationship between the brain and human nature.

Neurological systems serve different functions. Some are devoted to activating the distribution of blood in the body when a person is fighting to protect himself. Others alert us to cold or heat. They create a kind of super system that, with continued use, operates automatically. Furthermore, individual systems within a particular super system frequently are also parts of other super systems.

This is true of the NS. It is a part of many super systems that require it to homeostatically interact with many other genetically structured survival systems like hunger, fight or flight, mating, temperature control, and more. It, also as I described in Chapter 3, serves as one of the three systems that comprise the mind. The NS is one of three systems that interact with different information-processing systems which are experienced differently. Sensory information is experienced differently than nonsensory information. Despite the experiential difference between these functions, the NS's contribution in the different super systems is the same. It is a major survival system: orientation.

NS's Limited Orientation Process

Over eons of evolutionary growth, the NS and its homeostatic partner, the prefrontal cortex, from which a person is experienced, became able to differentiate disequilibrium in the body from disequilibrium in the person. The orienting process of the NS can discriminate the experiential differences between movement in the body, the senses, and in the prefrontal cortex.

The twenty-first-century NS automatically activates the same regulatory systems it used before the prefrontal cortex became the miraculously complex system it is today. For example, the NS distinguishes between the movement in the stomach of nutrient hunger or prefrontal cortex's need for the fulfillment of its affect hunger. In both cases, the NS orients itself to the source of disturbance. When hunger is experienced, the NS receives signals of systems needing either nutrition or exercise.

The mind (the interaction of the NS, consciousness, and cognition) identifies whether the source of disturbance is in the body, the senses, or in the person. If the disturbance is in the undernourished stomach, the person experiences a desire for food. The affect hunger of the prefrontal cortex is made more complex by cognitive operations of the mind and, therefore, the response to its affect hunger is more variable than a simple search for food. In my practice I have seen a high correlation between loneliness (affect hunger in the person) and obesity. But sex or work or other efforts developed in the person are also used to feed affect hunger.

Unlike the cognitive classification of feelings, the NS's similarity or analogical process has little or no explanatory component to it. It only uses structural similarity to react to information that is disequilibrating it. It mindlessly causes a bodily response when a prefrontal cortical dissonance seeks equilibration from the NS. This triggers the experience of emotion.

Emotion has a wide variety of analogical experiences of the body that range from "You give me a headache" to "I am hungry for you." Notice, that in the last two sentences describing intense emotional experiences the first-person singular pronoun locates the distress in the "I" of the NS, not in the head or genitalia. The "headache" or "hungry" are analogies describing the disequilibria of the person triggering a homeostatic response from the NS. From the top of the head to the bottom of the torso, experiences of the NS occur as primitive equilibratory operations, some of which are cognitively labeled.

When the "I" is attached to the experience of emotion, the person knows that the disturbance is not in the body.[1] This is the difference between the experience of a stomachache and the experience of emotion. Using the river analogy, when the river of homeostasis is flowing within its normative banks, a physically ill person simply experiences a stomachache, a chill, a fever, or another display of bodily malfunction. Under this condition, the person locates the difficulty in her body, cognitively categorizes the malfunction, and then comes to a decision about what to do about it. These experiences are not experiences of emotion. They are experiences of being sick. There are exceptions to this example in the case of persons who use physical illness for emotional purposes as in the cases of malingering or hypochondria.

Experiences of emotion are complex and are frequently intermingled with one another. Depressed people experience pain and anxiety as well as other uncomfortable bodily sensations in the movement of equilibration. I have never seen a person experiencing emotion from a single limbic site. Under conditions of extreme disequilibration that produce the mindstorms I described in Chapter 3, persons experience combinations of bodily sensations. Some of these sensations have culturally recognized labels, others do not and are experienced as distress or uneasiness, and some emotions are called feelings by some people.

The distressing experience of enduring cingulate (NS) dissonance underlies addictions, obsessive/compulsive behaviors, and other repetitive maladaptive behaviors or ways of thinking. This is the experience of disequilibrium. It is a generalized emotion without specific bodily origins. The experiential palette of the agonizingly destabilized NS drives people to drown its excruciating emotional "noise" with drugs, alcohol, cigarettes, sex, gambling, or whatever an individual person is trained to use to silence it. When the disequilibrium of the NS occurs in early childhood, anguished patterns of coping with it become habituated and become automated systems within the individual's character structure.

Frequently, the reequilibration of the NS occurs quickly. This is the moment Stern (2004) describes as the "now," which he estimates to be between six to ten seconds: the time it takes to restore the NS to its steady-state condition. However, when people are severely depressed or anxious, the disequilibrium of the NS can last for hours, days, or a lifetime.

Midbrain systems have long been known to mediate metabolic and survival processes that sustain the life of the individual. I have been told that Karl Pribram, the famed neuroscientist, once described the limbic system as the manager of the four F's of existence: fight, flight, feeding, and "sex." Orientation is the regulator of the limbic system. Without it, mammals could not find food, find mates, escape from danger, or defend themselves.

It is not my purpose to create a classification of the experience of limbic regulation. Using Pribram's classification, it is apparent that the experience of his four systems is displayed in awareness differently. The behaviors underlying feeding, fighting, fleeing, and sex use different systems in the body. The nonsensory experiential qualia of these systems are, understandably, different. The experience of fighting and fleeing is not at all like the experience of sexual arousal or sexual engagement, although they are known to interact passionately with one another. Obviously, different limbic systems have different experiential qualia. The experiential differences contribute to the mind creating different explanations about their meaning to the person.

Emotion and Character Structure

Allan Schore's (1994) "central thesis" of his book succinctly describes what I believe is the foundation of character structure. He says, "The central thesis of this book is that the early environment, mediated by the primary caregiver, directly influences the evolution of structures in the brain that are responsible for the future socioemotional development of the child" (p. 62).

The habituation of limbic process during infancy is, in large part, emotional, and, therefore, right-brained. This is the beginning of a description of change resistance that challenges psychotherapeutic effort. Character structure is the emotional soil from which the person grows. Character structure is emotionality in habituated movement.

Even before birth, the fetus interacts with his mother. In the womb, the orienting system of the infant is genetically responding to information about the mother and the environment to which she is reacting (Brazelton and Greenspan, 2000). After birth the infant is even more actively engaged with his mother and increasingly with the world around him (Siegel, 1999). The infant requires not only protection from the environment and food to feed his growing body but also sensory stimulation and emotional contact are needed to feed the affect hunger of his growing NS and his emerging person.

Touch and physical contact are major nutrients for the feeding of an infant's affect hunger (Eliot, 1999; Montagu, 1971; Gunzenhauser and Brazelton, 1990). The nourishment of affect is enormously important in establishing the foundations for a strong, stable NS. The emotional messages that are sent to children when they are touched and held and the kind of emotional contact that is made are highly complex and contribute to the formation of uniquely different personalities.

In previous chapters, I have pointed to the rich research literature about sensory and social deprivation documenting the enduring damage to the person and its emotionality caused by emotional starvation during infancy and early childhood (Harlow, 1974; Spitz, 1946; Zubek, 1969; Chugani et al., 2001). Anecdotal accounts of failed attempts to socialize feral children present dramatic evidence of the enduring negative effects of the absence of loving contact during early childhood experiencing. On the other side, there are equally dramatic stories about the skills children achieve to enrich their attachments with loving caregivers.

Young children learn patterns of movement from the emotionality they experience in their mother's arms. Parental character structures shape the emotional roots of their children. Mothers and fathers react to their children from the pains and joys of their own childhoods. Parents, for the most part, inadvertently and nonconsciously teach their children how to feel and react emotionally by modeling emotional patterning in their own behaviors and by requiring emotional compliance from their children. Since character structures are habituated, automatic emotional systems, most parents are not aware of how the subtleties of their emotional systems impact the emotional strength and skill of their children.

As children begin to walk and talk, they attend to the emotional reactions of those to whom they are attached. The information gathered from this attention becomes the template of the person's emotionality. In moments of stress or surprise, the child will look to her mother to know how to respond emotionally to a startling or novel situation. Both the strengths and weaknesses of personal development flow from the movement of family drama.

In the following discussion, I will be focusing primarily on the pain and distress of the human condition grown from the emotional difficulties parents have with their children, because they are the emotional conflicts with which I work. However, the love and beauty of human nature are also nourished in families who understand and cherish the developmental needs of their children.

I have worked with mothers who, being painfully mothered by their own competitive mothers, could not stand the daughters they bore. These women either physically tortured their daughters, in the name of training, or became so depressed that they could barely permit themselves to touch them. Some of these mothers, who could not make loving emotional contact with their daughters as they were growing into adulthood, grieved years later because they had lost the ability to make contact with their grown daughters.

Men, whose fathers beat them in their infancy, developed psychotic or borderline personalities. I have known men who were loved and accepted by their fathers during infancy and early childhood. After they became emotionally older than their fathers, they were painfully rejected. These sons bore the scars of rejection for the rest of their lives.

Adults and adolescents, who were raised under conditions of severe parental oppression, lived in the anguish of not being able to experience much of either emotion or feelings. They dwelled in a dreadful emotional emptiness: an emotional isolation cell permitting little or no emotional contact with others. I recall working with a 14-year old girl, who escaped the anguish of emotional emptiness by scarring herself with a razor blade from her wrists to the armpits of both her arms. The pain of the razor blade was better than helplessly living in the prison of anomie. It let her know that she was alive. She could feel "something." It also provoked pain and anxiety in her parents; that too was emotionally meaningful to her. Their distress about her self-mutilation provided some nourishment for her affect hunger.

Depression, pain, and anxiety arise from a person's inability to cognize these emotions into feelings. Frequently hidden in the fog of emotional emptiness are structures of anger and love moving outside of focal awareness. With patience, some people can sit still and look into their emotional fog banks and see vague forms of anger and loneliness moving about within them. By "emotional fog banks," I mean the wretched experiential mixture of anxiety/depression/distress emotions which contain few words of explanation. They have no cognitive labels to identify what is disturbing them. The ways children cope with the emotional patterns of everyday family life are practiced for years. Unfortunately, practice does not make patterns perfect. Practice makes them permanent (Gladwell, 2008).

The emotional skills practiced in childhood become habituated parts of the person's character structure. As such, they stabilize both the person and consequently the NS. Being habituated systems, they operate nonconsciously. The nonconscious nature of their operations underscores the automatic, unintentional, nature of the ways they function. They are self-perpetuating, functionally autonomous psychological systems. The processes of self-perpetuation and functional autonomy make them the challenging change-resistant systems with which people struggle in psychotherapy.

Feelings

I have the same difficulty with the word "feelings" that I have with the word "emotions." Feelings and emotions denote plurality. Using them in this way contains an implication that feelings are distinctive singular things. The term "the emotions" is assumed to contain a number of different distinctive emotions. Some theorists claim that there are usually between six and nine emotions.

The same is true of feelings. Using the plural assumes that there are different singular feelings (cf. Barrett's, 2006 discussion of "kinds" of emotions in the previous chapter). There is a specific number of names for feelings, which are needed for communicative purposes. It is important for one individual to verbally inform and influence another person about what he or she needs or wants. It should be recognized, however, that the names of feelings we use in everyday conversation simply denote cerebral processes that are commonly experienced. They do not denote "things." They are labels of nonsensory processes operating within a person. I will be using the terms "feelings" and "emotions" for heuristic purposes only.

Within the frame of the following discussion, I do not assume the presence of fixed entities that are as different from one another as footballs and lingerie. Feelings and emotions have culturally created cognitive labels roughly denoting the equilibratory movement of the NS. "They" are cultural labels of differently experienced equilibratory processes.

Feelings are a form of explanation. They are cognitive constructions that explain (not necessarily truthfully) the disequilibrium of a person. This is where explanation as a cortical process stabilizes the NS. Feelings also are attached to action programs designed to remedy the disturbance. These programs are genetically and individually designed to remediate the disequilibrium of the NS and its person.

The difference between a feeling and emotion is exemplified by the difference between fear and anxiety. They both have similar body experiential qualities. Anxiety is a word used to describe the bodily experience of adrenaline rushing through the body. When asked to talk about the reason for her discomfort, an anxious person will complain that she does not know the cause of her discomfort. It's been my experience that anxiety occurs when a person is unable to experience a feeling with which they do not have emotional skill or familiarity. A woman who has been taught to deny the experience of anger will experience anxiety rather than being angry.

On the other hand, fear is a feeling with an explanation. I have had the experience of a person to whom I was being introduced as a psychotherapist say that she was afraid of me. She wasn't afraid that I would attack her; she became anxious by the idea that I might see something about her that she didn't want me or anybody to see. This is where people conflate emotions with feelings. If a person cannot readily explain an experience of emotion (a body experience), his mind will seek to find a stabilizing explanation that is experientially similar to his bodily reaction. This is one of the reasons why feelings and emotions have not been clearly differentiated.

Feelings, as a form of cognition, are a system within the person. They stabilize the NS in two ways. First, they explain emotion. Explanations, meanings, and understandings are experiences of cognition that specifically equilibrate the NS. Cortical process equilibrates limbic activity. Anything confronting the person that is not understood or explained creates tension, the bodily part of anxiety. Tension and its anxiety are reduced by explanation or understanding. This is a major reason why explanatory systems, including psychotherapeutic interpretations, are so highly treasured, regardless of their truth value.

Second, feelings facilitate interpersonal engagement. The interpersonal expression of feelings is almost always used to, unintentionally and/or automatically, solicit validating feedback. Obviously, feelings are also used to deliberately influence the person or persons toward whom they are directed. This was discussed more intensively in Chapter 1 when I described dyadic communication.

No one experiences feelings in the same way that others experience them. We all sing the same song differently. While it is true that different bodily experiences are activated when the NS is in disequilibrium, the transformative movement of cognitive classification and cerebral autoregulation makes it impossible to create the same kind of fixed categories we create with physical objects.

The Double Duality of Feelings

Feelings are doubly dualistic. Persons have social and personal lexicons of feelings. There are feelings used in everyday social relationships that have little or no emotional content, and there are feelings used when a person is in an intense emotional relationship. Another way of saying this is that there are feelings used by the person's character structure and there are feelings used by the person who is part of the individual's personal identity.

My clinical understanding of feelings became most useful when I saw them as equilibratory systems, instead of seeing them just as disturbances that disrupted calm rational thought. It became obvious that the use of feelings is vitally important to the people with whom I work. It was also apparent that the personal meanings of feelings of an individual are frequently different from the cultural meanings of feelings that are used in everyday life in relatively unemotional, interpersonal transactions. The teller at the bank will smile at you and hope you are having a good day. This is an example of a relatively unemotional social transaction.

Under duress, when the NS overflows the banks of its river of equilibration, the individual's person is activated and becomes his central motivating system. Here, the person automatically, and therefore nonconsciously, falls back on the personal lexicon that she learned in childhood. Each individual has her own personal lexicon of feelings, conforming to the character structure of her person, which is used in a variety of different ways in different contexts to stabilize her NS. A woman with whom I was working, whose first language was German, but who spoke English for many years, reverted to German words for feelings when she was upset.

Also, when I worked with two women who each struggled with their multiple persons, I saw them revert to an alternate person when the current emotional moment was difficult and use the language of feeling that fit her alternate personal identity. In Chapter 5, I wrote about the time I suggested to a serious, multiple young woman, who was about to enter college, with whom I was going to lunch in San Francisco, that we jump on a cable car and have lunch at Fisherman's Wharf, she turned into a joyous boy begging for permission to stand on the running board of the cable car. It was easier for her to turn into her young boy than to be a delighted young woman. Persons have a system of feelings that are congruent with their self-concepts and personal realities.

The idiosyncratic use of feelings arises from the interpersonal context in which the person is engaged, the emotional intensity of that engagement, and the emotional skill of the persons who exist within the individual. Each individual usually contains two persons,[2] the early childhood one, and the more adult one who is used in everyday encounters.

Within the lexicons of both social and private feelings, there are dualities that create confusion and are counterproductive to emotional learning. The most common ones are the conflations of anxiety and fear, depression and unhappiness, envy and jealousy, and shame and guilt. These conflations frequently occur in ordinary conversation. If a person uses the word "fear" to label his anxiety, he is giving himself a misleading behavioral instruction. The word "fear" instructs him to either fight or flee when he is actually experiencing anxiety, and there is nothing in the external environment endangering him.

The complex prefrontal cortex/limbic system contains conflicting personal structures that disequilibrate the NS. When the mind is unable to classify cortical disequilibration, it is displayed in awareness as anxiety, depression, pain, or unnamed discomforts. The kind of emotion that is displayed in awareness is a result of the interaction of the general emotional default structure to which the person has become habituated and the social circumstance in which the person is engaged. For example, if a person has become habituated to a depressed characterological mood and is confronted with a personal rejection, he will become more deeply depressed. On the other side, when a depressed person is confronted with affectionate praise and/or respect, she will deflect or reject the positive feedback she is getting.

One half of the emotional duality focuses on the internal condition of the person and the other half explains a reaction to an external thing or circumstance. Anxiety and depression are experiences of internal disequilibria. Both are bodily experiences (emotions). They are labeled differently because their experiential qualities are different. They are similar in that, in and of themselves, they are bodily experiences which have little or no explanatory content. Anxiety and depression are like one another in that they occur within the person when he is unable to experience feelings that could equilibrate his character structure.

The explanatory content of feelings is also accompanied by sets of behavioral instructions designed to create behaviors that will change or relieve the disequilibrating circumstance. For example, by conflating depression, an emotion with little or no explanatory content, with unhappiness, a person has an immediate misunderstanding of what to do. If a person is unhappy, he is likely to search for the reason he is unhappy, in some way, in his external life to explain the unhappiness. "Looking out there" orients him to search in the wrong direction. If he is depressed, "looking" inside himself for the repressive structures that spoil his life would be more useful.

When I help "depressed" people experience a feeling, they are better able to deal with their life circumstances in more productive ways. For example, a man came to me complaining about his "depression." After he told me that his beloved mother died a few months back, I commented that he must be grieving her death. He was struck by the fact that he put her death in the back of his mind, but now that he thought of her death, he could see that he was in grief, not depression. His "depression" (unhappiness and grief) disappeared when I helped him recognize his loneliness and grief (feelings). The emotional withdrawal of depression compounds the anguish of depression. When a depressed person can make some emotional contact with others, the anguish of his depression can be relieved for short periods of time. Validating emotional contact sometimes alleviates the pain of depression, but momentary contact does not eliminate the emotional roots of depressive character structures. We spent a considerable amount of time on learning how emotional denial had served him in his life.

Another man, who was complaining about his anxiety, became angry with me when I did not show him the sympathy he was seeking. At an intense moment of his anger, I asked him if he was anxious. He stopped his bitter complaint about me and with surprise acknowledged that he no longer experienced anxiety.

This is one of the major reasons for the success of psychotherapy. Listening to a client with "unconditional positive regard" provides the help-seeker with respectful emotional contact and this alleviates emotional distress. This kind of psychotherapy is helpful, but it does not create a "cure." Because psychotherapy was born in the medical profession, symptom removal or relief became conflated with the medical idea of cure. Helping people with their emotional difficulties is not the same as getting rid of malfunctions of the body.

The Duality of Feelings

In the following discussion, I will describe commonly experienced social feelings that are frequently conflated. Envy expresses the desire to have something another person possesses. This is an experience of internal disequilibrium. It is about a person expressing a desire for something. Jealousy expresses the fear that a loved one will be taken from them. Jealousy is about the experience (real or imagined) of losing a loved one.

Guilt and shame are also frequently conflated. Guilt is about having done something "out there" that violates or invalidates the individual's personal identity. Shame is an explanation of why the person is angry at or disappointed with one's self for having behaved in a way that violates or invalidates his or her character structure or personal identity.

Fear, unhappiness, jealousy, anger, embarrassment, and guilt are all feelings explaining the bodily experience of emotion occurring within a person about something "out there." Fear states there is something dangerous is "out there." Unhappiness is about disappointment of a variety of sorts about conditions "out there." Embarrassment is about having displayed something "out there" that the person wants to keep hidden. Anger provides the person with an explanation to focus "out there" for the reason they are hurting. While it may be true that someone did hurt his feelings, it is also possible that the pain that triggered the anger was more significantly an enduring internal pain of which he is either unaware or does not want to face.

As a person develops skills in the experiencing and cognition of emotion, he can escape the confinement of painful childhood character structures and their automated behavioral programs. Behavioral "instructions" of feelings can increase the distress of emotions when they are automatically "obeyed." When a person, trained to avoid the expression of anger, tells himself to suppress that feeling, he will likely experience some form of anxiety and/or depression.

The structure of the person explains the uniqueness of the ways feelings are experienced within the individual. The emotional "shape" of the person determines the "tonality" of emotional experiencing. By the "shape," I mean the ways different experiential/emotional structures are integrated with one another in the course of the person's development. The emotional tonality of the person is the characteristic (habituated) mood that the person presents to others. Each person contains its own unique set of selves and feelings with their integrated personal realities. For example, a self that is constructed to relate to parents in a subservient manner with underlying unexpressed anger carries with it sets of feelings designed to stabilize his character structure. A person who was raised by an angry violent father, who could not stand the tears of his son, has a personal presentation that hides anger. His father promised him that he would "give him something to cry about" if he did not stop crying. The personal repertoire of feelings of this character structure is depressed and excludes the skillful use of anger. The emotional tonality of this person is depressed.

In another example, I know a man who, when he was four years old, teased his mother as she was rolling dough out for the apple strudel she was preparing as dessert for the evening meal. The experience of her playful response, by pretending to be upset, as he poked his forefinger through the paper-thin dough that was flowing over the sides of her enamel kitchen table, became an enduring part of his character. Her lovingly theatrical cries of dismay, expressed the pleasure and love she had for him. Teasing was integrated into the growing experience of his self, feelings, and personal reality that were in the process of forming his person. Throughout his life, he has playfully teased those he loved. Still another example of the integration of self, feelings, and personal reality is exemplified by a woman who wanted to give birth to a second daughter as a backup for her first daughter should anything "bad" happen to her. She, the second daughter, served as the family's Cinderella until she was 18 years old, when she left home. She found it difficult to recognize and easily accept the idea that she is an exceptional mother, business executive, and wife. The moment she is complimented, her personal reality tells her that something dreadful will happen. After a bit of investigation, she realized that in her childhood the safest place to be was to hide. When complimented, she tried to become invisible to avoid expected punishment. But hiding made it difficult for her to manage her anger at the unfairness of her mother. She believed she had greater control over events when she anticipated trouble, which, for her, was always around the corner. This was the way she learned to live at home when she was a child.

Early childhood ways of coping with parents and family become enduring parts of the character structure of the person. They are displayed in personal presentations and habituated ways of responding to others; they are behind the events and exchanges between people as they pursue the commerce of everyday living. While they influence the ways people experience one another, the emotional shape of the ways in which they do this happens, for the most part, without conscious awareness.

In another example, I worked with an extraordinarily beautiful, 29-year-old, tall, blonde woman, who dressed seductively and presented herself as an adorable five-year-old child. She had been this way for so many years that she thought that her presentation was her "true" self. After inquiring about the meaning of this presentation, she admitted, with a bit of reluctance, that she thought that she would be more successful in getting what she wanted by being this way. Unfortunately, she wanted to be happily married with children. Her presentation did not match her adult desires. She did get a lot sexual attention which, to her regret, was short lived.

Feelings and Selves

In order to meet the complexity of this discussion about the nature of feelings, I described the person's equilibratory relationship to the NS's equilibratory needs. This description is important because feelings are experienced differently than self-process. Feelings are almost invariably experienced with the bodily experience in the background of awareness. Therefore, the self is thought to be different from the feelings, which has led to the belief that the self is reacting to a feeling. Despite the differences in the way we experience feelings and self, I have come to the conclusion that they are different labels of nonsensory process that are functionally the same.

The Wedding of Self and Feelings

I was able to arrange this marriage when I shifted the basis of the classification of self and feelings from how they are experienced to how they serve the person. Because the psychological selves of everyday experience are displayed in awareness differently from feelings, they are generally classified as being different "things." I have found them to be functionally the same.

If we think of them as stabilizing cognitions, we have a clearer sense of their equilibratory role in both experience and behavior.

Feelings and the selves have traditionally been thought to be in opposition to one another. Both Plato and Freud thought that the self, as the controller and instigator of behavior, should hold sway over emotionality. My idea of their being the same is counterintuitive. They are cognitions about the NS in different conditions. Selves, as self-concepts, are cognitions about the NS in its stable-state condition. Feelings are cognitions about the NS moving to equilibrate itself. The presence of the bodily experience of emotion in the background of the experience of a feeling caused it to be classified as being different from self-process. The idea of the functional identity of the self and feelings simplified my understanding of what a person is. The person is the experience of stable state cognitions about the self (self-concepts), cognitions about the disequilibrated self (feelings), and cognitions about the self in relationships to the environment (personal reality).

Feelings and emotion are best understood as being experiences and expressions occurring within a relationship system. Understanding what the feeling behind the phrase "I love you" means makes sense only when it is cast in the moment of a relationship. The phrase has a different meaning when old lovers, in a moment of pleasure with one another say it, than when a horny young man wanting to have sex with a girl friend says it.

Three realizations encouraged me to continue my pursuit of this way of thinking about selves and feelings. First, I was liberated by knowing that experiential identity or differences were not compelling criteria for the tests of truth when it came to psychological matters. Just because a psychological phenomenon looks like a duck does not mean that it is a duck. Since I was looking at personality from the perspective of brain functions, the inside/out orientation, I am no longer bound by what culture, tradition, or what others say about the so-called "emotions."

Second, I found the logical structure of my theory compelling. The idea that everything psychological emerges from the interaction between the NS, cognition, and consciousness has a convincing simplicity for me. Furthermore, the classification of psychological phenomena from this paradigmatic stance leads to a system of definitions that are not only clear and distinct; they are functionally related to one another. No other psychological theory defines psychological phenomena with this precision, clarity, and dynamic relatedness.

Thirdly, even though there is little psychological experimentation that validates the truth of my hypothesis that the NS, cognition, and consciousness interact to produce personality, the underlying hypothesis of my theory is stated with sufficient clarity to permit experimental testing of it. The research reported in Chapter 4 supports my hypothesis that my theory can be tested within the traditional psychology laboratory and with the technology being currently created in the neurosciences.

Thinking of self and feelings as being identical within an equilibratory frame of reference not only brings the soul back into psychology, it enables the psychotherapist to help the people with whom she works get past confusions created by misleading conventional meanings or explanations about their emotionalities. The soul is returned to the person, when self-process is brought back into the heart of emotionality.

If feelings are the self in equilibratory movement, and if psychotherapy can enable a person to have greater skill in the management of that movement, then personality is changed. This is congruent with my clinical experience. Many people who have worked with me tell me that they are more competent in the use of their feelings than they were when they came into therapy with me. This increased ability is associated in a marked reduction in the discomfort of their anxieties and depressions.

Thinking about emotionality and personality as intimately related processes provides research with additional tools in the measurement of personality change. My theory brings clinical practice into a researchable relationship with scientific psychology.

Knowing that feelings are the self in transformative movement enables people to escape the rigidities of linear/sensory classification. In this way, persons can be known as creative, growing emotionalities that are celebrated in the beauty of art, literature, and music. Seeing the self as a moving, poetic process transforming herself as she dances through the complexities of loving relationships is what I meant when I wrote about bringing the soul back into psychology. Integrating brain dynamics with developmentally created personality dynamics promises to integrate psychological research with clinical practice.

The Phenomenology of Self and Feelings

The NS in its steady-state condition is never totally still. There is always some equilibratory movement within it, steadying itself. When riding a bicycle, one will stay erect as long as one keeps it moving. There are always minor adjustments that must be made to keep the NS in balance. The outside world moves, activating orientational activity. The internal structure of the complex relationship between the equilibratory prefrontal cortex and the NS with its affect hunger is constantly moving, requiring constant monitoring and autoregulation.

Internal and External Sources of Disequilibrium

For centuries, philosophers and psychologists have thought of humans as being primarily "reactive systems." Jaynes (1976) describes the ancient Greeks thinking that the motivations of people were being instigated by the gods. Freud, trained in the nineteenth-century neurology, thought of the stable-state neurological condition as being one of motionlessness (Sulloway, 1979). As the Duchess could say, "And the moral of this is that we only move when we are pushed."

One of Freud's great contributions was calling our attention to the internal dynamics of personality as being a major motivational system guiding our life. The "stimulus-response" paradigm that dominated the early years of scientific psychology is another example of the intellectual tradition that conceptualized human nature as one that primarily responds to external stimulation. It is obvious; we are not automatons whose buttons are simply pushed by external conditions.

Of course, we do react to external circumstances. However, we react even more to the dazzling complexity of our being: the personality systems. Internal equilibratory process triggers experience and behavior more than stimuli from the external environment; most of these experiences and behaviors become habituated (Wyer, 1997). The affect hunger of the NS, a major source of internal disequilibrium, gives rise to both the creative energy of human nature and its anguish. Internal sources of disequilibrium are the fountains of the creativity and agonies of human nature.

Situations in the external environment that destabilize the NS are classified as external sources of disequilibrium. A word of caution! Let me reiterate, the term "disequilibrium" should not be construed as being either pleasant or unpleasant. The cognitive constructions of "pleasant" or "unpleasant" are judgments about the nature of the experience.

As I noted earlier, individuals are differentially skilled with the display in awareness of both their self-process and feelings. The ways an individual experiences her feelings are dependent upon the emotional skills that individual develops in early childhood, her orientational skills, and the degree of compatibility that exists between the individual's character structure and personal identity.

The clinical vignettes I have presented illustrate the internally generated disequilibrium of the NS. People suffering from character disorders, where character stabilization dominates their experience of feeling and shapes the kinds of relationships they are able to endure have a uniquely organized variety of feelings and range of emotional intensities they can tolerate. While they, for the most part, can experience and express commonplace socially used feelings, they have difficulty experiencing feelings that are incongruent with emotionality that is habituated within the core of their character structures. They all experience loneliness, the experiential display of affect hunger. Affect hunger is the emotion. Loneliness is its explanation, a feeling.

In relatively unemotional conditions, people struggling with character disorders experience feelings largely within left hemisphere formats. I recall working with a severely depressed woman, who told me she could not experience feelings. Instead, she said she understood what the social/emotional protocols of most social situations were. With that knowledge, she knew what the appropriate emotional response should be, and she would then play it out. In effect, she would "go through the motions" of social engagement without much in the way of emotional contact with others.

This is also true of others, whom I have previously described. Each of them has their own unique script to which they are bound. They play out their emotional relationships in ways that conform to the habituated emotional structures created in their childhoods. Feelings that violate character structures create confusion or trigger pain and are unintentionally avoided.

This is especially true with respect to loving feelings. When a person is confronted with the need to experience or express a feeling that is incompatible with his character, he will regress. I am using the term "regress" to denote a return to an emotionality with which she has greater skill. I described this earlier when I described the person as having its own unique system of feelings. Characterological emotionalities created in childhood are practiced and rehearsed over long periods of time and, therefore, are more highly skilled and durable than personal identity emotionalities developed later in life. As such they have more highly automated relationships with their Neurological Selves than feelings formed in the later stages of childhood.

Emotional Skill

Emotional skill is measured in the range and intensity of feelings that can be experienced and cognized. People are trained, both within the family and the culture, to use feelings native to these traditions. Families and cultures also train their people to use and avoid different kinds of feelings. Expressions of anger are different in Japan than they are in Italy. The emotional traditions of families also have "rules" about which feelings are acceptable and which are not. Within that frame, each individual shapes his emotionality to meet the requirements of his caretakers and family.

Emotional skill is defined as the ability of the person to experience, think about, and express a broad range of feelings and intensities that stabilize the NS without having to act. I have previously defined emotional skill experientially (Gross, 1992). In that definition, I described emotional skill at five different levels.

The first level of skill is the ability to display the bodily aspect of an emotion in awareness. People can have a bodily disturbance without experiencing it in focal awareness. In my previous book, I described myself as discovering that I had emotional aches, when I attended an American Psychological Association convention, which receded into the background of awareness during the hurly burly of convention business. Finally, once in the solitary quietness of my hotel room, I paid attention to an ache in my body. At first, I thought I was physically ill, but that did not jibe with the rest of the experience of my body. My orientation process did not locate the ache in my body as an illness. I had a disturbing experience in my body but did not know what it meant.

The second level of skill occurs when the person is able to experience the bodily movement (emotion) with a label. When I discovered that the ache in my body was loneliness, I had achieved the second level of skill with regard to loneliness. I am reminded of the biblical injunction, "In the beginning was the Word." The power of labeling and explanation has long been known to reduce emotional distress.

The third level of emotional skill occurs when the person experiences the bodily distress, labels it, and then constructs an explanation of what is happening to her. Then she has a feeling. In my case, I realized that I was missing emotional contact with someone who was lovingly or affectionately meaningful to me, someone who could feed my affect hunger.

The fourth level occurred when I was able to think about my feeling and decide what to do about the condition that was disequilibrating my NS. The feeling was then associated with a behavioral program. When I realized I was lonely, I went to the bar at the conference I was attending and made friends with some of my colleagues. There, I was partly relieved of my ache of loneliness.

And finally, the fifth level of emotional skill occurs when the person can experience a feeling with great bodily intensity and retain the ability to think. At this level, the person is liberated from the automaticity of engaging behavioral programs habituated to feelings. This kind of thinking resists the automaticity of behavior. Resisting automaticity leads to changing habituated character structures. The ability to think while in the throes of intense emotionality can be learned. Learning this skill takes repetitious practice.

People raised in families organized around bland, monotonic emotionality have great difficulty with emotional intensity of any kind. Others raised in families where anger was used as a means of coercing obedience or as a way of masking pain become skilled with anger intensity and use it similarly in their adult lives.

Nonconscious Self-Presentation

The emotionality of character structure is not only played out in the choices one makes in adult loving relationships or the avoidance of them, it is also displayed in the emotional tonality of the person. As I said earlier, I use the metaphor of "tonality" to describe the stable characteristic emotional experience and display of it that resides in the background of all self-presentations: the person's disposition.

In the center of a self-presentation are the smiles, frowns, body movements, speech characteristics of the person. These and other behaviors are designed to elicit a validating response from others with whom the person is engaged. Behind personal presentation, which stabilizes the personal identity of the person, are enduring emotional tonalities. They can be playful, sad, dour or whatever. All of these are like violas or cellos played in the background of the melodies of self-presentation.

Self-presentation is a nonconscious behavioral habit, mindlessly repeating itself in its solicitation for emotionally validating feedback to satisfy the affect hunger of the NS and neurological structures underlying the person. All self-presentations invite a response that is congruent with the smile, charm, complaint or whatever is presented. Ordinarily, in everyday relatively unemotional circumstances, people respond to the invitation obediently, with the same nonconscious automaticity presented in the invitation. The friendly greeting of the cashier's presentation at a supermarket is an example of social lubrication of a routine interaction. The validation of presentation reinforces the habit strength of the emotional structure issuing the invitation and the NS. This is what contributes to making the personality structure self-perpetuating and change resistant.

The invalidation of self-presentation invariably triggers emotionality. It disequilibrates the NS. The NS then activates varieties of different responses depending on the nature of the character structure, personal identity, and/or the person on the receiving end of the invalidation. The recognition of this process instructs the psychotherapist about the emotional skills and dynamics of the person with whom she is working. This will be discussed more fully in Chapter 9.

The Integrity of the NS

By integrity of the NS, I mean the inherent stability of the orienting system to remain in contact with the full array of its autoregulatory systems under the impact of intensely disequilibrating information and the ability to rapidly recover from disequilibration. I am using the phrase "integrity of the NS" instead of the commonly used "ego strength" to avoid ambiguity of definition that commonly exists in these terms. In part, these capacities have genetic roots and are shaped by the ways the infant and child are trained. It is reasonable to believe that neurological structures have inherited characteristics that affect their ability to remain in a stable-state condition under extraordinary destabilizing circumstances. Some inherited neurological systems are better able to withstand changes in metabolic or diseased conditions than others.

The nature of the NS's structural integrity also plays a role in how character structure is formed. Different systems of autoregulation will be constructed depending upon the ability of the NS to resist or recover from deprivation or shock. Rapid recovery of the NS enables the creation of a character structure that actively seeks validation from challenging engagements. Lengthy periods of disorganization encourage the creation of character structures that avoid engagement and enable the growth of more flight systems.

We do not yet know with any specificity what is meant by genetic contributions to personality organization. The research literature is beginning to explore the interactions between genes and the environment that effect psychopathology. However, they have not yet ventured into the territory where they could contribute to an understanding of how they affect the orienting process (the self-process).

Kagan's (1989) work points to temperament as a genetically based aspect of personality. It is interesting to note that he describes temperament as the emotional orientation of the child to the external environment. It is logical to believe that there are other factors such as reliability of neural transmission and stability of neural systems, which could provide a neural basis for biologically based ideas about a strong, resilient NS. In this area of speculation, I think that there may be neurological systems that have inherited capacities to engage a nonsensory system of the brain more effectively than a sensory one, or vice versa.

Damage to the NS

Studies of sensory and social deprivation during infancy and early childhood describe the profoundly negative and enduring effects on the stability and character of adult behavior. Under conditions of severe deprivation, the young fail to mature into effective adulthood. However, there are some adults who, under great deprivation over long periods of time, continue to function effectively, and can remain cognitively intact in their relationship with the stressful situation. Wiesel (1960) and Bettelheim (1943) dramatically describe the operations of strong NS's that enabled some Jews to survive Nazi concentration camps. Child development studies attest to the growth of stable personality structures, when children experience consistent respect for their developmental needs and emotional validation during infancy and early childhood relationships (Eliot, 1999).[3]

The Transformative Nature of Feelings

Recognizing the transformative nature of feelings enables the therapist to help the person with whom he works escape common definitions of feelings that exist in the social lexicon of emotionality. The therapist is aided in doing this when he attends to both the background process of what is happening in the therapeutic interview and what the person is telling him about herself. She is telling him what she is thinking, which is at the center of her attention, while, at the same time, in the background of her awareness, she is sending behavioral signals seeking validational feedback.

In moments of emotional distress, the person tells her therapist about her difficulties, hoping the therapist will be helpful. However, if a person does not recognize that she is using her social vocabulary of feelings, she may be using an explanation that compounds her pain and confusion rather than achieving clarifying relief. Unfortunately, many equilibratory purposes are simply reinforcements of painful character structures that are age inappropriate.

My work with a woman, with whom I had been working on and off for about ten years, exemplifies this. At one point, she called me in great distress asking for an extra appointment. She came in demanding that I tell her she is crazy because she believes her husband is planning to leave her to live with one of her girlfriends. I had no difficulty with that. I agreed saying, "Yes. You're crazy."

I did this to call attention to her desire to quarrel with me because she assumed I would disagree with her about her suspicion of husband's infidelity. After she recognized she was convinced about the truth of her jealous belief and wanted me to get into a debate in which I would have been bound to lose, she settled down to tell me in a more focused way the evidence she had been gathering that caused her to come to this very painful conclusion. None of her "evidence" convinced me. Furthermore, the evidence was entirely focused on the affection for their friend that she and her husband both shared.

At no point did she look at anything that had been going on in her relationship with her husband. I suggested that if this is what she believed; she must also be very angry with him. She agreed. Then I asked if she had been angry with him before she came to believe in his infatuation with her friend. She acknowledged that she had been irritable for weeks before that. She also recognized that she had also been fighting with a colleague at work. I asked (even though I knew from previous discussions with her about her marriage what her answer would be) what her husband did when she was angry. "He withdraws!" she said with pain and anger. After some discussion, she saw that she had been very lonely despite living with him. She recognized her anger from which he withdrew and diminished his contact with her, which increased her loneliness, which was then transformed into jealousy.

As a matter of fact, that was the major difficulty in their marriage. He was a sweet, kind companion. Not great in bed but interested in pleasing her. Her husband had never been a man interested in or capable of much emotional contact in any relationship. She realized it was much easier for her to transform the loneliness into jealousy, which gave her a reason to be angry, than it was to confront the loneliness.

She was also dimly aware that her anger was a mask for a deeper pain that resided in her character. The exploration and elimination of painful anger is a major therapeutic task for her. Jealousy was an easier, immediate, externalizing emotional solution. In that way the focus of her attention could be solely on him and she would not have to face the "bargain" that she had made to be with a decent reliable man who was emotionally distant. That bargain enabled her to avoid the difficult therapeutic task of coping with her characterological loneliness. She could blame him and not face the loneliness imbedded in her personality.

This is but one of many, many examples of how feelings are transformed from one kind of feeling experience into another. In other chapters, I have written about how the pain of love can be transformed into feelings of anger. I have also mentioned how feelings of guilt are used to avoid experiences of anger.

The governing principle in the transformation of feelings is skill. If a feeling is a mismatch or in conflict within an individual's character structure, he will automatically transform that feeling into another with which he has greater skill or one that matches the individual's character structure or personal identity. Skilled feelings are automatically activated regardless of the pain or pleasure that accompanies the activation. I know a man who is very skilled with his anger. At one point, we were discussing the pain that resided beneath his experience of anger. He explained that even though his anger devastated his wife, "It doesn't hurt so much, when I am angry!"

Hemispheric Emotionality

Left hemisphere emotionality is experienced as feelings without much in the way of a bodily experience in focal awareness. As I have said before, whenever, the NS is activated there is an accompanying bodily reaction, which usually resides in the background of awareness. I think about the emotionality of a depressed woman who used her analytic understanding of the social conventions of emotional exchange required to give her the appearance of being "normal," "like everyone else." However, the repression of right hemisphere rage and loneliness drove her to suicidal despair.[4] Depression, anxiety, and pain are experienced primarily as a kind of right hemisphere anguish. When they are experienced with intensity, left hemisphere logical, analytic cognition is severely impaired.

In psychoanalysis, the duality of this experience has been seen as the difference between emotionally experienced insight and intellectualization. William James (1890/1950) recognized this kind of emotionality in the following quote.

> I now proceed to urge the vital point of my whole theory, which is this: *If we fancy some strong emotion, and then try to abstract from our consciousness of all the feelings of its bodily symptoms, we find we have nothing left behind*, no "mind-stuff" out of which the emotion can be constituted, and that a cold and neutral state of intellectual perception is all that remains.
>
> (Vol. II, p. 451) (original emphasis)

My guess is that although James was not aware of it, what "remained" was his depression. His description of emotionality fits present day recognitions of the roles of the left and right hemispheres of the brain in the experience of emotionality. The distinction between left and right hemispheric emotionality has important implications for the therapeutic engagement. It has been my observation that those who rely upon left hemisphere explanations or solutions to problems have great difficulty accessing their right hemisphere emotionality.

I worked with a very bright young man, Harvey, who recognized that he had difficulty in accessing feelings about his father. He told me, with some satisfaction, that he realized he had this difficulty. In a previous session, he had been able to experience some sadness about the tragedy of his father. However, he said that today, he was past that and doubted that he would ever again be able to feel that way about his father.

His father, at one time many years earlier, had been a relatively successful talent agent in Hollywood. But since the divorce from Harvey's mother, he had been going downhill. Now, but for the grace of Harvey's dutiful caring, he would be living on the street.

Harvey, who was living on a tight budget, was infuriated when his father overdrew his checking account and Harvey was forced to pay his father's overdraft. At that point Harvey, who, devotedly, had dinner with his father once a week, terminated this gesture of filial obedience. In that session, Harvey told me his father had called the previous week and was surprisingly caring. He had inquired about his granddaughter, Harvey's newborn child. He inquired about the health and welfare of Harvey and his wife. In general, he was not his narcissistic old self. Harvey went on to tell me this was just a passing phase. His father had not really changed. I commented that his father's inquiries must have felt good to him. He acknowledged that they did. But he knew that his father was an old con man. I then said, "And he loves you very much." Harvey's eyes welled with tears. I had pushed him into his right hemisphere emotionality. That was helpful.

I worked with another man, who has many feelings about his father and an almost total absence of feelings about his mother. Whenever we get close to him having a feeling about her, he goes blank, complains about his inability to remember her, or starts yawning and wants to go to sleep. Loving feelings about her are extremely difficult for him to experience but he is masterful with anger, sorrowful complaining, and loneliness.

I am describing him to illustrate the relationship between emotional skill and the hemispheric specialization of the experience and expression of emotionality. I have observed that when one is able to construct a classification about a repetitive ongoing process that the classification takes on a unitary character permitting the ongoing process to be treated in a logical left hemispheric term as a "thing." This is a form of intellectualization.

In short, right hemisphere experiencing of body and cognition about the bodily process has been thought to be the "gold" of psychotherapeutic experience. Left hemispheric thinking enables emotionality to become change resistant but some find it most satisfying because it helps them escape the pain of change.

I am reminded of a sad story, which was told to me as a joke, about a stuttering man who searched the world over for someone to help release him from his disability. Finally, he spent five years with a German therapist. On his arrival back home, his friends looked at him with astonished disappointment and expressed sorrow that he was still stuttering. The stuttering man responded to them with great satisfaction and said, "Yes, but now I know the reason why."

I have seen people react emotionally without having an experience of a feeling or emotion. It is not unusual for some people, who are embarrassed to be surprised when another person tells them he is blushing or that the vein of embarrassment is pulsating on his forehead. Recall, my body ached with the pain of loneliness before I became aware of my feeling of loneliness.

The blended experience of physiological activity and the cognitive explanation about that activity informs us of the genuineness of the feeling. The terms "true" and "genuine" should not be thought of as meaning that the feelings are "really" true or right. The terms indicate only that the feelings come from "the heart" of the NS. They are not fraudulent or intentional acts. When my blood rushes, I am really feeling something as opposed to pretending to be intense about something without a bodily reaction associated with my intention.[5] Left hemispheric emotionality is another way for people to avoid the pain of experiencing the emotionality of early childhood pain. It is not unusual for a person to come into psychotherapy seeking a linear logical explanation rather than experiencing the embarrassment and pain of learning how to know about and use full-bodied emotionality.

The Complexity of the Experience of Feelings

The expressions of feelings are externally stabilizing in the sense they are attempts at changing the external environment to respond in a way that removes or changes the disrupting events. The experience of feelings as cognitions is internally stabilizing. They explain what is happening and have a set of behavioral instructions about what to do about the disturbing situation. This duality of life creates an emotional process that is constantly moving. It is this movement that prevents the classification of feelings as static elements.

The learned cognitive matrix about the operations of midbrain structures managing the life of the individual is enormous. Feelings are a part of the complexity of the person. For example, some persons use different feelings more readily than others. Recall the man I described earlier who used his anger extravagantly; his person could accommodate anger better than it could the expression of pain. Another man found that his suffering was much more stabilizing than anger. Anger, suffering, and all of the other feelings listed in the social lexicon of feelings are experienced with background displays of bodily process.

Rarely does anyone experience a single feeling. People ordinarily experience quietly moving mists of different feelings in the passage of daily living. When the NS becomes severely destabilized, the gentle winds of feeling can turn into gales of emotion. These mixtures of eemotions and self-experience reflect the complexity of emotional reactions to the situations in which humans are engaged. In an emotional moment, a person not only experiences an emotion; she also experiences herself having feelings and adjusting to them.

Her experience is a chord played by an orchestra. The experience of feeling arises from the interaction of the homeostatic operations of the NS in relation to other systems in the limbic system and the prefrontal cortex that contains the character structure and personal identity of the person, which thereby helps the individual navigate the complex interpersonal terrain of civilization.

I recall a time working in group therapy when I made an absurd but incisive observation. I felt a rush of excitement about being clever and I was delighted and pleased with myself. At the same moment, I felt the blush of embarrassment on my face, and then I was chagrined at having exposed a private part of myself to group observation. Later, I sat back and reflected on my multihued reaction and realized how multifaceted the experience of feelings is.

What we experience as feelings are cognitive end-product displays of complex, interactive neurological systems displayed in behavior and awareness as personality. Despite the conventional wisdom of feelings as disturbers of mental tranquility, the psychobiological function of feelings is to steady the person's passage through life.

Emotional Intensity

Emotional intensity is a paradoxical phenomenon. Humans both abhor and crave it. The internal/external dynamic and the validation/invalidation of the structures of the NS and its person explain our positive and negative reactions to emotional intensity.

An impending head-on car crash terrifies us. Being insulted by an employer humiliates us. Invalidating internal emotional intensity is experienced with a variety of what are commonly called "negative" feelings or emotions. When invalidating external intensity is experienced as threat or danger coming from something dangerous happening, we abhor it.

The mindstorms I described in Chapter 3 are internal disrupting experiences of intensity. The experience of self-hating feelings, particularly when a person is unable to escape them by focusing on sensory systems, can be terrifying.

Validating internal intensity is a source of great pleasure. Recreational sex is a common example of this aspect of intensity. Creative work validates the creators of all forms of art. I will discuss this more fully in the last chapter of this book, "The Art of Psychotherapy."

The validating external emotional intensity, like fighting the "bad guys" or escaping "danger," is craved. Violent and/or horror motion pictures produce the largest revenues for the motion picture industry. The excitement of danger in the safety of a movie theater validates the affect hungers' neurological fight/flight systems. This is particularly true when the audience knows that the hero will survive the most horrifying dangers.

We don't think clearly when we are emotionally aroused in ways that are unfamiliar to us. The confusion and the distress of intense emotionality, with which we have poor experiential skills, have led to the belief it should be banished or be controlled by intention (Becker, 1932). Neither of these wishes can be reliably or successfully fulfilled in our lives. Furthermore, the failure of our wishes or intentions to think and behave *rationally* confuses us and supports self-recrimination, at which too many of us are very skilled. On the other hand, when the intensity is "out there" in battle on the screen, in literature, or on a punching bag in the gym, it feeds the affect hunger of neurological survival systems, which also need validating exercise.

It is abundantly clear that emotional intensity also resides at the center of love, beauty, passion, and creativity. It has, from the beginnings of psychotherapy, held a favored place in the theories about the nature of personality change. Insight without intense emotional accompaniment has always been seen as a relatively weak therapeutic achievement.

The structural integrity of the person rests upon the tripod of love, work, and play. The emotional intensity of the engagement of the person in each of these areas of living is an important part of creativity in the life of the person. In each of these rich sources of validation, the person learns to cope with and is personally enriched by the exciting intensity of his or her engagement in them. "Creativity" is another word for the growth that is essential for living the good life. Intimately related to growth are experiences of beauty and excellence that nourish the cognitive structures of the person, which in turn enhance the strength and stability of the NS.

The human need to feed the affect hunger of personal systems in the brain with emotional intensity can be seen in the fact that, in American culture, it is one of the major economic foundations of the motion picture industry, amusement parks, the alcohol industry, and pornography. All of these commercial enterprises feed the person's affect hunger for emotional intensity. The emotional intensities we pursue with billions of dollars and endless amounts of time are generated by external situations that have socially institutionalized explanatory systems. The "good" and "bad guys" of action movies provide validational feedback not only to our cultural moral values, they also provide ways of experiencing and validating internal emotional structures of rage and anger for which there is no acceptable place in everyday social life.

We dread the pain and anguish of internal invalidating emotional intensity. When a person does not have cognitive skills to accommodate the intensity of affect hunger, the "noise" within his head becomes unbearable. By "noise" I mean the dissonance that can exist between the private (character) and public (identity) persons of the individual. The next chapter will describe this duality of personality. The inability of some to cognitively classify the mysteries of the emotional conflicts of a painful childhood causes emotional intensity to become a dreadful presence in their mind.

It drives them to seek change that will emancipate them from the tortured "prisons" of their childhood. Habituated childhood personal structures that prevent persons from enjoying the freedom and creativity of their adulthoods are the prisons from which psychotherapy seeks to liberate people. Internal emotional intensities are difficult because humans have impoverished emotion vocabularies making emotions difficult to explain. The explanatory skills of psychotherapy contribute to the relief from the pain caused by emotional cognitive incompetence.

Like the cognitive structures that shape the experience of feelings, there are neurological structures that accommodate emotional intensity, partly with cognition but also with systemic relations among themselves to maintain the steady-state condition of the NS. As neurological systems, the neurological structures too require exercise to feed their affect hunger. The ability to accommodate emotional intensity is a major part of emotional skill systems.

From the beginning of modern psychotherapy, in the ecstatic confusion of the first psychoanalytic case of Anna O., emotionality has been a central presence in the pursuit of what Anna O. called the "talking cure." The passionate intensity of their work enlivened Breuer, her doctor, for a period of time. But when it became intensely sexual, it drove them away from further engagement in the psychotherapeutic adventure.

Freud's courage, genius, and ambition pressed him to continue on the path of psychotherapeutic exploration. I empathize with him about the reasons that compelled him to take refuge behind the couch. He needed to reduce the emotional intensity of psychotherapeutic work enough to enable him to continue his exploration of it.[6] It was an intensity for which he was culturally and personally unprepared.

At the center of my theory is the proposition that both stability and growth reside at the center of human existence. Evidence of the growth of the human brain is testimony to the human talent for change as it resides in the "bed" of its equilibratory stability.

Change

Of all the creatures on this earth, humans are champions of change and growth. Through the centuries, the rate of change of social complexity and knowledge has been causing the growth of our brains. This astounding movement of human change and creativity has been accompanied by both tragedy and beauty. In my eyes, the growth of knowledge about both technology and human wisdom has been worth the tragic price that has been and is continuing to be paid for it. In the long view there is a promise of bettering the human condition and reducing the tragedies that scar our history.

From the perspective of psychotherapy, growth and change illuminate the beauty of human nature. Persons are like other beautiful phenomena. One has but to recall the delight and enchantment one feels watching a year-old infant looking around the room taking the world in. Children learning to walk and talk and clamoring for affectionate attention fill me with awe as I watch them in their ceaseless growing complexity. Observing the charm of adults interacting is an experience of the beauty of personality. The delight of good ideas is another kind of experience of the beauty of intelligence. For the therapist, personal beauty is experienced in the unique, creative complexity of the psychological selves and emotionality in the ways adults enable the NS to maintain its structural integrity.

It is this complexity that facilitates the growth of personality. The complexity of newly forming personal systems frequently collides with other earlier and more habituated childhood personal systems during the maturation of the person. The collisions of personal systems interrupt the automaticity of their habituated operations. They, too, can be "corrective" emotional experiences. Interruptions of habituated personal cognitive systems permit cerebral structures to regroup in new, more age-appropriate, creative ways. The observation of this creativity in adults is as beautiful as is the beauty of the personal growth of children. Therapists who participate in this beauty are privileged.

I devoutly hope the theory I have presented expands the range of creativity of both therapists and the persons with whom they work. It is an introduction to a way of integrating emotionality into the immediacy of psychotherapeutic work. It awaits further work to develop a more explicit description of personality process.

I can now turn to the description of the person. The next chapter will describe it in greater detail. Another example of the duality of this theory resides in the fact that personal identity is, also, emotionality in habituated movement. I will be discussing the personal and social lexicons of the two persons inhabiting the individual. Character structure uses the personal lexicon and personal identity uses the social lexicon. This issue will be discussed in greater detail in the next chapter.

Notes

1. When people are unskilled with the experience of a given emotion, they experience the bodily process but are unable to label it. In my previous book (Gross, 1992), I described having aches in my body until I realized that I was very lonely.
2. I will describe the persons of character structure and personal identity in the next chapter. There is a voluminous literature on infant care, attachment theory, and

parenting that relates to this issue, but it is beyond the scope of this work to enter into it.
3. There is a voluminous literature on infant care, attachment theory, and parenting that relates to this issue, but it is beyond the scope of this work to enter into it.
4. This sentence raises the question of interhemispheric inhibition that I am unable to answer. The answer to it will clarify the nature of repression. The idea of repression suggests the notion that consciousness is inhibited from displaying information from the right hemisphere. The answer to this question will also clarify the nature of depression and anxiety.
5. I am using "intention" here in its colloquial form. It is a shorthand way of describing the complexity of the social situation, which activates personal structures to engage in ways that invoke the idea of intention. I still regard intentionality as a form of ex post facto explanation.
6. In my consultation with other therapists, I have found that most of them are unprepared for the intensity of the work. See my discussion of the Wolf-Man in Chapter 1, which describes Freud's reasons for going behind the couch.

Chapter 8

A Portrait of the Person

The Equilibratory and Destabilizing Systems of Personality

Personality is a genetically structured homeostatic system serving the equilibratory needs of the rest of the brain. Despite their homeostatic duty, personality systems become so complex they also destabilize themselves and the brain they are genetically organized to stabilize. In addition to the stabilizing and destabilizing nature of personality, there is another duality within it. Like Janus, the god of beginnings, changes, time, and duality, the biological foundation of personality evolved to stabilize the Neurological Self (NS): the brain's orienting system, which is further cognitively classified to meet different kinds of relationships the brain encounters in its life. These classifications become organized into neurological structures that are experienced as "the person." It emerges into experience from different classifications of the NS; they are experiences of self-process.

A Definition of the Word "Person"

In conventional usage, the word "person" is simply there; motionless, like a stone on the side of the road: just a word to designate a human individual. The Latin word "persona," from which the English "person" is derived, means mask. It, too, is a motionless thing. But behind the person's mask is a mysterious nonsensory "something": personality.

The stillness of the word "person" hides the dynamic role it plays in the ways we conduct our lives. We use the word person so frequently that, like most psychological terms with which we are familiar, we think we know what it means without being able to define it. In this chapter, I will move behind the mask of the person and describe its cognitive equilibratory role in personality dynamics.

As it is with all living process, persons are self-perpetuating systems that are in constant equilibratory movement, changing to meet changing circumstances that destabilize the brain. Personal identities change as they move through the various stages of the person's life. We have a structural definition of the person, when we use Piaget's (1970) definition of psychological structures as self-perpetuating wholes and add Allport's (1955) recognition that psychological systems become functionally autonomous.

The person is the integrated experience of the four different cognitive systems. They are the "I," psychological selves, feelings, and personal reality. The person regulates prefrontal/limbic systems, primarily the NS, to maintain their normative operating conditions. Because the "normative operating condition" operates automatically and nonconsciously, it has been frequently construed to be a static-state system. I have seen it as a constantly moving neurological process.[1] The "I" of the person was described in Chapter 5 as the experience of the biological orienting function of the person. It is used as a cursor, locating the person to whatever the brain is unable to automatically process. In its stable-state condition, the NS is classified as the psychological self. When it is disequilibrated and is in the process of homeostatically restoring itself to its stable-state condition it is experienced as feelings. And finally, when the NS is engaged in the external environment, both social and physical, it is experienced as personal reality.

Character Structure and Personal Identity

Like the duality of dialogue, the person is dualistically organized for similar purposes. Character structure and personal identity become the Janus head of existence. Character structure is the face that serves the internal equilibration of the brain. The other face, personal identity, is the psychological system used by individuals to engage the physical and interpersonal worlds. Both serve to stabilize the rest of the brain. Underlying both of these psychological systems are massive neurological networks.

The word "person" fits the idea of a face that lies in front of neurological personality systems. It is a masklike system looking out at the interpersonal environment with which neurological personality structures must cope and engage. Faces express emotionality and seek emotional feedback. The flexibility of the human face can nonverbally influence others emotionally. Our faces are major homeostatic operators.

The characterological face begins its existence in relation to the infant's caretakers. The early care of the infant is largely physical and emotional. It is predominantly a nonsensory, right-brained system (Schore, 2003). Faces change as the individual matures. They become parts of the persons that exist within the individual. The person of character structure is called the private person. Personal identity is colloquially called the public person.

As the infant learns to walk and talk she encounters her mother, a father, grandparents, siblings, and other caretakers. The brain creates a face enabling the growing child to cope with the complexities of her relations with the outer world. During infancy, the baby learns to cry and make faces to communicate with her caretakers about her needs. With repetition, she becomes habituated to facial behaviors that are reinforced. They are right-brained structures that increasingly retreat to the background of awareness as the individual matures. The face of personal identity is, primarily, a sensory, left-brained system that contains beliefs, values, cultural standards of conduct and emotionality. It acts as a guide helping its person navigate in the social world and ways of eliciting validating emotional feedback to exercise the NS.

Character structure and personal identity have different psychological persons. This idea is different from common usage, where it is generally believed that we only have one person. I frequently engage with the two persons of the people with whom I work. On rare occasions, I have found myself working with people who use more than two persons to stabilize their personalities.

The Structural Dynamics of the Person

The diagram of the person that follows illustrates its cognitive dynamics. It shows the relatedness of its four psychological systems. The linear/nonlinear

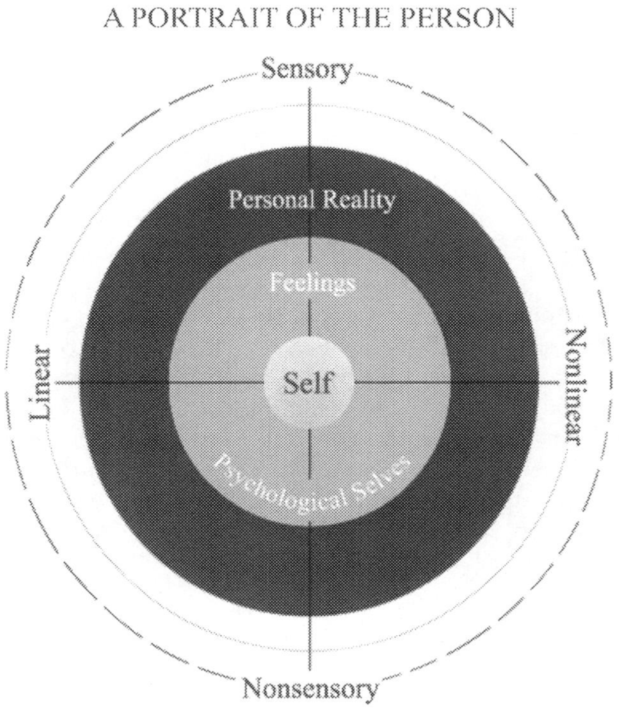

A PORTRAIT OF THE PERSON

Figure 8.1 A Portrait of the Person

and sensory/nonsensory labels at the sides of the diagram of the person indicate the kinds of cognitive formatting used to shape the experience of the person. In the following discussion, I describe the four cognitive systems within the context of their roles in personality.

First is the "I" of the NS, which resides in the center of these systems. It is in the center of the diagram as it does in the center of the individual's life. It functions the same way in both the persons of character structure and of personal identity. It is the focal point of the homeostatic orientation process. It is the cognitive label of the anterior cingulate cortex and other neurological systems related to orientation.

Recall, the "I" is the "cursor" of orientation. It establishes the relationship of the individual to any information she is unable to automatically process. At that moment, both cognition and consciousness, as processes of the mind, enable the person to respond to the disequilibrating information. The person experiences the disequilibrating information and her mind provides her with an "understanding" (a cognition) of her relationship and what to do about it. Behavioral programs can be drawn from behavioral programs described by Miller, Galanter and Pribram (1960).

The "I" of the Selves

The NS mindlessly activates limbic systems designed to return physiological systems to their steady state conditions. This is a major source of human pain and confusion. The NS as an evolving neurological system, doesn't always clearly discriminate between error signals from personality systems in the prefrontal cortex and those from the body. I knew a man, suffering from an obsessive-compulsive disorder, who compulsively complained about his abdominal pains, which drove his wife to avoid him, which in turn depressed him. The psychological functions of his complaints were based on both his childhood anger at his narcissistic mother and his demand that his mother take care of him or in his adulthood, that his wife take care of him. He could not recognize the difference between his emotional pain and the pains of his body. The pain and confusion resided in the vicious cycle of complaint and avoidance that he experienced in his childhood. Pain as well as love can become habituated emotional experience and expression. His wife avoided him too, but for different reasons, which reinforced his complaints; this in turn, resulted in a self-perpetuating misery between them. It was a folie a deux.

The Psychological Selves

The second system, the psychological selves, is a complex of cognitions which classify the NS in its steady-state condition. Like the "I," they are cognitive labels of the NS. They are commonly known as self-concepts.

"This is me when I am at a cocktail party." "This is me when I am in my office." "This is me when I am playing with my children." I am somewhat different in all of these and other situations. The psychological selves, unlike feelings, are not accompanied with emotion. They are the "saturated" selves (Gergen, 1991) that we experience when the NS is residing within the normative bed of its steady-state condition.

These selves are parts of the cognitive foundations of both character structure and personal identity. Because they have different equilibratory functions (internal and external), they are experienced differently and have different meanings. Usually an individual, in ordinary everyday relationships has a stable balance between his public (personal identity) and private selves (character structure). An individual projects his public self figurally with his private self-expressing emotionality seeking validation. It is usually displayed in the background of awareness.

The psychological selves, like emotionality, are experienced in both linear/sensory and nonlinear/nonsensory formats. Being developed at different stages of the maturation of personality, the psychological selves frequently have contradictory and conflicted validational needs. They operate in both the public and private persons to aid in managing both social and intimate relationships. Therefore, instead of being simple equilibrators of the NS, they also disequilibrate the NS when they are confronted with invalidating information—that is, feelings—and they mindlessly seek homeostatic regulation from the disequilibrated NS.

Feelings

Feelings, the third system within the person, are cognitions about the NS when its automaticity has been interrupted and it is restoring itself to its steady-state condition. In other words, feelings are cognitions about a disequilibrated NS.

This idea provides an explanation of the relationship between emotionality and personality change. When a person develops increased emotional skills, her/his personality changes. In Breuer's work with Anna O., the two believed that remembering experiences of feelings was necessary for personality change. Remembering past conflicts or emotional pain does little to change personality structure. I have found interrupting age-inappropriate personality habit systems facilitates structural change in personalities.

Reiterating from Chapter 7, feelings, as cognitions, are explanations about what is disturbing the person with behavioral programs telling her what she should do about the disturbance. Ordinarily they are displayed in focal awareness, while emotion resides in the background of that awareness. Feelings, as systems of explanation, are homeostatically designed to stabilize the NS in its relationships with both its persons and the outer world.

Unfortunately, there are occasions when the feelings of character structure conflict with the organization of personal identity.

Personal Reality

Fourth, personal reality is a system of cognitions about the NS's relationship to its external environment. It is a system of explanations about what the individual is or should be in the world in which she lives. It is incorporated in beliefs about religion, moral values, political values, and cosmology. The devotions of millions of people to the great explanatory systems of Confucianism, Buddhism, and Monotheism testify to their deep meaningfulness to human existence.

Personal reality is a system of ideas/beliefs/faiths about how the psychological selves should relate to the world in which they live. Within the linear/sensory format, it is organized in ways that are similar to the ways in which physical objects are classified. Many people have rather rigid rules about who they think they should be and how they should live their lives. In everyday terms, there are those who know that they must be kind and considerate under all circumstances. This knowledge is like the sensory/linear knowledge that the ignition of an automobile must be turned on to start the engine. When both formatting conditions operate in conformity with the ways they are "supposed" to operate (they are structurally compatible), the NS remains in its steady-state condition.

Personal reality and emotionality used in everyday social relationships conform to one another. Personal reality can become habituated to ways of warding off the experience of emotionality that is not congruent with its person. For example, a severely depressed individual has a person who does not experience anger or love in an intimate relationship because he became habituated or fixated to pain with these experiences. If he is confronted with feelings of warmth or praise, he will brush the warmth aside with a deflecting comment.

The triad of psychological selves, feelings, and personal reality has a rough resemblance to Freud's ego, id, and superego. Both models describe the dynamics of personality operations. The major difference between Freud's triad and mine is that mine are experiences of mindlessly operating neurological structures. None of my hypothetical structures has a homunculus hiding within it.

The Duality of Personality

The duality of the personal systems has an experiential dynamic that is structurally the same as the figure/ground illusion. Visual information displayed in focal awareness has the "appearance" of being in front of other kinds of information displayed behind the central figure. The background display of information is most often processed automatically and is, therefore, not usually experienced focally. Nonetheless, the background display of information affects the ways that the entire display of information is cognitively structured and experienced.

This is true of both personality process and visual perception (Shepard, 1990). The nonsensory display of one of the two persons is experienced in the center of attention, while the other resides in the background of awareness. Nonetheless, it significantly influences what the person experiences in focal awareness.

Not only do the persons alternate in awareness, they also alternate in the ways they are called upon to stabilize the NS. Both persons sing a duet of living. They each sing their own songs in the lives of their individuals. Sometimes they harmonize beautifully and other times the dissonance of their melodies creates an unbearable noise of emotional pain.

Initially in the life of the individual, character structure has a right-brained equilibratory relationship with the NS. As I said in the last chapter, character structure is emotionality in habituated movement. With habituation, it functions automatically to stabilize the NS. It is frequently recognized as the "child" within us. As such it is a major source of emotion. It is the internal dynamic of personality.

Personal identity with the emergence of self-consciousness and its relationship to others is more of a left-brained process learning the rules of speech, social engagement, everyday relatively unemotional relationships with other persons, and the nature of the world within which he is living. With repetitive use it, too, becomes habituated and it, too, operates automatically.

This description of the two persons existing within the same individual has a kind of neatness and symmetry. Character structure emerges from the right side of the brain and is primarily centered on internal emotional dynamics, while the public person manages the individual's relationships of her external environment with the logic and reason of the left side of her brain. I have no doubt that as the interaction between the hemispheres becomes neurologically better known, the left/right dichotomy will be understood in a more complex way.

The Double Duality of Personality

When I talk to myself, I am debating, discussing, quarreling, or just simply trying to figure something out by dialoguing within the duality of my personal systems. I frequently have to turn off my linear, logical person, my personal identity, to allow my relational, nonlinear character structure to come up with a way of transitioning from one topic to another in the description of my theory. Looking at myself while in inner dialogue, I became aware that there is a double duality within my brain. I (as a self) am talking to my (other) self. Here again we have the duality of linear/nonlinear and the duality of sensory/nonsensory cognitive dynamics that enables my description of personality to be more complexly described.

Transitioning from one topic to another is a nonlinear relational cognitive process. Making a transition is a right hemisphere function. Logical left hemisphere cognition interferes with that kind of cognitive work. Turning off that part of me is no easy task. Similarly, when emotionality is intense (right hemisphere intensity), it is impossible to think logically and rationally (left hemisphere process). There is no ready intentional switch I can use. When my logical self impedes solutions to problems that confront me in my theoretical work, sleep or meditation help me. The literature is rich with descriptions about discoveries that are made during the night and are preserved in memory the next morning (cf. Polanyi, 1958; Bronowski, 1956).

Margaret Atwood's (2002) description of personal duality is so illustrative and congruent with my thinking that I will quote a small section of it here.

> I grew up in a world of doubles. My generation of children had no television—ours was the age of comic books—and in these, a superhero was nobody unless he had an alter ego who really was nobody. Superman was really the bespectacled Clark Kent. Captain Marvel was really the crippled newsboy Billy Batson, Batman was really a Scarlet Pimpernel sort of fellow who acted a playboy twit in real life or was it the other way around? The superhero, large and powerful and good, was what we wished to be; the one who lived dans le vrai and was small and weak and fallible and at the mercy of beings more powerful than us, was what we really were.
>
> (p. 31)

The duality of personality is portrayed in the great modern fantasy tale of Harry Potter in his life and death struggle with the evil side of his personality, Lord Voldemort. One interpretation of the duality in this tale is that lovable young Potter is more powerful than his evil self, Lord Voldemort, which would be an upside down way to the way the struggle is usually portrayed. The Jekyll/Hyde duality of personality is another story of how the self-loving/self-hating personal duality is played out in fiction. Mr. Hyde is the self within which the almost universal self-hatred of the person is played out. Here again we see the self-hating and rational selves engaged in the painful argument born of emotional ignorance. Anna O., in the beginning of psychoanalysis, recognized that she had two persons in her personality; the sweet, intelligent, giving person and the angry, disagreeable one (Breuer and Freud, 1893/1895).

The Paradoxical Nature of the Person

In Chapter 3, I described personality as a biological, cognitive, stabilizing function designed to restore the NS to its stable-state condition. I also discussed the developmental contradiction to this mandate. As personality engages into the world, it becomes more complex than the simple duality of character structure and personal identity.

Character structures, with abuse or trauma, become habituated or fixated. Biologically, they are required to elicit behaviors from others to feed their affect hunger. This is where the "child" in our adult personality becomes operative. Like other neurological systems, it engages the environment to feed its affect hunger. Doing this reinforces the integrity of neurological structures from which a child-like personality emerges. When the "young one"[2] is fixated by trauma or abuse, it becomes the dominant feature of character structure. Fixated personality structures, being created in early childhood and repetitively reinforced over longer periods of time, are more stable and durable than personality structures emerging later in life. As a result, they more effectively control behavior. This results in a characterological personality system, which resides behind personal identity and which dominates the behavior of the individual. It does so in pursuit of feeding the affect hunger of childlike character structures.

My work with George, a 50-year-old man, exemplifies this condition. His adult personal identity was governed by a fixated childhood character structure. He suffered a disastrous childhood. His psychotic father beat him, while his mother urged her husband to be careful to not bruise George's face. When George would hear his father coming home, he would jump into a closet, hiding under old clothes.

He escaped from his home in his late teens and learned a trade to support himself and three wretched and painful relationships with two wives and a lover. His work life carried the same theme of pain and confusion. Although he hadn't graduated from high school, he was very intelligent and creative in his work. He came up with various interesting business projects, all of which came to naught because he used his projects to try to persuade his partners to give him the love and appreciation that was absent in his childhood. He was aware of how smart he was and valued his contributions more highly than they did, which contributed to his failures. He was in constant pursuit of the love he experienced in his very early childhood before his father's psychotic break. His childlike grandiosity and his search for love confused his colleagues, who were unaware that George's primary agenda was healing "little traumatized" George.

The confusion and mystery of the paradox of a habituated childhood character structure governing personal identity have created the agony and belief systems that have confounded human existence. Habituated structures are immune to persuasion, verbal abuse, logic, or any linear cognitive manipulations. They continue perpetuating themselves unless their habit strengths are weakened by persistent interruptions.

These structures operate automatically and, therefore, the individual is not aware of their operations. Being nonconscious, they have been regarded as dreadful mysteries. Saint Augustine's confusion about the disobedience of his penis to his intentions contributed to doctrines about sexuality that have caused great confusion and pain (Pagels, 1988).[3] There is a pernicious belief that "out of sight is out of mind." Asleep or awake, personal systems mindlessly perpetuate themselves.

The Private Person of Character Structure

The cognitive systems of the private person are more frequently accompanied with experiences of bodily sensations (emotions), which cause them to be thought of as being "real," "true," or "genuine" feelings (James, 1890/1950). In adulthood, the private person of character structure emerges primarily into awareness as idiosyncratic thoughtless emotionality.

An example of childhood structures emerging thoughtlessly can be seen in the dilemma of a woman I know, as a friend, who told me about a therapist she was seeing with whom she was discontented but attached. As she spoke about her relationship with her therapist, it became apparent that she was angry with her therapist. I asked her about how she dealt with those feelings. She wept and complained that she felt helpless in her work with her therapist. Whenever she expressed dissatisfaction with her lack of progress in therapy, her therapist told she was wrong and that her complaints were expressions of resistance to the work of therapy. As we spoke, she became more and more anxious. I finally asked her if she was angry with me for pressing her to talk about how angry she was with her therapist. She returned to her tears and said that it was extremely difficult for her to experience and/or express her anger. She then told me about how, in her childhood, her mother beat her when she became angry. Her anger was not tolerated. It was extraordinarily difficult for her to feel it in the now and even more difficult to express it when it emerges into awareness and is felt. I encouraged her to speak to her therapist about this impairment.

In my practice I see the private person as being much more volatile than the public person. Its development in the early life of the individual is frequently incongruent with the more adult and socially adaptive systems of the public person. Two- and three-year-olds have only the rudimentary beginnings of a private person. And therefore, are more readily triggered into intense emotional expression.

The range of emotional intensities of the private person is much greater than those permitted to the public person. The private person's emotionality is flexibly transformative and is not as rigidly bound by the definitions contained in the public lexicon of feelings. It is here that individual differences between people are most vividly seen. Anger can be used to conceal pain. Sexuality can be used to express anger. Guilt is, at times, used to conceal anger and so on. Unlike the public person, the private person is uncomfortable with public inspection. There is an exception to this shyness; in loving relationships, a well-loved private person appreciates the loving, validating expression of another loving person. However, as I mentioned earlier, feelings of acceptance are not always greeted with pleasure by persons who were raised in abusive childhoods. The exposure of the private person to public observation can generate feelings ranging from pleasant embarrassment to humiliation, depending on the structural stability of the private person and the congruence (friendliness) of her relationship with her public person.

The Private Person and the NS

The private person's psychological selves, feelings, and personal reality are developed in relationships with the child's caretakers. It then becomes functionally autonomous and no longer needs the originating relationships to stabilize and reinforce its existence. It moves about in the world, nonconsciously seeking validation to perpetuate its neurological underpinnings.

The emotional intensities of the infant are centered on loving touch, pain, nutrient hunger, affect hunger, and a whole bodied pleasure. The care and attention paid to these conditions determine the nature and security of the infant's attachment to mothers and other caretakers (Siegel, 1999; Stern, 1985). The attentive and skilled care of the infant in the first months of life is responsible for the creation of Winnicott's (1972) "secure base." The secure base makes a major contribution to the stability and strength of the individual's personality. Genetic factors also contribute to the NS's integrity.

The secure base is the cornerstone of the kind of loving relationships the individual is able to make. Securely based psychological selves have a greater ability to grow out of childhood attachments. A secure base also minimizes difficulties encountered during the period when a person begins emerging into awareness in childhood.

The experience of separateness in psychological selves that are deprived of secure attachments by physical and/or emotional abuse can be dreadfully painful. Abuse and/or deprivation of the nurturance of affect hunger in early infancy weaken or distort personality development in individuals. They become prisoners in isolation continually suffering the pangs of affect hunger. These people share a fate like David Levy's (1937) puppies, who were deprived of suckling and who continued to compulsively suckle in adulthood.

There is substantial evidence that isolation during infancy and early childhood has debilitating physical and neurological consequences in the development of children (Spitz, 1946; Reisen, 1975; Chugani et al., 2001). In addition to emotional deprivation, traumatic or severe emotional intensity creates personal systems fixated in childhood structures. Bryck and Fisher (2012) report that "there is increasing evidence that exposure to stress at levels that overwhelm the organism's ability to manage that stress may negatively affect brain development" (p. 56).

I worked with a man who was raised by uneducated, childlike, well-meaning parents. When the man was eight, his father, a day laborer, in a gesture of "generosity," gave his son a cigarette to smoke. Unfortunately, he was unable to play with or talk to his son. His mother, an obese woman, sexually cuddled with him until he was 12 years old. When he could no longer stand the confusion of his sexual feelings with and about her, he would wander the streets of his city at night avoiding his family. His parents were kind, silent, and emotionally younger than their son. Their kindness contributed to a sweetness and charm in his personality. Their inability to relate emotionally was reflected in his emotional immaturity. The incestuous experience he had with his mother fixated his emotionality in early childhood. His "young one" (his characterological person) created the agenda of his life.

When he was 14, he met a girl who was being sexually abused by her father. Theirs, too, was a silent relationship. Neither had the ability to talk to the other about anything significant that was occurring emotionally between them. In their teen years, after they had sex, Nate was unable to spend time with Sheryl and would drop her off at her house and go to a bingo parlor. For years, he escaped by gambling at bingo. Eventually, he became a champion horseracing handicapper.

Their relationship helped them leave their families and start one of their own. Sheryl became pregnant in the third year of their marriage; unfortunately, their child was stillborn. They were unable to talk to one another about the meaning of their child's death. Their inability to share feelings deepened the loneliness that existed between them from the beginning of their relationship. Their marriage ended in her despair and his guilt.

Throughout all the years of his work and the relationships with his wife and lover, his private person dominated the conduct of his life. He remained trapped in a character structure whose only excited stimulations were sex and gambling. Eventually, because of his inability to relate to his women emotionally, he alienated both, which left him a lonely gambler. Believing his penis was small, he was not willing to risk seeking another relationship with a woman. This belief survived within him because it gave him an explanation and rationale to avoid confusing feelings that would inevitably arise in a relationship with another woman.

Individuals coming into intensive psychotherapy do so because they are plagued with highly unstable maladaptive relationships between their private and public persons. When the NS receives conflicting information from either or both the private and public person, the individual suffers anxiety, pain, and depression.

The Public Person of Personal Identity

The public person carries the many "faces" that everyone tries to save. It is not an immobile Greek mask. It is an active personal presentation seeking validational feedback from others. When it is in its steady-state condition, it uses the social lexicon of feelings to let others know who he is and what he wants in his relationship with them. For the most part, in everyday living the public person resides in the center of awareness.

The public person is shaped by familial, culturally conditioned emotionalities, the cultural ethos, community, and economic traditions within which the person is raised and socialized. All of these personality-shaping venues create the public person through repeated practice with others and by validation when socially approved behaviors are exercised.

Common sense is the primary cognitive process used by the public person to stabilize itself. Most of its cognitive categorizing process is formatted within the left brain's linear structures. Linear personal reality suppresses and/or represses the experience of nonlinear feelings.

Personal identity is shaped to accommodate to or assimilate information coming from the social environment into which the person is being acculturated. Cultural emotionality and personal reality guide the experience and behavioral shape of personal identity. In turn, it engages the social environment in ways designed to meet the needs of the affect hunger of the NS and its two persons. There are times under conditions of severe abuse in early childhood that an individual will develop more than two public persons.

The rules of personal identity are learned with the increasing contact a child has with everyday living in an increasingly complex social environment. As the child's engagement with others becomes more complex, she develops a set of emotional rules about how she "should" be in the world. I place quotes around "should" to indicate that these rules are idiosyncratically generated and are not universal mandates governing individual relationships with the rest of the world.

The social environment can be likened to the climate environment shaping the look of trees. The trees of Nova Scotia have a look that is different from the trees of the Sierra Nevada Mountains in California. This person's self-concepts (another term for psychological selves), feelings, and personal reality are closely congruent with the ways their society sets standards of propriety and normalcy.

In some ways, personal identity, in its use of personal reality, resembles Freud's superego. It is a system of automatic adaptations to the social situations within which the individual is engaged. It automatically, for the most part, follows the rules of the society into which she has been acculturated. If she does not follow the rules, she realizes that she is "different" from the norm. The task of the socialized public person is to accommodate the affect hunger of the NS to the social world within which it lives. Unlike Freud's superego, the public person is not a tyrannical homunculus that oppresses the id and the ego. However, there can be and frequently are severe mismatches between the personal realities of the private and public persons.

Recall a man I mentioned in the last chapter, a member of one of my groups, who was consistently pressed by other members to deal with his hurt feelings about his wife instead of simply complaining about what she did or did not do. He suddenly declared, "Now I get it! The job of this group is to turn us all into wimps." He went on to realize that if he acknowledged he felt hurt when his wife rejected him, he would appear weak and vulnerable, for which his father and friends on the street would have ridiculed him. This is an example of conflict between one's private and public persons.

The emotionality of the public person is based on the lexicon and behavioral styles of cultural emotionality. Argentineans dance the tango very differently from Finns who also love the tango. Not only does each culture have its own dictionary of emotional meanings, each has a distinctive stylistic way of expressing them. This is the social vocabulary I described in the last chapter.

The impress of culture is also seen in the way people hold themselves as they move about in everyday living. When I was a lieutenant in the American Army Air Corps on a few days of relaxation in Rio de Janeiro, I could spot American sailors on the street even though they were dressed in civilian clothes. The ways they dressed and moved clearly showed they were not Cariocas (residents of Rio).

Each culture has its own distinctive emotional traditions. It is not difficult to distinguish between Irish and Italian, or Finnish and Arab, or Korean American and African American emotionalities. My point, here, is that personal identity uses the cultural language of feelings, which facilitates public communication about feelings and interpersonal relationships. In the last chapter, I described the difference between the lexicons of public and private emotionalities. The cultural language of feelings contains the behavioral rules of social appropriateness for the culture in which its persons dwell.

Following the rules of a culture is part of the equilibratory role of the public person. When she is highly skilled in complying with the emotional and social conventions of her culture, she experiences ease, comfort, and success living in it.

"Face" is an example of the search for validational feedback through social conformity. Face is the presentation of self to the social environment that demands validating feedback. The invalidation of face creates pain and/or embarrassment. The public person is in a position similar to Snow White's stepmother demanding that she be told she "is the fairest one of all." The validating moment stabilizes not only the neurological systems underlying the personal identity but also creates pleasurable experiences of the NS being stabilized. "Saving face" is closely related to systems of personal reality. Much of the person's face is a reflection of its understanding and commitment to conform to the conventions of its culture. "Face" has surplus meanings in different cultures that are different from its meaning in the United States.

In the last chapter, I described the anxiety, depression, and pain that arise from the processes of suppression and repression. If a feeling cannot be suppressed or repressed, the private person is likely to be activated. When that happens, the idiosyncratic lexicon and intensity of feelings of the private person emerge into awareness and are expressed, frequently to the dismay of the public person. The emotional discrepancy between the public and private persons is a frequent source of the experience of embarrassment.

I have worked with people who yearn to find something in their lives which fits their "interests" in order to be able to know and be responsible for the ways they will live out the rest of their days. I worked with a man who had been successful in almost everything he did. He succeeded in his profession. Wonderful women loved him. His children adored him. Yet there was always something missing, something that did not fit. He complained that his profession did not really do it for him. His present wife did not really fit his interests or needs.

At one point in a discussion with me, he thought of a project that could really do it for him, and before he got the words out his mouth, he thought of reasons why it probably would not work. I then suggested that he had already found his way of life. It was to complain. In this way he could maintain the stability of the home he never wanted to leave. He began yawning, which was an indicator, about which we both were familiar, that I had said something emotionally disturbing. He went on to complain that I was difficult and that he had a hard time being with me. He resented me for turning his gaze inward. And then he realized he wanted to remain on the "dock of his life" waiting for "a ship of good fortune" to rescue him from his ennui about which he could comfortably complain.

The Origin of Personality Disorder

The theoretical symmetry of character structure and personal identity stands in sharp contrast to the chaos and pain that can arise from the different ways they interact with one another and the external environment. Personality disorder arises from the dissonance between character structure and personal identity. Persons suffering with personality disorders have character structures that dominate emotional experience and conduct.

A man with whom I was working told me that a part of him enjoyed "feeling sorry for myself." I asked him if that was the reason he complained so much. He protested that he was not a complainer. In the midst of his protestation, he stopped and exclaimed, "Of course! They go together." He had never seen the connection between complaining and feeling sorry for himself. "Feeling sorry for myself" was a way he comforted the very young boy in his private person, who had been severely physically abused. That was his way of validating and perpetuating structures of pain in his childhood. They were parts of his character structure.

His personal identity carried the image of a capable, self-sufficient adult male who should be able bear the burdens of adulthood. And he made sure those burdens "unfairly" existed in his life. Therefore, all of his complaints were "legitimate." He had been unaware of the dialogic interaction between his character structure and his personal identity. With this realization, he turned to me and said, with a smile on his face, "What will I do if I can't complain anymore?" How could he take care of and nourish his "young one," his private person?

Pain and confusion arise from the disequilibration of the NS caused by interactions between (1) information arising from the external environment and (2) the incompatibility of the operational differences existing between character structure and personal identity. The complexity of these interactions is compounded because these conditions organically continue to reverberate among themselves.

There is no start/stop mechanism in their operations, as implied in the stimulus-response theory. Recall in Chapter 7, I described feelings as being functionally the same as selves in the process of restoring the NS to its steady-state condition. The only difference between them is the experience of emotion in experiential ground of the equilibratory process. Feelings, for the most part, are experienced as explanations accompanied by a background display of some body process. For example, if one is embarrassed, she is telling herself that she is exposing something about herself that she did not want to be seen by others. Associated with that explanation, she blushes. In this case, her NS is flowing over the banks of its steady-state condition.

We do not start behaving simply because someone says something to us. Much of the time, the disequilibration of the NS has the look of a small stone dropped into a still pond. Under the worst circumstances, the disequilibration of brain dynamics resembles wave action when weather fronts collide in a perfect storm over an ocean.

In Chapter 3, I described the mindstorms. The continuing disequilibrium between the NS, character structure, and personal identity arises from the NS's mindless autoregulatory responses to its persons—which are designed to stabilize the NS. The complexity of the persons also requires them to seek homeostatic regulation, and they call upon the NS, already in disequilibrium for stabilizing information. A mindless vicious circle of mutual invalidation between the persons and the disoriented NS produces the mindstorm.

For many the mindless homeostatic pursuit of NS's equilibrium occurs nonconsciously when they are in a glazed condition. A person is in a glazed condition when her awareness is focused internally on displaying nonsensory information about her mind or the affect hunger of parts of her personality structures. In the glaze, her attention is focused on the internal movement of her mind. Sensory processes of sight or hearing may be displayed in the background of her awareness. This produces poor retention and a diminished ability to think.

If the disequilibrium between the NS, character structure, and personal identity endures over a long period of time or occurs with great intensity, the emotional reaction to the disequilibrium becomes habituated, and the individual suffers a continuing experience of anxiety, depression, and/or pain. An enduring, self-perpetuating pattern of emotion then becomes a theme in the personality structure of an individual.

I worked with a financially successful man who lived in constant anxiety about not having enough money. He was clear—there was nothing to worry about today. But he was plagued with a thought: "What if something goes wrong, will I be able to make it?" In the course of our work, other emotional problems, which brought him into therapy in the first place, were resolved. As his life became more peaceful, he became more miserable about the financial situation of his business. Could he meet his payroll? Did he have enough cash reserves to meet future obligations? I knew from other sources that his worries were groundless.

At one point when he was stressed about the cash flow of his business, I asked him if he knew whether his accounts receivable would cover his obligations. He looked at me with embarrassment and said that he did not keep track of that. He had a computer program that could readily access that information, but he kept it away from himself. It became clear from our discussion that he needed to avoid information about money that would be coming into his business in order to give himself a good reason for his anxiety. At that point, he became curious about his erroneous explanation of his characterological anxiety. As we explored this interesting question, he realized that he had always been anxious, and that it was rooted in his relationship with an explosively critical father. This is an example of a self-perpetuating emotional process that had become functionally autonomous. This person also exemplifies the intimate relationship between behavior and emotional and cognitive systems of the person.

Psychotherapeutic Implications of My Theory of the Person

The idea that personal and emotional systems can be thought of as systems of habits helped me to see the psychotherapeutic meaningfulness of repetitively interrupting the automaticity of these personal systems.[4] It was apparent such interruptions weakened habit strength. When this happens, de-automated brain structures have an opportunity to reorganize themselves in ways that are currently more age-appropriate and adaptive.

Thinking of personality systems as habituated neuropsychological systems has two therapeutic implications. First, instead of seeing personality problems as expressions of unresolved childhood conflicts or traumas—even if that is their source—the therapist can recognize them as habituated systems operating in the here and now, and liberate his therapy from the endless and frequently fruitless searches for the "reasons why" a psychological difficulty persists.

Second, by regarding personality systems as habits, the therapist can focus his attention on what the person is doing and not be blinded by what the person is saying. For example, I consulted with a therapist who worked with a man who was married to a beautiful woman. He diminished the importance of her beauty by complaining that she did not love him caringly enough. Despite his complaints, he was deeply attached to her. He constantly complained that she did not love him enough because she would not dress the way a former lover, a Las Vegas stripper, dressed. If only she would be more passionate by losing three more pounds. He engaged his therapist with incessant irrational complaints about the "external" things of the marriage, which validated his complaint that he was perpetually doomed to never be loved enough.

His complaints and demands confused and offended his wife. Whenever his marriage improved, as when his wife touched him tenderly and he had a glimpse of himself avoiding a deeper pain within him, he embraced his complaints with renewed ardor, which confused and dismayed his therapist. Her attempts to help him see the delusional nature of the "reality" of his deprivations simply reinforced it.

It became clear that all of this was done in order to keep the loving experience between his wife and himself at bay. His complaints about not getting enough from his wife were designed to keep her and his therapist just far enough away from warm emotional contact, but not too far. Warm emotional contact triggered the pain of his childhood.

When the therapist saw his complaints as flights from pain, she could acknowledge his pain and not get involved in debates with him about the "reality" of his "terrible" dilemma—debates he was devoted to because they helped keep him in the left hemisphere of his brain and away from the painful emotionality of his childhood.

When a cognitive process consistently classifies information of any kind, it becomes a construct, a well-practiced idea. Persons are constructs. As expressions of and the experience of neuropsychological systems, they have all the fluidity and changeability of neurological process. They change to accommodate or assimilate new information that demands neuropsychological integrity and growth. Persons grow and change with the changing circumstances of their lives. Like all living systems, persons either grow or die (Ainsworth-Land, 1986). Psychotherapy helps persons break emotional habits that are age-inappropriate, and which are behaviorally and emotionally dysfunctional.

My work with Raymond, the man I described in Chapter 2, exemplifies what I mean by the habituation of a self-presentation. Because of his sour personal presentation, he had great difficulty finding and keeping jobs and close friendships. Also, close relationships are painful to him. At one point, I asked him if he was able to see how miserable he looked when he was interviewing for a job. He said he had not thought about it. I suggested he smile. He looked pained and withdrew from me. I urged him to look at me and give me a smile. My invitation deeply offended him. In this period of our work, I had no idea how painful it would be for him to like me. He accused me of wanting him to be fraudulent, which would be especially true if he smiled at me. To smile would be dishonest. Most of his personal systems were structured to not experience interpersonal pleasure. Moreover, he took great pride in being "honest"; his personal identity demanded it. He was unhappy and miserable and, in all honesty, he had to show it. In addition, nonconsciously, his angry presentation was designed to keep others at an emotionally safe distance.

Smiles are not simply reactions of pleasure. They are also emissaries reaching out into the social environment seeking validational feedback. They are subtle, mostly nonconscious messengers of affect hunger soliciting reinforcing information from others to stabilize and perpetuate neurological structures underlying personality systems. Although intentional solicitation is disdained in polite society, we all do it, for the most part unintentionally. It is a form of interpersonal manipulation. Unfortunately, manipulation is frequently conflated with intentionality and the person can be thought of as a deceitful schemer.

I am not using the term "manipulation" pejoratively. Some manipulations may be deceitful; others are just automatic behaviors to get something done without duplicitous intent. I manipulate a screwdriver to fix things and I am straightforward about it. On the other hand, when I get angry with my wife, I am not so sure about my straightforwardness. The manipulations of my emotional equilibrations often betray my duplicity.

To suggest that the person seeking validational feedback is being manipulative frequently creates embarrassment and denial. Nevertheless, it is a constant presence in all interpersonal engagements. The psychoanalytic literature has numerous references to this aspect of human nature. Sandor Ferenczi's (1931) discussion of affect hunger helped me understand Hellmuth Kaiser's (Fierman, 1965) concept of the "universal symptom"; the search (or demand) for validational feedback. The background solicitation for validational feedback is what Theodore Reik (1948) was hearing when he was "listening with the third ear."

This request does not mean that the person is seeking pleasant feedback. The kind of feedback a person seeks is shaped by character structure. For some, pleasurable feedback sends shivers of anxiety through their bodies. Others are pleasantly tanned in the sunshine of warm approval. In short, emotional habits are not simply automatic behaviors or experiences with no functional content. They are calls for feedback to reinforce the stability of neural systems underlying their existence.

The Influence of Nonconscious Behavioral Solicitations

The story of Clever Hans illustrates the subtle unintentional nature of the ways in which interpersonal feedback is solicited and to which it is responded. Clever Hans was an Arabian stallion purchased in 1900 by Wilhelm von Osten, a retired schoolteacher who believed that animals were as intelligent as humans. To prove his point, he tried to teach a cat, a horse, and a troublesome bear to solve simple arithmetic problems. The bear and cat were not interested. But Clever Hans responded beautifully. Von Osten taught him to recognize numbers from one to nine. Or at least von Osten thought that was what he was doing. Soon, Clever Hans was able to "solve" more complex problems including the square root of some numbers. Clever Hans and von Osten became famous.

O. Pfungst, a psychologist from Berlin, was skeptical. When he called to Clever Hans the numbers of a simple arithmetic problem, while hiding behind a blackboard, Clever Hans failed every test. Pfungst concluded that Hans was taking subtle visual clues from his questioners. Hans was able to detect slight head movements and signs of tension of his questioner as he came close to a desired answer. These clues signaled Hans to stop tapping his hoof.

Pfungst went on to test this hypothesis in his laboratory. The students were instructed to ask questions like those which were asked of Clever Hans. Pfungst, like Clever Hans, responded to their questions by tapping his "hoof." The results were spectacular. Over 90% of his subjects provided him with unintentional visual clues telling him when to stop tapping. Presumably, these clues were the same as those noted by Clever Hans when he was "questioned." Interestingly, for the purposes of my theory, the subjects of Pfungst's experiment were unaware of sending clues. This phenomenon became known as the "Clever Hans effect."

Robert Rosenthal (2003) has spent his professional life studying and demonstrating the influences of intended and unintended interpersonal expectancies on the behavior of humans and animals. In the later part of the twentieth century, due to his efforts, the phenomenon has become known as the "Pygmalion Effect." There is a biological purpose in this subliminal, unintentional, information exchange. One thing is common to each of the phenomena I have described: the repetitive exchange of validational feedback, which reinforces the stability and integrity of psychological systems.

Being on the receiving ends of smiles and pats on the back, for most people, is stabilizing and pleasant. Over time and repeated rehearsal, these reinforcing experiences create stable, change-resistant, psychological structures, physical behaviors, and experiences. "Practice doesn't make perfect. Practice makes permanent." In the next chapter, I will describe the creative ways psychotherapy enables people to escape the limitations of emotional habituation.

Notes

1. It is unfortunate that the word "homeostasis" has "stasis" in it that connotes a static condition rather than a dynamic steady-state condition.
2. This is the way I refer to characterologically immature personalities in my practice.
3. I am using St. Augustine only as an example. The confusion about sexuality is worldwide. It exists equally in the monotheistic religions of Christianity, Islam, and Judaism.
4. It is beyond the purpose of this book to unravel the relationship between the NS and the reinforcement of habits or the distinction between increasing the habit strength of a personality structure by intermittent interruption and weakening its habit strength by repetitiously interrupting it. This is one of the theoretical places where the meaningfulness of my theory can be experimentally tested.

Chapter 9

The Art of Psychotherapy

The End of the Journey

Any discussion of "art" involves the loving production of "beauty." The art of psychotherapy as I see it is also interlaced with love. This chapter will describe how love and beauty emerge in psychotherapy for both the therapist and the persons she serves.

In this chapter, I will describe psychotherapy as an extremely diverse social institution proclaiming the existence of 600 different therapies and with dyadic practices of psychotherapy that are remarkably similar within that diversity. Then I will describe psychotherapy based on the theory of personality I have been describing in this book. This is unusual because theories of psychotherapy and theories of personality have never been integrated. Mine is! And finally, I will comment on the art of a psychotherapy enriched by a brain-based theory of personality.

While my theory is paradigmatically different from conventional theories, it has a similarity to a good wine that is composed of different flavors. Wines have combinations of flavors; like dry, sweet, and a hint of lemon, peach, spice, and so on. My theory has the flavors of psychoanalysis, cognitive behaviorism, constructivism, Gestalt psychology, and nondirective psychotherapy. There are also very distinct flavors of Piaget, the Theater of the Absurd, and Zen in it.

The Different Goals of Psychotherapy: Feeling Better Versus Personality Change

From the very beginning of psychoanalysis, analysts wanted to do more than help people feel better. They wanted to help people change their personalities, especially their character structures (Reich, 1933/1945; Kaiser in Fierman, 1965), in order to enable them to live the rest of their lives with greater ease and personal productivity.

The differences between the goals of helping people feel better and helping them change their personalities have different psychotherapeutic consequences, a distinction not clearly recognized in today's psychotherapy research literature. Epistemologically, present day psychological research does not conceptualize personality variables in ways that are either researchable or relevant to the work of characterologically oriented psychotherapists (Barrett, 2006; Beutler, 2009; Gross, 2001; Roediger, 2004).

Despite the differences in psychotherapy techniques and explanations, I have found similarities in psychotherapy relationships of different persuasions that explain why psychotherapy research has not found significant differences between them with respect to how effective they are. Rosenzweig (1936) called this finding the Dodo Bird Verdict. In Alice's Wonderland, it declared that all of the contestants, starting at different places and times in a caucus race, were winners. But research has found that there are significant outcome differences between therapists. Some therapists are more effective than others. I believe the effectiveness of therapists is highly correlated with their ability to make contact with their clients.

The Luxurious Therapeutic Dyad

Regardless of what theoretical orientation a therapist uses, most psychotherapy relationships are emotionally luxurious. The interpersonal engagement of any kind of well-practiced psychotherapy ameliorates personal distress. In May 2000, I attended the annual meeting of the Society for the Exploration of Psychotherapy Integration (SEPI) in Washington, D.C., and later in that month I went to the conference on the Evolution of Psychotherapy in Anaheim, California. At these meetings I became aware of the behavioral similarities of experienced therapists of different persuasions who conducted their demonstrational therapeutic sessions. This led me to an understanding of why people seeking help feel better regardless of different psychotherapeutic orientations.

At both meetings, presenters talked about psychotherapy in different languages. They had different conceptions about what the nature of help was or should be. Underlying these differences were disparate assumptions about the nature of personality and the tasks of psychotherapy. The presenters described what they thought psychotherapy looked like, and it looked different to all of them.

This is not an unusual observation. Salvador Minuchin, at the Evolution of Psychotherapy conference, commented on the fact that the diversity of explanations about the nature of psychotherapy was both enormous and intelligent. He went on to say that he and all the presenters believed that they were "effective" therapists. He also noted that it was remarkable that so many dedicated and talented men and women who have participated in the therapeutic relationship have come up with so many different explanations about its nature. Furthermore, he said that regardless of their explanatory differences, they were all helpful (the Dodo Bird Verdict).

I agreed. I saw it with my own eyes. As part of the Evolution of Psychotherapy conference, several of the presenters conducted a demonstration interview with a volunteer from the audience. Each presenter conducted his interview in his own way (they were all males). All the interviewees left their 20-minute sessions expressing gratitude for the "help" they received.

The bedlam of the different theoretical voices caused me to think they were talking about different interpersonal enterprises. This observation puzzled me. If they were different kinds of relationships, why, then, did all the interviewees express the same appreciation for the different kinds of help they received in their 20-minute sessions? The clatter of explanations had a dizzying effect on me. I turned the sound off. The quieting peace that followed allowed me to look at what these different therapists were doing with their client/patients. Without being distracted by the noise of their different explanatory systems, I was struck by how much alike they looked.

Of course, the therapists were different in their personal presentations. Albert Ellis's aggressive assertiveness was different from Eugene Gendlin's gentle empathy or Leslie Greenberg's Santa Claus geniality. But they were all authoritative and had a presence and wisdom that comes with years of practice and teaching. They were all respectful and comfortable with their interviewee. They were clearly interested in being helpful. At the beginning of each demonstration, the presenters gently took care to put their clients at ease. All of this was done without asking anything in the way of personal validational feedback back from the interviewee. They made eye contact and continually sent nonverbal signals of approval and understanding to the client/patient. They were all quiet, warm, nonjudgmental, and intuitively empathic. It was obvious they wanted to have a clear understanding of how their interviewees experienced their distress. Each therapist asked penetrating questions until he understood his client's problem. Their questions demonstrated the intelligent interest of the therapist and conveyed to the client that he or she was in competent hands. The therapists carefully proceeded to reframe their interviewee's problem in their own terms. The therapists' restatement of the problem caused the interviewee to think about his or her problem in a new way. The clients were given a new cognitive perspective on the nature of her/his distress. It is easy to see why they felt better after the demonstration, being the recipients of all this dedicated intelligent interest and warm intuitive attention. Moreover, they all felt helped by being given a novel validating explanatory perspective on themselves.

The psychotherapeutic benefit of feeling better does not explain how the therapeutic dyad contributes to the intensive hard work of changing personality structures created in early childhood. Feeling better for some people may be enough to change some meaningful aspects of their personalities and their behaviors, but these aspects are not the habituated structures that cause unending difficulties for many seeking psychotherapeutic help. It is the repeated intense emotional interaction between the therapist and client that enables deep-seated characterological change to happen with varying degrees of completeness.

My increasing recognition of the importance of the interpersonal relationship between therapist and client as a major source of psychotherapeutic change led me into the exploration of the great mystery of human existence: the experience of the selves and feelings (a condition of the self) of the person. Intensive psychotherapy, intentionally or not, is involved in helping people untangle this mystery.

The solution to this mystery, to which I have been referring throughout this book, resides in recognizing that the orientation of the NS interacting with the cognition of the prefrontal cortex and the neurologically distributed systems of consciousness produces the experience of the mind. In my theory, the mind's prime imperative is the maintenance of the rest of the brain in its homeostatic condition by reducing complexity or by interrupting the automatic operations of maladaptive neural systems that destabilize the brain.

This leads to a theory of psychotherapy that includes the recognition of cerebral dynamics as important neurological systems that produce personality disorders. Nerves repeatedly interacting with one another form stable cell assemblies. They react automatically and become functionally autonomous. They are reinforced by information that exercises their current operating systems. In other words, if they occur in the prefrontal cortex, they are habituated self-perpetuating structures: personality structures. When, over time, they become age inappropriate, they are the neurological underpinnings of personality disorders.

The work of psychotherapy is the interruption of these habituated personality structures by disrupting their automatic operations, which reduces their habit strength. This work, in addition to explanation and insight, adds a major dimension to the art of psychotherapy. The interruptive process involves the therapist's person. With this explanation, we have a description of a relational psychotherapy that integrates brain dynamics with personality processes.

The Unique Psychotherapeutic Dyad

Psychotherapy, historically, is a new kind of interpersonal dyad. It is different in four ways from dyads that have existed before. First, it is an abstract, emotional relationship devoted to helping people escape from the prisons of their childhoods and helping them to learn new more age-appropriate emotional skills. It contains no physical objects around which the therapist and client engage. I can think of no other dyadic relationship where there are no "things" around which members of the dyad engage. Alice Miller's (1981) felicitous phrase "prisoners of childhood" encapsulates this psychotherapeutic goal, and, when rephrased states, that psychotherapy seeks to help people escape from the prisons of their childhoods.

The uniqueness of the psychotherapeutic dyad resides in the fact that the relationship creates a kind of emotionality between therapist and client that does not occur in conventional relationships. All human relationships up to the late nineteenth century had some physical things around which ordinary dyads were engaged. In intensive characterologically oriented psychotherapy, the primary task of this relationship has no crucially relevant external object. Psychotherapy is not about the fee the client pays in private practice, nor finding solutions to the practical problems of living. These may be important parts of what happens between members of the therapeutic dyad, but they are secondary to the therapeutic work.

The primary tasks of intensive characterologically oriented psychotherapy are changing the habituated emotionality of the person (her character structure), and facilitating the creation of new, age-appropriate ones.

Second, another primary task is the alleviation of emotional distress. In previous chapters, I described the fact that the experience of nonlinear/nonsensory process is a recent human development. Because of this, humans do not have the cognitive skills with nonsensory process they have with sensory process, especially vision.

Third, the therapist refrains from seeking personal validational feedback from the help-seeking person. With practice the therapist learns to avoid his personal search for reciprocal feedback in his therapeutic relationships. This creates a free "space" in the therapeutic relationship. Refraining from asking for emotional validation simplifies the emotional process, freeing the therapist and client to more easily focus on their therapeutic work.

And fourth, helping people become more skilled emotionally changes those people's personalities. In Chapter 7, I proposed that emotionality was the self in the process of stabilizing itself. Therefore, if emotionality is changed, personality is changed. This is where my theory is integrated with practice. Helping people increase emotional skill is different from changing behaviors and/or the way they experience themselves. This kind of change not only relieves anxiety and depression; it enables them to interact with others more productively for themselves.

The Nonsensory/Nonlinear Nature of the Therapeutic Dyad

In the earlier chapters of this book, I described the evolutionary growth of the prefrontal cortex as the autoregulatory system of the rest of the brain. The interactions of the anterior cingulate cortex (the orienting system), the cortex (cognition), and consciousness created the mind. Over evolutionary time, humans could experience nonlinear/nonsensory process of the frontal areas of the brain. They became self-conscious. At first, ancients found it difficult to fathom the constant presence of something in their experience that they could not see, but which significantly affected the ways they related to one another and how they lived their lives. The experience of emotionality, a form of self-experiencing, has been the great mystery of human existence.

From the beginning of self-awareness, humans have been plagued with an unnamable and unfathomable experience of a strange movement occurring in their brains and bodies. Over the centuries, humans have learned to experience and classify this experience as their selves, and their selves in autoregulatory process (feelings), with increasing competence. For a theological description of this historical, emotional growth let me refer you to *The gift of the Jews: How a tribe of desert nomads changed the way everyone thinks and feels* (Cahill, 1998).

In the three Western monotheistic religions, there is a belief that self-experiencing resides at the heart of mystical experience. Armstrong (1994) describes this in the following quote:

> The mystics have long insisted that God is not Another Being; they have claimed he does not really exist and that it is better to call him Nothing. This God is not in tune with the atheistic mood of our secular society, with its distrust of inadequate images of the Absolute. Instead of seeing God as an objective Fact, which can be demonstrated by means of scientific proof, mystics have claimed that he is a subjective experience, mysteriously experienced in the ground of being. This God is to be approached through the imagination and can be seen as a kind of art form, akin to the other great artistic symbols that have expressed the ineffable mystery, beauty and value of life. . . . Like all art, mysticism requires intelligence, discipline and self-criticism as a safeguard against indulgent emotionalism and projection.
>
> (p. 396)

Throughout her *History of God*, Armstrong reports that many theologians believed the experience of God was the experience of self. Many theologists declared that God was either in them or is a presence in all of mankind. With research on the limbic system, we are coming closer to a way of validating the belief that this mysterious experience is, indeed, within us, whether or not we believe in the existence of a supernatural being.

As we have lived with these "unnamable" experiences, humans have gained greater skills in bringing emotion into awareness and have an increased ability to classify experiences of emotion into feelings, which have become less mysterious. Throughout the ages, we have been wedded to the tradition of projecting the mysteries of our emotionalities outward onto gods or a God as a way of stabilizing ourselves.

We no longer need to project self-experiencing outward in the physical world. We have narrowed this mystery down to finding a solution in a theory of cerebral autoregulation. With that knowledge, we recognize that humans have become more skilled with the experience of emotions and their feelings. When a person is unskilled with his emotional experiencing, he experiences confusions about where he is in his relations with others. This is the mystery people bring into therapists' offices.

It is not surprising, therefore, that until the nineteenth century, humans did not or could not establish relationships that dealt solely with nonlinear/nonsensory process. At the beginning of modern psychotherapy, emotionality was a mystery that confounded the Breuer/Anna O. relationship and still does for many therapists (de Oliveira and Vandenberghe, 2009). It was in this time that Martin Buber (1958) published his book on the emotional awesomeness of the "I–Thou" relationship. This is the mystery into which the psychotherapeutic dyad delves by interrupting the automaticity of maladaptive personality structures and facilitating the creation of new ones to liberate the person.

The Absence of Dyadic Reciprocity in Psychotherapy

Under ideal circumstances, the therapist's person is neither validated nor emotionally nourished by the client. He does not seek affection, respect, or admiration from the person with whom he is working. Humans require validational feedback to stabilize the affect hunger of their Neurological Selves. Most validation-seeking self-presentations are learned in childhood. By the time a person reaches adulthood, her self-presentations have been honed by practice for so many years that they become habituated and therefore operate outside of awareness.

It takes years of work for the therapist and anyone else to break that habit and relate to the person with whom they are working without requiring anything from them besides therapeutic work and a fee. The therapist is nourished by his love of the client's work and talent. And much like other artists, therapists are also nourished by the creativity of their own work. The therapeutic relationship is additionally luxurious for the client because the therapist is attentive, nonjudgmental, empathic, and holds the person with whom he is working in "unconditional positive regard." Carl Rogers's injunction to work with people with "unconditional positive regard" is therapeutically necessary. When one judges something, he has come to a conclusion. Coming to a conclusion is cognitively limiting because there is no need for further curiosity. If a therapist becomes enamored of his theory or an interpretation, his blindness causes him to miss essential therapeutic information that occurs on the baseline aspects of his relationship with the person who is seeking his help. In addition to his nonjudgmental stance, the therapist enjoys being with a client. How much more luxurious can a dyadic relationship get? These skills take years to develop.

In this relationship, the client, within conversational limits, can be any way she wants to be and continue to be listened to with respect and with an enduring desire on the part of the therapist to be helpful. Nowhere else in life can a person have this freedom except in infancy and, unfortunately, even there many infants are punished for not being obedient to the validational needs of their caregivers.

Interrupting Automaticity

While these unique conditions of the therapeutic relationship undoubtedly play a role in interrupting emotional automaticities, they do so accidentally. The very nature of the therapeutic dyad interrupts the expectations of many people who enter psychotherapy. For them, the normal expectation in intimate, primary relationships is to be disrespected, not listened to, and subjected to the emotional needs of the other person. These are the underlying emotional reasons that bring most people into psychotherapy. It is a small wonder that people feel better talking with an experienced psychotherapist who holds them in "unconditional positive regard."

Chapter 1 described the reasons why therapeutic validation on the baseline of the dyadic triangle is necessary for the relationship to be psychotherapeutically productive. Psychotherapy, using baseline dialogue, has a marked resemblance to the nonlinearity of Eastern mystical traditions. Sufi tales and Zen koans and metaphors are cast into nonlinear cognitive constructs. They illuminate previously unexperienced emotional and interpersonal relationships. In both traditions, the client is confronted with nonlinear information that does not make linear sense. When this happens, she is encouraged to make "sense" out of a disturbingly unfamiliar emotional moment.

This reminds me of the Zen tale of "two men from the land of fools" who heard there was a visitor in their village called the "polite man." They agreed that it would be a good idea to meet with him. At the village, they saw a stranger sitting by the well in the center of the village. One of the "fools" asked the other if the stranger was the polite man. His friend said he didn't know but he would go and ask the stranger. The friend approached the stranger and asked, "Are you the polite man?" The stranger looked up and said, "Get away from me or I will break every tooth in your head." He fled back to his friend, who asked, "Is he the polite man?" "I don't know" he replied, "he didn't tell me."

When confronted with an "I-Thou" observation or confrontation by a therapist, the client very often is confused because she has been taught to ignore emotional process that lies in the background of awareness in conversations. Observations of this kind trigger right-brained activity, which is neurologically closer to the emotional center of the person than linear explanations about the emotional effects of family dynamics. The client is left with the disturbing discomfort of not "knowing" what to do or how to linearly think about the conundrum with which she has been confronted. To escape her confusion, she will ask the therapist to explain what or why the confrontation confused her, just like the "fool" in the Zen story who couldn't read the Polite Man's nonlinear hostility.

This is one of the places where emotional intensity arises in psychotherapy. Instead of explaining, the therapist takes the person through the process she triggered. A man, who is caught in a miserably attached marriage, complained to me about how his wife, upon whom he was financially dependent, was consistently demeaning and insulting to him. I asked him how he reacted to her when she tore him down. He said it made him furious and he would attack her back. "How long has this been going on in the marriage?" I asked. "It's been going on for years," he said. "And it hasn't gotten any better?" I asked. "No! In fact, it's gotten worse. We haven't had sex in years," he replied. With that, I congratulated him and suggested that he didn't need my help. He was confused and asked me what I was talking about. "You and your wife have created a perfect life for yourselves." "You are crazy. We are miserable." "Exactly" I replied.

He was puzzled and annoyed. "But we love each other." "That's right. I don't doubt that," I said. After a few moments of uneasy silence, he said, "I have never been happy in a relationship with a woman." Realizing this he became curious about the nature of his unhappiness with women, which led to an exploration of his very painful relationship with his narcissistic mother who disliked him. He bypassed understanding and began experiencing both his anger and pain with his mother, which had become a habituated part of his character structure. He became interpersonally more skilled as he was able to experience how the pain of his relationship with his mother affected his relationship with his wife. His increased emotional skill resulted in personality change.

When the therapist and client agree to the task of increasing her nonlinear cognitive skills, their task changes from helping her person feel better or understanding a relational dilemma, to bringing about personality change. From this point on the goal of therapy is primarily but not exclusively oriented toward helping the person break painful and conflictual emotional habits and learn new emotional skills. The art of the therapist is more actively engaged in this effort.

Throughout this book I have been using the terms "automated structures" and "habits" synonymously. Psychological habits, unlike physical ones, are functionally autonomous, self-perpetuating structures that continue to exist in the present by unintentionally (nonconsciously) being validated in interactions with others that maintain and reinforce their existence.

This is a more accurate description of the change-resistant nature of personality structures than thinking of emotional reactions as unresolved unconscious conflicts in loving relationships of childhood, or disturbing childhood memories that have been repressed but continue to unconsciously disturb personalities. The vignette about the man with a perpetually miserable marriage that I described earlier is an example of mindless self-perpetuating habituated psychological systems. Moreover, this point of view opens the door to more innovative ways of participating in the psychotherapeutic adventure.

I have found it simpler and more direct to help a person to participate with me in the interruption of a maladaptive emotional habit, than to encourage the person to recall a childhood conflict in the hope that the recall would erase the psychological disability. The active work of the client in recognizing the impulse to act, think, or feel in a habituated way and then to stop the behavior or experience resembles a cognitive behavioral exercise. Being mindful of maladaptive emotional habits is very helpful in deconstructing troublesome personality structures.

In an initial interview with a man who told me that he was suffering from anxiety, he impressed me with how deeply he had been suffering. In fact, his pain was so compelling, I commented, without much sympathy, that it must be awful to live with such agony. He looked at me with confusion. I asked him to tell me how I had confused him. His face turned red and was furious with me, asking me what kind of a heartless therapist was I that I couldn't commiserate with his distress. In the midst of his complaint, I asked him if he was anxious at that moment. He looked at me with surprise; recognizing that he, in fact, was not anxious, but furious. I suggested that his anger with me might be a clue to a way of getting rid of his anxiety. Much of our work centered on his difficulty with anger, which was a deeply imbedded part of his character structure and which he continually tried to suppress. In place of his unwelcome anger, he experienced anxiety and suffering. As he developed increasing skill with angry feelings, he no longer needed to seek sympathy and support for his suffering. He stopped suffering and began experiencing himself more respectfully.

Shortly after the transference hypothesis was proposed, analysts became aware that the insight or explanation had to be "worked through." Working through an interpretation involves constantly repeating it. The aphorism "practice makes permanent; not perfect" explains the work of habituating emotional/personality structures. In other words, with repetition the insight or explanation becomes a habituated belief. As such it can provide the person with the relaxation that reasonable, well-practiced beliefs provided.

This is exemplified by a man I worked with who loved his constantly complaining mother. In his childhood he tried to accommodate her distress by taking care of her and his chronically sick older brother. After college, he escaped from home and became a successful businessman. He married a woman who, like his mother, constantly complained. It was extraordinarily difficult for him to see the similarity between his efforts to placate his wife's complaints and his mother's. He had even greater difficulty in recognizing that his compliance with his mother's reality operated in his efforts to accommodate his wife's complaints about him. I consistently called attention to how readily he agreed with his wife without any accompanying recognition of his desire to make her happy with him. He tried to accept her personal reality even when it violated his own reality. Gradually the fight invaded their sex. At this point, he recognized that his efforts had been fruitless. He realized that he couldn't make either his mother or wife happy. He was liberated from a childhood-habituated system dedicated to get his mother to appreciate how much he wanted to make her happy.

In another example, I worked with a woman who, in the beginning of our work, had great difficulty saying what she meant about her emotional experience. At the outset, when she tried to explain the frustrations she felt in her marriage, she confused me and her comrades in group therapy. She was unaware of the emotional difficulty she had articulating her confusion and pain. Over time, we were able to help her to become mindful of this emotional and cognitive difficulty by demanding and encouraging her to focus on her emotional experience and then to articulate that experience. As time went by, in both individual and group therapy, where much of her therapeutic work was centered on baseline communication, she expanded her emotional vocabulary and developed greater skills in experiencing and expressing her feelings. With this, she became much less anxious/depressed and much more autonomous in her marriage.

Helping people alter inappropriate emotional habits enables their brains to reorganize the autoregulatory systems of the Neurological Self. In so doing, the person can experience a greater range of feelings, and their intensities, and have more age-appropriate cognitive appraisals of them.

Having described the theoretical nature of my therapeutic work, I will now describe the way I practice it in greater detail.

The Psychotherapeutic Journey

Initially people come into psychotherapy to be relieved of painful confusions caused by the operations of childhood "realities," which are shaped to cope with the pains, anxieties, or depressions of their families during their formative years. In effect, their goal is to feel better or to solve some emotional problem. I do not recall anyone seeking psychotherapy in my practice who simply wished to indulge in the philosophical and/or aesthetic pursuit of self-knowledge. That desire can come later. The turning point in therapy comes after the person begins feeling better both because of the nourishment of the therapeutic relationship and because aspects of the presenting problem no longer are as disturbing as they were at the beginning of therapy.

I liken the psychotherapeutic journey to a trip on a train, where the help-seeking person decides on a particular "feeling better" destination but then, after reaching it, may discover that there are other important destinations to visit. For example, a woman might begin therapy by declaring, "I want to be able to stop fighting with my boyfriend." When she gets there, she becomes aware of other troublesome issues in her personality such as not tolerating the loving aspects of her sexual experience. With this awareness, she may or may not decide to get better acquainted with a confused or tormented sexuality, which underlies the pain/anxiety/anger that caused her to fight with her boyfriend. Her decisions to go further on the trip are based on the nature and quality of her relationship with her therapist and on the economic and emotional circumstances of her life. If she decides to enter the work of learning more about her emotionality, she is aware and appreciative of the nonlinear, metaphoric engagement of her therapist. When she is meaningfully informed about the ways her therapist works, she does not feel misled when confronted with the sometimes very painful discomfort of emotional experiences induced by her therapist. I have never seen a final therapeutic destination . . . not in my practice nor in myself. Now, here in my old age, I still find myself changing.

The Therapist's Person in the Therapeutic Process

I have found it most helpful to develop a therapeutic contract with the person with whom I am working, as close to the initial session as possible. The contract contains the easily negotiated fee, appointment schedule, insurance cooperation, and payment schedules. Next, it is helpful to get some initial indication about the emotional difficulties that bring the person to see me, although there are times when it takes several sessions for me to have a clear idea of this. When I do, I translate that into a therapeutic experience of what the work will be.

As mentioned earlier, in the initial interview it is helpful for the therapist to have some ideas about the emotional difficulty the person is bringing into therapy. These ideas are a kind of psychotherapeutic diagnosis. It is an assessment of the emotional skills of the person seeking help. The therapeutic diagnosis is not a DSM-V labeling. I begin the diagnostic process by seeking to understand the kind of emotional response the client is trying to elicit from me. What kind of impression does that person want to make? What are the emotional constituents of that impression? For example, is that person trying to impress the therapist with how bright he is? (As I did with Hellmuth Kaiser.) Does she want me to find her physically attractive? Is he asking to be taken care of? And so on. Presentations provide clues about the nature of the emotional skills of that person. Some people find the experience of being angry to be difficult, loathsome, and/or embarrassing. On the other hand, there are those who find great comfort in being angry. For those who detest anger, becoming angry impairs their ability to think. Those who are comforted in anger, find their intellectual abilities enhanced when they are angry or find a reason to be angry. This is true of other feelings. Those suffering from depression find feelings of being loved difficult. Whatever kind of emotional organization a person presents, it has become habituated and is functionally autonomous and self-perpetuating.

Answers to the questions leading to the psychotherapeutic diagnosis describe the functional nature of the emotional structure of the person seeking help. The therapist continues a search for an understanding about the adaptive purposes of behavioral and/or characterological repetitiousness. In this exploration, the work of the therapeutic dyad raises questions that have been hidden in the habituation of an emotional pattern that is maladaptive.

In Chapter 7, I discussed the social and idiosyncratic lexicon of feelings that an individual uses. What kinds of feelings emerge when the person is unable to use the social lexicon of feelings that are conventionally available? What kinds of feelings are most easily experienced and used? What feelings are avoided? Within the frame of my theory, personality is the habituated organization of the emotionality of the person.

And finally, regarding the diagnostic effort, the therapist wants to know about the person's childhood history. The person's relationships with primary caregivers are the templates upon which emotional structures are built. The early emotional foundations of personality are constructed from the intrauterine conditions of the individual's fetal environment, to the ways infants are held, fed, and cared for, and to how the emotional needs of parents impact their children. These then become elaborated into rules of conduct in the early childhood years of the person's development. Emotional habits emerge as the person copes with the complexities of social life. The therapist learns about the emotional habits of the person with whom she is working by observing the patterns of emotionality that arise from the person she is helping. What feelings are easy or difficult to express or use in different kinds of relationships? What emotional ranges of intensity are available? How intelligent is the person about the uses of her "feelings"? Connecting these observations to the person's relationships with caretakers enables the therapist to develop a plan of treatment.

In the first session, the client describes his/her reasons for coming for help. They are about love, family, occupational relationships, physical disorders, emotional confusions, and other behavioral or emotional complaints. Whatever distresses the person is usually cast into some external relational explanation. The description of the present life of the person carries with it information about how the person experiences feelings in these relationships. Most often they contain repetitious themes about how they are being treated. There are those who experience themselves as perennial victims. Others talk about wanting to achieve some standard of success and being frustrated in these efforts. And still others, in the retirement years of their lives, confront the dilemma of meaninglessness in their existence.

Clients are introduced to the nature of their work and the nature of his/her relationship to the therapist. It is important, in an initial interview, to engage the person emotionally. This serves two purposes. First, I am introducing the person into a way that I work by engaging them on the baseline of our dyadic triangle. In my practice, I very frequently see persons who have been in therapy before. By engaging the person on the baseline, I inform him about what to expect of me and the kind of psychotherapy I practice, which is different from his other therapeutic relationships. Second, I interrupt a habituated personality structure, which becomes a very important part of our therapeutic work. At this moment, my client experiences something new about his self, which creates a sense of understanding the work of psychotherapy accompanied with hope. The client is then prepared to begin his work with me. Then there are no unexpected surprises.

In relational psychotherapy, the therapist's person becomes a powerful therapeutic instrument. Instead of trying to be reactively interpretive, the traditional psychoanalytic stance, the relational therapist actively engages the person with whom she is working in five ways.

First, is the diagnostic effort. Lying behind the social feeling lexicon, which is usually employed in casual conversation, are habituated emotional structures set up in early childhood and elaborated as the person grows to accommodate adulthood. Psychotherapeutic diagnosis about the idiosyncratic feeling lexicon of the person provides the therapist with rich understanding of the emotional environment in which the person was raised.

In the second, therapeutic mode of engagement, the therapist interrupts the client's automatic behaviors and emotional reactions in a variety of ways. He may explain developmental emotional dynamics, as in describing the repetitiveness of the client's avoidance of conflict because his father tormented him when he fought with his mother, to his present-day avoidance of his wife when she gets angry with him. Or he may disagree with his client's depressive self-criticisms. Or he may confront the person working with him with some absurd observation to evoke an unusual emotional reaction.

I recall working with a woman who would alternately present herself as an authoritative assertive adult or a manipulative injured child. On one occasion she made an abrupt shift from aggression to manipulative injury, to which I said, "You poor baby." She was astonished by both the tears and laughter that automatically came out of her. She was crying about the pain of her childhood and laughing at the absurdity that her "child" created in her life. The simultaneous experience of both her characterological person and her personal identities person was dramatic and startling to both of us.

A third type of engagement, explanation, is useful in limited doses. At the beginning of therapy, it helps to explain the nature of the dyad and emotionality to facilitate an understanding of the therapy in which the person is engaged. Too much explanation encourages expectations that understanding and rote learning lead therapeutic effectiveness. This creates a serious difficulty because it is too easy for the client to appreciate linear explanations rather than do the work of confusing nonlinear emotional experience.

The fourth kind of engagement, consultation, is not psychotherapy. But it is useful in maintaining the meaningfulness of the therapeutic relationship. A therapist has knowledge that can be important in helping the client with a difficult problem. But here again, consultation risks becoming so central to the therapeutic relationship that psychotherapy is destroyed. The linearity of consultation makes it difficult to move into the confusion and uncertainty of nonlinear emotionality, which is the primary area of psychotherapeutic work.

And finally, the fifth, the most difficult skill the relational therapist must learn, is to monitor and therapeutically use the here-and-now emotionality of the therapeutic relationship and be aware of and therapeutically use his or her own emotionality in the therapeutic session. I have rarely lost control during a therapy session, but in the early years of my practice, I have been hurt or so confused that I couldn't use my feelings therapeutically. However, an early failure called my attention to learn more about this aspect of therapeutic work.

I earlier described the man with whom I lost control as the man who wouldn't smile because it would be dishonest for him to do so. The incident occurred at the beginning of a group session. When the group settled in, he turned to me, this time with a malicious smile, and with clear deliberation, poured his cup of coffee on to the carpet in front of me. It was perfect. I was obedient. I did exactly what he wanted me to do. I was furious and told him to get out. I missed an opportunity to interrupt his habituated desire to alienate me. Had I been able to turn to him with compassionate curiosity and ask what he wanted from me; I would have been much more effective. With practice, I have learned to sit and listen attentively to whatever the client was saying to or about me and with whatever volume it was being delivered. These are therapeutic moments where dramatic corrective emotional experiences can happen.

It is both a part of the learning of the therapist and her capacity as an artist to remain true to her therapeutic commitment. It is a nonlinear form of learning, taking hours of practice and a willingness to endure the personal pain of invalidating confrontation that can occur when a therapist interrupts the client's automated emotionality.

The therapist experiences pain, embarrassment, and/or anxiety when his automated childhood structures are invalidated. I recall a session from which I emerged deeply hurt. In this session, a woman challenged my honesty and integrity. I was so hurt, I lost sight of her. On the way home after work, I found my thoughts going to some of the major difficulties in my life, like a painful divorce. As I scanned my ruminations, I became aware of the residual pains of those events, which were still operating. This is where much of the emotional learning of the therapist occurs.

The attachment of the therapist to the therapeutic process is based on both the aesthetic of therapeutic work and the monetary compensation she receives for it. The therapist under the best of circumstances does not become attached to the person with whom he is working. Because he is attached to the work and art of psychotherapy, he does not seek validational feedback from his clients.

After years working with actors, it struck me that therapists and actors use their emotionalities in similar ways. We both attend to the text and subtext of dialogue when we work. Actors use their emotionality at the service of their dramatic work. Therapists use theirs to create "corrective emotional experiences" in the therapeutic hour with their clients. This not only interrupts maladaptive emotional habits; it also helps clients to learn new age-appropriate ones.

The similarity between actors and therapists reminds me of an apocryphal story about a conversation that Dustin Hoffman had with Laurence Olivier. While waiting between filming on the set of the movie *Marathon Man*, Dustin turned to Laurence saying that he admired Laurence's acting and asked to what he attributed his great ability. Laurence reached out and grabbed Dustin's shirt front, put his face toward Dustin's, and said with great intensity, "Look at me. Look at me." Even though Laurence Olivier was noted for the meticulous care he took to dress, from his shoes up, like the character he was portraying, he was showing Dustin his active use of passion.

The difference between actors and therapists lies in the tasks to which they put their emotional skills. Actors use their feelings to facilitate the emotional drama of character they are performing, not their own person. It is not a personal interaction with the other actor with whom they are acting. Therapists, on the other hand, expose their own persons to the emotional reactions of their clients when they react to the subtext of their client's presentation. If a therapist responds to the unintentional, but habituated, appeal for a childhood need in her client, she interrupts an old need and triggers an emotional reaction in her client to herself, for having intentionally disturbed him.

Related to the separateness of the therapist is her ability to remain alone. The aloneness of the therapist bears a superficial resemblance to the old analytic belief in the "objectivity" of the analyst. Also, I should comment, aloneness does not mean loneliness. This is one of the most difficult emotional positions for beginning therapists to learn. When I learned to appreciate being alone, I was enabled to more freely engage on the baseline with the people who worked with me. With it, I became able to welcome a client's emotional reactions to me without being vulnerable to the personal invalidations of his reactions to me. Moreover, since I needed less validational feedback, it liberated me from actively soliciting feedback to emotionally stabilize myself. When I needed validation, my therapeutic effectiveness was markedly diminished. My learning to be alone was based on my ability to distinguish being separate from being lonely. When I recognized my loneliness, I knew what to do about it. When I became anxious due to the experience of aloneness, I learned to care for the little boy in the character structure of my personality.

I recall working with a man who for many years "knew" that I was lying whenever I admired his work and respected his intelligence. On one occasion, he was describing how painful it was to be with his sisters, who were older than he, because he "knew" they looked at him with pity and contempt. The evidence he gave was equivocal, at best. They were extra "nice" to him because they "pitied" him. At the time of the interaction, both his sisters were in relationships with men, and even though he would never be in a relationship with a woman who was like the characterologically impaired men with whom his sisters were married, he "knew" they felt sorry for him because he was alone. He also believed they were better educated than he was. He had a medical degree; they did not. However, his sisters, in their own occupational fields, were also very talented.

I commented that it seemed as though he was reacting to them as he reacted to me when I told him how much I admired his work. He broke into tears and said, "I know that you lie when you tell me that." I said,

> I know you believe that, but you also know that I don't lie about other issues in our work. I'm not telling you that you're mistaken about me here, but for a moment, try to think about your tears. What makes you cry when I "lie" to you?

At this point he spoke at length about his narcissistic mother and how dangerous it was for him to respond with warmth to his mother's insistent demands for unreciprocated affection. If he believed me, he would feel warmly affectionate toward me, and that would be painful and dangerous. I did not tell him he was wrong about my belief and feelings about him. I did not have to defend my personal integrity and tell him I was not a liar. Instead, I asked him to review his experience with me and explore other possible meanings for his feelings.

Note, several paragraphs earlier, I said I needed "less" emotional feedback. I do not believe any therapist is completely liberated from the need for some personal validational feedback. But it is a major talent that therapists can develop as they practice the art of psychotherapy. When I am in good form, my attention and therapeutic focus remain stable, enabling me to respond creatively in our baseline dance.

The Emotionality of the Therapeutic Relationship

Humans have gradually improved their ability to experience, categorize, and verbalize the experience of their emotionalities. This improvement is limited, however, by the overlearned social lexicon of feelings. The repeated usage of socially constructed meanings leads many people to believe that they have no trouble experiencing and knowing what they feel. It is only when they are engaged in an intense emotional experience in which their social lexicon of feelings is unable to explain the emotional disturbance with which they are confronted that they realize the limitations of their understanding of their feelings. This is seen in fights between lovers where they can both retreat to childhood emotional structures and relate to one another in terms of the family systems in which they matured. The different family backgrounds create different private emotionalities, which if they are not recognized causes the loving dyad to become confused. This frequently results in an irretrievable alienation between lovers.

It also happens when a therapist engages a client's presentation that triggers an emotional reaction within that person. A frequent emotional reaction is embarrassment. Then, if she is asked to tell the therapist how she felt about the therapist for having spoken to her that way, she will have difficulty talking about the immediate experience of feelings she was having about the therapist who upset her.

Humans are relatively unskilled with the experience of their idiosyncratic emotionality: the emotionality of childhood that forms parts of their character structures. Like the experience of smell, the experience of intense emotionality does not have the stability or reliability of the experience of vision. Speaking on the baseline to the people with whom they work, psychotherapists trigger the deeply personal emotional experiences with which clients are unskilled.

Transferential emotional structures exist in any emotional encounter because emotional structures are learned in childhood and endure in varied forms as the person matures. The idea of transference is embedded in Freud's explanations; he believed that the recovery of repressed emotional experiences of past events caused the removal of "hysterical" symptoms. This led to the idea that the pain and confusion of past relationships caused emotional distress.

Classical psychoanalytic theory hypothesizes that these coping "ways" emerge in the therapeutic session intact, relatively unaffected by experiences of everyday life. It proposes that, like Anna O.'s (Breuer and Freud, 1893/1895) remembrances, the experience of the transference of childhood ways of coping within the analytic session relieves the person from the regressive features of their personality. Unfortunately, it did not happen as simply as that. Interpretations alone had a limited therapeutic effect. Early in the development of psychoanalysis, analysts realized that transference interpretations and/or insights about past relationships had to be "worked through." As I said before, the idea of working through is very much like breaking old habits by interrupting their automaticity.

The repetition and rehearsal of insights or recovered memories is very much like the process of making or breaking habits. Working through in relational psychotherapy not only provides the repetition of rehearsal but also facilitates the practice of newly formed personality structures because it occurs in the moments of active engagement with another person who is oriented to call attention to the reality of an emotional encounter with a real person: the therapist.

This position is congruent with Wachtel's (2008) description of a two-person psychology of psychotherapy. In this description he says,

> In a fully two-person psychology, the affective exchange between *actual people* takes center stage, and one comes to see and understand the profound ways in which moods, fantasies, *desires*, perceptions, and expectations of each intersect with, create, transform, and recreate the moods, fantasies, desires, perceptions, and expectations of the other. It is not a psychology that *ignores* those "inner" states or qualities. Rather it aims to deepen and expand our understanding of them by looking not only at how they are structured and manifest themselves in each individual's psychological economy but also how they are dynamically and mutually elicited in the living transactions with *other's* inner lives.
>
> (p. 49) (original emphasis)

This way of explaining personality integrates both the past and present without getting caught up in the confusions of transference theory. It also shifts the explanation of personality change from liberating the person from past traumatic relationships by interpretation and working them through emotionally to interrupting the automaticity of habituated personality structures. Having discussed the emotionality of the therapeutic relationship and its relation to habituated emotionality, I will now describe some of its dynamics.

The Therapeutic Dyad; Its Intersubjectivity

In conventional relationship theories, the dyad is simply regarded as two separate people emotionally interacting without describing the dyadic function of this interaction. Recent theories of "Intersubjectivity" (Orange et al., 1997; Aron, 1999, 2006) and "immediacy" (Hill et al., 2008) recognize and describe the internal experiences of each member of the therapeutic dyad about the other member, but they do not recognize the functional impact of the baseline process as part of the holistic dynamic of the relationship and where the art of the therapist is practiced.

Whether therapists are aware of this dynamic or not, it is a major current in the creative flow of therapeutic art. With the emergence of knowledge about the meaningfulness of emotional relationships, both in the psychotherapeutic professions and in parenting, there is now a growing awareness of the power of the emotional relationship that facilitates growth and change in persons.

Freud was unable to escape from the emotionality of the therapeutic relationship because he used explanations based on a nineteenth-century theoretical paradigm. His inability to explain the dynamics of dyadic interaction led to his attempt to escape from it by developing the "blank screen" rationale to explain the "curative" effects of the psychoanalytic relationship. Hiding behind the couch upon which his patients were encouraged to freely associate, he could not completely escape their emotionality or his own.

At the same time, the power of the therapeutic relationship compelled some analysts to experiment with the relationship itself. Sandor Ferenczi was most notable among these early experimenters. In the shadow of psychoanalytic orthodoxy, many analysts in various ways questioned the blank screen model. From the mid-1970s, analysts have been shifting the emphasis of psychoanalysis from its strict interpretation to an increased recognition of the intersubjectivity of analytic treatment.

As I was beginning to write this chapter, I attended an afternoon conference at which Dr. Robert Stolorow was presenting his ideas about intersubjectivity. Before I went to the conference, I had some ideas about it and wanted to get the straight dope from the horse's mouth. In doing so, I was confronted with an interesting paradox. His ideas about intersubjectivity were congruent with mine. Of course, there were differences, but his clinical understanding of the covert emotional exchange between therapist and patient (intersubjectivity) was almost identical with mine. Here, I felt right at home with him.

However, despite similarities in our views about the nature of dyadic interaction, it took us in dramatically different theoretical directions. He insisted that brain functions were irrelevant to psychoanalysis. He said that when reading about the relationship of the brain to psychotherapy, he would "glaze over." I knew exactly what he meant. I agree that much neurologizing about personality is simplistically reductionistic. On the other hand, I glaze over while reading about psychoanalytic concepts of emotion and insight. We think in different paradigmatic traditions. Translation between them is difficult.

My experiences engaging on the baseline with people in my practice (another way of describing intersubjectively) called my attention to the brain. And as the Duchess in Alice in Wonderland might say, "The moral of that is that different birds fly in different flocks." While both Dr. Stolorow and I found the interpersonal process of psychotherapy compellingly useful in psychotherapy, the differences in our personalities took us on different theoretical flights.

Epistemologically, Dr. Stolorow resides within the current psychoanalytic paradigm and contributes to its theoretical growth. I, on the other hand, entered a different paradigm and found myself speaking a different "language" (Gross, 2001). The terms "intersubjectivity" and "baseline process" denote this difference. It should be clear; I prefer my way of thinking because it solves some of the shortcomings of the psychoanalytic paradigm based on nineteenth-century empiricism.

It is in the "intersubjectivity" of the therapeutic engagement that the therapist practices her art. The key to the meaning of this sentence resides in the meaning of "subjective." The dictionary definition (*Random House Dictionary of the English Language*) of "subjective" is

> 1. existing in the mind belonging to the thinking subject rather than to the object of thought (opposed to objective). . . . 3. placing excessive emphasis on one's own moods, attitudes, opinions, etc. . . . 5. relating to properties or specific conditions of the mind as distinguished from general or universal experience.

These are phenomenal definitions saying that subjectivity is a nonsensory experience of an undefined mind. Within the terminology of my theory, "subjectivity" is a right-brained mental process that integrates both linear cognition about relationships and nonlinear, emotional cognition of a relational process that disequilibrates the Neurological Self. In other words, with respect to the psychotherapeutic dyad, both persons are responding to one another rationally and emotionally, hopefully, in an integrative way. When this frequently occurs in the therapeutic relationship, loving feelings happen.

Love and Attachment

Attachment is the emotion that occurs in any relationship where the person's NS is repeatedly validated. Much of the time, the feelings that emerge from attachment are loving ones. This is true about any kind of relationship a person has. It occurs in work, play, and human relationships. In human relationships, attachment is defined as an emotional bond that occurs when one person repeatedly provides emotional support to another person. Ordinarily, this occurs for both persons supporting one another. The therapeutic dyad is unusual in that attachment is a one-way street. I will discuss this more fully in what follows.

Bowlby (1969) recognized the significance of attachment in children who had been separated from parents during World War II. Attachment of children arises from repeated parental, nourishing validation. As we have seen in earlier chapters of this book, children suffer when they are deprived of emotional nourishment. The Neurological Selves of children become attached to parents who care for them. Parental attachment is formed in infancy prior to the development of the child's person. At its inception, it becomes part of the emotional structure of the child. It is a foundational part of the emotionality of personality. In adulthood, the absence or loss of attachment is experienced as the experience of loneliness and/or the dread of being alone. As such, these experiences are classified in my theory as feelings.

Dependency is a feeling system initiated and nourished during a person's childhood. It, too, is rooted in the person's past. Attachment and dependency are frequently conflated. Attachment is a dynamic in the individual's character structure. Like my definition of emotion, it has little cognitive content. Dependency feelings have both cognitive content and a complex system of behavioral instructions. Dependency is a feeling explanation of the emotion of attachment. As a feeling, a person can use it manipulatively for the furtherance of some, usually emotional, goal. In this case it can be experienced without an accompanying attachment.

If, at the beginning of psychotherapy, the person develops a sense of hope that her work with the therapist will be of help, then a therapeutic dyad is created. And when the therapist feels that progress is being made, she recognizes that an attached dyad has been created. A mutually validating engagement then occurs. But a skilled therapist can contain and use the emotionality of the dyad at the service of the task without requiring the help-seeking person to conform to the personal (emotional) needs of the therapist.

The skilled therapist, then, remains unattached to the person with whom she is working because she is trained to monitor the intersubjective dynamics of the dyadic system of which she is a part and, as I said in the beginning of this chapter, because her affect hunger is not fed by the help seeker's person. This enables her to remain free of the need for the validation of her personality structures.

With these skills, therapists can have the pleasure and excitement experienced by other artists in different art forms. Moments of creativity inspire experiences of beauty and love. This brings me to the conclusion of this book with a brief discussion of love and the art of psychotherapy.

Love and the Art of Psychotherapy

Throughout this book there has been a theme of complexity and the growth of our brains to create skills to cope with that growth. Coping with complexity created opportunities for discovery and creativity, which has led to human experiences of art and love.

Unlike the arts of theater, painting, music, and dance, which are experienced through our senses, the art of psychotherapy is primarily displayed emotionally on the nonsensory screen of our awareness. Despite this important difference, all arts are experienced with a kind of love. It is a love that grows from the beauty and excellence of the artwork nourishing the stability and growth of the Neurological Self of the observer of the art and of the artist who creatively produces the work.

The richness and beauty of the ways in which the therapist and client encounter one another in psychotherapy creates an unexpected growth experience for the client. It also enriches the therapist's ability to find exciting new ways of enjoying the creativity of his work. Each therapeutic endeavor is singular in its emotional complexity. Like any other art form, the excitement of creative psychotherapeutic work holds both the therapist and client in its thrall.

Most of the artists with whom I have been acquainted and who love their work tell me they find it exciting, meaningful, and express pleasure and/or a (sometimes not too joyous) compulsion to be in it. This is true of the musicians I have known, painters, motion picture and television actors, gardeners, and business executives. All of them who loved their work are in one way or another, enlivened by it. They experience the beauty of their work and the beauty of their selves in it. The same is true of psychotherapists.

However, there is a complication with psychotherapy that does not exist in the other arts. In psychotherapy, love of the work occurs in an intimate relationship with another person. This creates an emotional dilemma for many psychotherapeutic dyads. When the therapist and client are caught up in the throes of loneliness, the affection and admiration they experience arising from the excellence of their work can get confused with romantic sexuality. Musicians and actors also experience this confusion in their work. In this condition, they sometimes fall in "love" with the person with whom they are working.

Artists love their work. Therapists, too, love their work. And we love artists. We appreciate the hours of dedication, practice, and the pain it took for them to be able to reach the level of excellence that enabled them to create the work that stirs an aesthetic loving experience within us. While we treasure the artist's effort and talent, we do not love the artist's person; we love her work.

Similarly, people who work with therapists can love the therapist's work, but they do not love the therapist's person. Loving another person, beyond infatuation, grows with the intense emotional encounter of a mutually engaged relationship. Psychotherapy possesses a mutuality that is different from that encountered in romantic loving partnerships.

Like the love experienced in art appreciation, the therapist loves the creative effort expended by the people with whom she is working. As in any effective team effort, the client loves the therapist's talent and dedication. As it is in all forms of art, the artist and the appreciator of art have incomplete knowledge of one another. The therapist is not conventionally engaged in the validational process of dyadic interaction because he does not require reciprocal feedback. If he does, he has left his therapeutic task and responsibility. Depriving the help seeker of this crucial knowledge about the therapist's personality prevents the client from having meaningful knowledge about the therapist's personality.

Love and Sex in Psychotherapy

Love and sex have always been bewilderingly present in psychotherapy. An example of this confusion occurred in the early history of psychoanalysis. Wolf-Man (1971) reported that Freud told him that his flight behind the couch was to avoid the sexual advances of a woman patient. More than likely, Freud's emotional confusion about the sexual situation with which he was confronted had to be avoided for him to maintain the rational observational stance that was necessary in the empirical medical tradition of his time. Even though he avoided an interpersonal encounter with sex in his therapeutic work, it was so compellingly present in his experience that he made it a centerpiece of his early thinking about the nature of neurosis.

As we have seen throughout other chapters in this book, emotionality has been a great human mystery. Within this mystery, sexuality has reigned as its queen. She is a major source of anxiety that plagues and confuses humanity, not just psychotherapists. Unfortunately, anxiety has been and is conflated with fear.

And following the instructions contained in feelings of fear, humanity has fled from confronting this mystery. In fleeing from it we have perpetuated ignorance about the meaning and beauty of sexuality. Many cultures have coped with this confusion by simply confining it solely as a procreational activity and condemning other meanings or relational purposes for it (cf. Diamond, 1997 for a learned description of the biological and evolutionary nature of human sexuality). These cultural traditions generate parenting rules that primarily instill anxiety and fear into the sexual lives of people. This creates one of the major areas of work for psychotherapists.

Unfortunately, therapists are still trained to regard sex in their practices with fear and loathing (Pope and Bouhoutsos, 1986). Koocher, in his foreword to the second edition of *What Therapists Don't Talk About* (Pope et al., 2003), says, about the nature of training psychotherapists, that, "we have historically done a poor job of teaching psychotherapists about our own intrapsychic complexities" (p. xxiv). Not only are therapists poorly trained to deal with their "own intrapsychic complexities," but they also do not have an adequate clinical theory of emotionality to help them escape prejudices of the past.

The literature of sex in psychotherapy does not recognize the transactional, intersubjective process, which exists in any mutually agreed upon sexual encounter. The emotional theory used by most therapists does not recognize the purposive, expressive dynamics of neurological emotionality (cf. Chapter 7).

Also, there is no recognition in the relational psychotherapy literature of the influence of baseline dynamics (cf. Chapter 1) on the sexual behavior and experience of dyads. As I mentioned earlier, when baseline process is ruptured, members of an attached dyad lose sexual interest in one another.

Without these theoretical understandings about the complex emotional nature of sexuality, it is extremely difficult for a therapist to do anything more about the frequent experience of sexuality in psychotherapy than to avoid it. In doing this, they miss opportunities to become therapeutically effective with the people whom they serve who almost universally live with sexual difficulties of one sort or another.

These social and conceptual confusions about sexuality are exemplified in a recent study of "therapist immediacy" (Kasper et al., 2008). This was Case Study One of two in the same journal studying the effects of immediacy. Immediacy within this study is similar in structure to the I-Thou relationship I described in Chapter 1 but is used in a very different interpersonal way from the way I use it. They also explain therapeutic interventions differently from the language I have been using in this book.

In this study, Dr. N., a 51-year-old male therapist, worked with a young female graduate student, Lily, about the difficulties she was having with men. In this study, Dr. N. used his person very actively. He initiated all of their sessions with inquiries about her feelings about him. The therapist indicates he was unaware of how his solicitations might have affected their work. The study points to the desirability of educating the help-seeking person to the meaning and therapeutic purpose of baseline encounters before it can be used with therapeutic effectiveness. I quote from the article:

> In his post-treatment interview, Dr. N. acknowledged the impact that sex differences might have had and noted that he should have raised the topic with Lily. It is possible that if Dr. N. had discussed their sex differences, Lily might have felt less confused about Dr. N.'s intentions in using intimately self-involving statements and, therefore, been more involved in response to these in treatment. When reading the paper, Dr. N. wrote, "I am more and more convinced that not talking about the sex differences was a crucial mistake on my part."
>
> (p. 294)

This study did not have a theory of dyadic interaction to inform it. The history of psychotherapy is fraught with an ignorance compelled by fearful avoidance. To simply close our eyes to the significance of sexual expression in psychotherapy blinds us to the meaningfulness of sexuality in the therapeutic relationship, which expresses important information about the emotionality of both members of the therapeutic dyad.

I attended a Risk Management Program organized by the American Psychological Association, designed to help psychologists avoid being sued, to aid in keeping malpractice insurance costs down, and to fulfill a continuing education requirement enabling me to renew my license to practice. At the beginning of the program, the lawyer/psychologist conducting the program announced that he was there to "frighten" the attendees about sexuality in their practices. This may be a prudent tactic to keep insurance costs down. It also has the disastrous side effect of keeping psychotherapists ignorant of an enduring dynamic in psychotherapy.

It is obvious that sex is a "many splendored thing" used for a huge variety of emotional purposes in an equally huge variety of social settings. The intimacy and luxury of dyadic psychotherapy generates a kind of love that can become confused with conventional loving genital experiences, which are tightly tied to sexual desire.

I agree with the Hippocratic Oath and Sigmund Freud about the destructiveness to the therapeutic relationship when sex happens between therapists and the people they serve. However, I disagree with their reasons for proscribing sexuality in psychotherapy.

First, therapists are limited in their ability to see sexuality as a meaningful emotional experience in their therapeutic relationship. If therapists are limited in their knowledge of emotionality, especially sexuality, the intensity of sexual arousal prevents the therapist from recognizing the baseline meaning of their sexual experience and prevents him from fulfilling the terms of his therapeutic contract.

Second, sexuality always fulfills some intense emotional need of the person, whether it is the client or the therapist. In the therapist's case, he violates the therapeutic contract. If he engages sexually, he is requiring validational feedback from the person he is serving. In doing so, he is abandoning the therapeutic contract, which prescribes that he does not require reciprocal feedback from the person with whom he is working.

Third, when the therapist gets lost in his sexual experience, he will not be able to see what the person in therapy is saying to him about her feelings about their therapeutic work. The moment a therapist requires validational feedback from a person she serves she is unable to see baseline process clearly or use it therapeutically. She is looking at the person with whom she is working through the eyes of her loneliness.

In over 60 years of practice, I have seen sexuality being used by therapists and the people they serve for a variety of different purposes. Within the frame of my theory, these purposes are activated by the affect hunger of different parts of the personalities of the sexually involved dyads. In one way or another, sexual partners are seeking emotional validation from one another and it is not always loving feedback that is being sought. The affect hunger of the Neurological Self mindlessly operates to stabilize itself in sexuality in whatever ways its stabilizing structures require. Commonly, sex is thought to be a "loving" experience. It is not unusual for a person to say, "Let's make love" when he means, "Let's have sex." Sex is also used to humiliate, assuage loneliness, or whatever was emotionally important in the early years of an emerging person who, for a variety of reasons, finds sexuality useful for the moment. This is true of all people, including psychotherapists.

I believe a better way of serving psychotherapy would be to provide therapists with a more complete training in the emotionality of their work and to teach them how to recognize the meaning of the sexuality they experience within a psychotherapeutic frame. This would truly reduce malpractice insurance rates. It is beyond the scope of this book to describe a psychotherapeutic way of treating the sexual experience in psychotherapy, but I will describe some examples of how I dealt with it in my practice.

For example, a woman, who was successfully working with me to save an alienated marriage, at one point turned to me and asked when I was going to have sex with her. This question came out of the blue. This was the first time sex entered our relationship. She had discussed her sexual relationship with her husband, which due to their alienation was infrequent and not satisfactory. I had never been approached that directly or in that way before. "Do you want to have sex with me?" I asked. She replied, "No, but I thought that this was expected of me." Her expectation was congruent with what she had told me about her childhood. In previous sessions, she told me that her mother wanted another child later in life (my client was ten years younger than her sister) in order to have a child who could take care of her in her old age. Her childhood was a loveless, duty-ridden existence, full of rules and punishments for disobedience. For her, sex was a requirement that had to be fulfilled. In the following sessions, she began to see that sex could be more than reluctant compliance. It could be a sweet way of expressing love with her husband.

At other times, I found myself being sexually invited in seductive nonverbal ways. Let me hasten to say, this happened rarely. But over time I learned how to recognize that sexual expression had psychotherapeutic meaning. I learned that sometimes addressing it directly meant the person with whom I was working wanted to stop being in psychotherapy, was trying to control our relationship with sexual power, or was terribly lonely in their marriage or life.

In Conclusion

I am ending this book with a discussion about the importance of creating a theory of personality based on brain functions. As we have seen, ideas about the significance of a pleasure principle, intentionality, understanding, meaning, or any other form of explanation that is not based on brain functions, do not take into consideration homeostatic processes of the brain that effect all of the psychological processes that are of concern to mental health.

Today the relationship of the brain to personality is increasingly recognized throughout our society. Most psychology departments in the university system have robust neuropsychology scholars attempting to fathom the brain/mind relationship. However, they are doing this without a personality theory to guide them. The mindsets they use are influenced by a theoretical paradigm that assumes an unbridgeable difference between material and immaterial experience. The theory I have presented here is a way of integrating sensory and nonsensory experiencing.

It brings psychology, more fully, into research laboratories. Not only is the theory researchable but it also contains definitions of psychological phenomena, like feelings, emotion, and the self that are based on homeostatic operations of the brain. In the following discussion, I will again describe how the mind emerges from these functions to explain the intimate relationship between brain research and psychological process.

Three evolutionary steps will take us to an understanding of how the brain's growth results in the experience of the mind. First, the entropy-resistant brain is in the automatic, constant process of restoring itself its homeostatic condition. This is the cerebral imperative that affects everything we do, think, and feel. The nerves of the brain, like the muscles of the body are similar in their physical restorative functions. Both respond to the rule of "practice makes permanent." They need to be exercised or their neural or muscular structures deteriorate. And they both need to grow or die. They differ to the extent that over centuries of growth, nerves create a complexity within their systems that enables them to activate muscular exercise (behaviors). These behaviors respond to genetically developed survival systems in the paleomammalian brain (the limbic system).

Within the limbic system is an orienting process, the Neurological Self (NS), enabling humans and many other creatures that move in their environments to orient themselves to its assets and dangers. In humans, this system is called the anterior cingulate cortex. It resides in the midbrain. The surface cortex of the brain grew with its ability to cope with increasing complexity. It eventually became the neurological foundation of what we now call self-process. It grew so complex that it developed structures increasing connections between the prefrontal cortex and the limbic system.

The second step describes the prefrontal cortex modulating limbic activity. It developed ways of simplifying information by grouping similarities into single categories. We call this function cognition. In early evolutionary times, it simplified sensory information enabling humans to cope with the external environment more and more effectively. As the brain became the most complex, it also grew in size: grow or die. The human brain grew larger per body weight than the brain of any other creature on earth. With this size the brain's complexity also grew. The prefrontal cortex and its intimate relationship with the limbic system began regulating the internal complexity of the brain itself. This relationship became so complex that the brain constructed a way to hold information in place (consciousness) within the brain, giving cognition time for the brain to either accommodate or assimilate the information.

Step three. When the orienting system (self-process), cognition, and consciousness interact with one another we have an experience, which we call the mind. The NS monitors the brain for any information in its structures that it is unable to process automatically. It then interacts with the cortex, which attempts to either accommodate or assimilate the disequilibrating information. If it cannot do either of these two processes quickly, consciousness holds the information in awareness. At this point, psychology begins.

How Homeostasis Influences Personality Process

In the following discussion, I will argue that it is necessary to understand homeostatic process as a part of personality dynamics. I have described the origin of the mind as a homeostatic development of the brain. The mind's biological purpose is to serve the brain's homeostatic needs. It is not the "mind over matter" explanation, which assumes the mind is superior to and fundamentally different from the brain. It presumes that the mind is an immaterial process. The neurological structures underlying cognitive explanations are homeostatic operations. As such their truth value is suspect. Their purpose is homeostatic.

This idea throws an interesting light on our understanding of emotionality, especially feelings. In Chapter 7, I described them as a kind of explanation, whose truth value is also suspect. At times, feelings provide a helpful explanation of what is happening in a relationship with someone, but at other times they create unintended conflict and/or create confusion in the mind of the person who is experiencing the feeling explanation.

The art of psychotherapy involves the repeated interruption of maladaptive emotional habits while, at the same time, facilitating the creation of new age-appropriate ones.

Two Afterthoughts

First, from the beginning of my psychotherapeutic training, I was confronted with the mysteries of therapeutic work. Being a disbeliever of magic, I felt compelled to make sense out of what I was doing with my clients. None of the existing theories gave me much comfort. In the early years of my work, psychoanalysis both supported and confounded me. Eventually, my realizations about the duality of dyadic dialogue gave me hope for a better understanding of psychotherapy and encouraged me to explore the nature of the ways people spoke to one another. It took many years to put it into the form of this book. Having made enough sense of the work of psychotherapy to escape my compulsion, I feel finished with it. I can close this book, while seeing the vast amount of work that lies ahead on which I will not be able to work.

Second, I am concluding this book by opening the door to a much larger issue, which awaits future generations of clinicians and research workers. I am calling attention to the social necessity of increasing the emotional intelligence, not only of psychotherapists, but of infants and children emerging from early childhood to adulthood.

Helping a person become emotionally intelligent is another way of saying they would no longer suffer painful confusions about who they are, or suffer suicidal depressions, or suffer heart-rending anxieties. With these talents, they are better able to chart the course of their lives and to stay on course. Wouldn't it be wonderful if we made it a social priority to begin helping our children, from infancy, to become emotionally brilliant persons? Think of the economic savings we could have in our mental health programs, addiction programs, and jail systems if we had generations of emotionally intelligent people.

We are on the threshold of achieving these goals. More and more programs explore ways of helping psychotherapists become emotionally skillful. When therapists are able to manage their own emotional skills, they are better able to help their clients break age-inappropriate emotional habits and create new ones.

There is an increasing recognition of the benefits of pre-school education where children are helped to become more intelligent and better students. There are even early education schools that enroll, not only two-year-old children but enroll the families of their children. This enables parents to learn and share with one another emotional skills that enrich the lives of themselves and their children.

This is a huge agenda for the future to meet the demands of the technological revolution in which we are all engaged. I have always been accused of wearing rose-colored glasses. Nonetheless, when I look through the lens of evolutionary development of *Homo sapiens*, I can see a hopeful future for humankind.

Appendix

Glossary

Definitions of psychological variables based on homeostatic functions.

affect hunger An emotion. The need of nervous tissue for exercise.

cognition Cerebral simplification (CS). The cortex stabilizing the limbic system. Cognitive classification. See Ch. 3

consciousness The display of information (DI). Enabling cognitive classification. See Ch. 3

contact Two persons holding each other in focal and background awareness.

emotion The experience of the Neurological Self homeostatically activating sites in the limbic system. See Ch. 7

emotionality The interaction of emotion and feelings.

feelings The experience of the cognitive classifications of emotions. See Ch. 7

formatting systems Cerebral organization of information into linear/nonlinear and sensory/nonsensory formats. See Ch. 3

"I" The cognitive label of the Neurological Self. See Ch. 5

information Anything that creates changes within or between systems.

mind The interaction of orientation (the Neurological Self), simplification (cognition), and display of information (consciousness).

neurological self (NS) The orienting system of the brain. The anterior cingulate cortex and associated limbic structures.

perception The transport of information between systems.

person The interaction of self-systems, emotionality, and personal reality. See Ch. 8

personal reality Cognitive classifications about the NS's relationships with the external environment.

psychological systems Cortical structures stabilizing the NS.

self-systems (the selves) Linear and nonlinear cognitions about the NS.

The Use of the Therapist's Person

1. The therapist compassionately uses his/her person by actively making *contact* with the client.
2. The therapist holds his/her client in "unconditional personal regard"; respect.
3. The therapist *avoids* seeking validation of his/her *affect hunger* from the client. The therapist is *not* the client's friend.
4. The therapist *interrupts* the *automaticity* of age-inappropriate requests for *validation* from his/her client using personal engagement and/or observation.
5. The therapist *validates* newly emerging emotional skills using personal engagement and/or observation: "corrective emotional experiences."

Bibliography

Ahalya, H., Davidson, R. J., & Rozin, P. (2000) Exploring Hindu Indian emotion expressions: Evidence for accurate recognition by Americans and Indians. *Psychological Science*, 11, 183–187.
Ainsworth-Land, G. T. (1986) *Grow or die: The unifying principle of transformation.* New York: John Wiley and Sons.
Alexander, F. (1963) The dynamics of psychotherapy in the light of learning theory. *American Journal of Psychiatry*, 120, 440–448.
Alexander, F., & French, T. M. (1946) *Psychoanalytic therapy: Principles and application.* New York: The Ronald Press.
Allman, J. M., Hakeem, A., Erwin, J. M., Nimchinsky, E., & Hof, P. (2001) The anterior cingulate cortex, the evolution of an interface between emotion and cognition. *Annals of the New York Academy of Sciences*, 935, 107–117.
Allport, G. W. (1937) *Personality: A psychological interpretation.* New York: Henry Holt and Company.
Allport, G. W. (1955) *Becoming: Basic considerations for a psychology of personality.* New Haven: Yale University Press.
Allport, G. W. (1960) *Personality and social encounter: Selected essays.* Boston: Beacon Press.
Appy, C. G. (2004) *Patriots: The Vietnam war remembered from all sides.* New York: Viking.
Armstrong, K. (1994) *A history of God: The 4000-year quest of Judaism, Christianity and Islam.* New York: Alfred A. Knopf.
Arnett, J. J. (2008) The neglected 95%. *American Psychologist*, 63, 602–614.
Aron, L. (1999) The patient's experience of the analyst's subjectivity. In S. A. Mitchell & L. Aron (Eds.), *Relational psychoanalysis: The emergence of a tradition.* Hillsdale, NJ: The Analytic Press.
Aron, L. (2006) Analytic impasse and the third: Clinical implications of intersubjectivity theory. *International Journal of Psychoanalysis*, 87, 349–368.
Atwood, M. (2002) *Negotiating with the dead: A writer on writing.* Cambridge: Cambridge University Press, p. 31.
Averill, J. R. (1994) In the eyes of the beholder. In P. Ekman & R. J. Davidson (Eds.), *The nature of emotion: Fundamental questions.* New York: Oxford University Press.
Averill, J. R. (2003) The future of emotion. *Contemporary Psychology: APA Review of Books*, 48, 782–783.
Baars, B. J. (1997) *In the theater of consciousness: The workspace of the mind.* New York: Oxford University Press.
Baddeley, A. (2007) *Working memory, thought, and action.* Oxford: Oxford University Press.

Badenoch, B. (2008) *Being a brain-wise therapist: A practical guide to interpersonal neurobiology.* New York: W.W. Norton and Company.
Bargh, J. A. (1994) Environmental control of goal-directed action: Automatic and strategic contingencies between situations and behavior. In W. D. Spaulding (Ed.), *Integrative views of motivation, cognition, and emotion: Nebraska symposium on motivation,* Vol. 41. Lincoln: University of Nebraska Press.
Bargh, J. A. (1997). *The automaticity of everyday life.* In R. S. Wyer, Jr. (Ed.), *Advances in social cognition,* Vol. 10. *The automaticity of everyday life: Advances in social cognition, Vol. 10* (p. 1–61). Mahway, NJ: Lawrence Erlbaum Associates Publishers.
Barnard, K. E., & Brazelton, T. B. (Eds.). (1990) *Touch: The foundation of experience.* Madison, CT: International Universities Press.
Barrett, L. F. (2006) Are emotions natural kinds? *Perspectives on Psychological Science,* 1, 28–58.
Barrett, L. F., Mesquita, B., & Smith, E. R. (2010) The context principle. In B. Mesquita, L. F. Barrett, & E. R. Smith (Eds.), *The mind in context.* New York: The Guilford Press.
Baumeister, R. F. (2002) Religion and psychology. *Psychological Inquiry,* 13, 165–247.
Beck, A. T. (1995) Cognitive therapy, past, present, and future. In M. J. Mahoney (Ed.), *Cognitive and constructive psychotherapies: Theories, research, and practice.* New York: Springer Publishing Company.
Becker, C. L. (1932) *The heavenly city of eighteenth-century philosophers.* New Haven: Yale University Press.
Beitman, B. D. and Nair, J. (Eds.). (2004) *Self-awareness deficits in psychiatric patients: Neurobiology, assessment, and treatment.* New York: W.W. Norton and Company.
Beitman, B. D., & Soth, A. M. (2006) Activation of self-observation: A core process among the psychotherapies. *Journal of Psychotherapy Integration,* 16, 383–397.
Benson, D. F., & Zaidel, E. (Eds.). (1985) *The dual brain: Hemispheric specialization in humans.* New York: The Guilford Press.
Berkowitz, L., & Harmon-Jones, E. (2004) Toward an understanding of the determinants of anger. *Emotion,* 4, 107–130.
Berlyne, D. E. (1966) Curiosity and exploration. *Science,* 153, 25–33.
Bettelheim, B. (1943) Individual and mass behavior in extreme situations. *Journal of Abnormal Psychology,* 38(4), 417–452.
Beutler, L. E. (2009) Making science matter in clinical practice: Redefining psychotherapy. *Clinical Psychology: Science and Practice,* 16, 301–317.
Biello, D. (2007) Searching for god in the brain. *Scientific American Mind,* 18, 39–45.
Bion, W. F. (1977) *Seven servants: Four works by Wilfred R. Bion.* New York: Jason Aronson.
Boswell, J., Hill, C. E., & Castonguay, L. G. (2008) Insight in psychotherapy: Toward a consensus about definition, process, and future research directions. *Psychotherapy Bulletin,* 43, 21–27.
Bowlby, J. (1969) *Attachment,* Volume I in Attachment and Loss series. New York: Basic Books.
Brazelton, T. B., & Greenspan, S. I. (2000) *The irreducible needs of children: What every child must have to grow, learn, and flourish.* Cambridge: Perseus Publishing.
Breger, L. (2009) *A dream of undying fame: How Freud betrayed his mentor and invented psychoanalysis.* New York: Basic Books.
Breuer, J., & Freud, S. (1893/1895) *Studies on hysteria.* New York: Basic Books.
Bronowski, J. (1956) *Science and human values.* New York: Julian Messner.

Brothers, L. (1997) *Friday's footprint: How society shapes the human mind*. New York: Oxford University Press.
Brothers, L. (2001) *Mistaken identity: The mind-brain problem reconsidered*. New York: State University of New York Press.
Bryck, L. R., & Fisher, P. A. (2012) Training the brain: Practical applications of neural plasticity from the intersection of cognitive neuroscience, developmental psychology, and prevention science. *American Psychologist*, 67, 87–100.
Buber, M. (1958) *I and Thou* (2nd edition). New York: Charles Scribner's Sons.
Buber, M. in Kaufmann, W. (1970). *I and Thou*. New York: Charles Scribner's Sons.
Bugental, J. F. T. (1987) *The art of the psychotherapist*. New York: W.W. Norton and Company.
Buller, D. J. (2005) *Adapting minds: Evolutionary psychology and the persistent quest for human nature*. Cambridge: MIT Press.
Burns, B. D. (1968) *Uncertain nervous system*. London: Edward Arnold.
Cacioppo, J. T., Amaral, D. G., Blanchard, J. J., Cameron, J. L., Carter, C. S., Crews, D., Fiske, S., Heatherton, T., Johnson, M. K., Kozak, M. J., Levenson, R. W., Lord, C., Miller, E. K., Ochsner, K., Raichle, M. E., Shea, M. T., Taylor, S. E., Young, L. J., & Quinn, K. J. (2007) Social neuroscience: Progress and Implications for mental health. *Perspectives on Psychological Science*, 2, 99–123.
Cahill, T. (1998) *The gift of the Jews: How a tribe of desert nomads changed the way everyone thinks and feels*. New York: Nan A Talese, Anchor Books.
Cannon, W. B. (1932). *The wisdom of the body*. New York: W. W. Norton & Co.
Capra, F. (1976) *The tao of physics*. New York: Bantam Press.
Carroll, L. (1965) *Alice's adventures in wonderland*. New York: Avenal Books.
Carver, C. S. (2001) Affect and the functional bases of behavior: On the dimensional structure of affective experience. *Personality and Social Psychology Review*, 5, 345–365.
Caspi, A., Harrington, H., Moffitt, T. E., Milne, B. J., & Poulton, R. (2006) Socially isolated children 20 years later: Risk of cardiovascular disease. *Archives of Pediatrics and Adolescent Medicine*, 160(8), 805–811.
Casteneda, C. (1961) *The teachings of Don Juan: A Yaqui way of knowledge*. New York: Simon and Schuster.
Chalmers, D. J. (1996) *The conscious mind: In search of a fundamental theory*. New York: Oxford University Press.
Chugani, H. T., Behen, M. E., Muzik, O., Juhasz, C., Nagy, F., & Chugani, D. C. (2001) Local brain functional activity following early deprivation; A study of postinstitutionalized Romanian orphans. *NeuroImage*, 14, 1290–1301.
Churchland, P. S. (1996) *Neurophilosophy: Toward a unified science of the mind-brain*. Cambridge: The MIT Press.
Cohen, R. A., Paul, R., Zawacki, Moser, T. M., Sweet, L., & Wilkinson, H. (2001) Emotional and personality changes following cingulotomy. *Emotion*, 1, 38–50.
Colvin, G. (2008) *Talent is overrated: What really separates world-class performers from everybody else*. New York: Penguin Group.
Constantino, M. J., & Castonguay, L. G. (2003) Learning from the basics: Clinical implications of social, developmental, and cross-cultural study of the self. *Journal of Psychotherapy Integration*, 13, 2–8.
Cotton, T. J. (1974) *The development of a methodology to examine the experience of embarrassment during experiential confrontation in the psychotherapeutic session*. Doctoral Dissertation, California School of Professional Psychology.

Critchfield, K. L., & Knox, S. (2010) Conceptual skills needed for evidence-based practice of psychotherapy: A few recommendations. *Psychotherapy Bulletin*, 45, 10–13.
Cronkite, K. (1994) *On the edge of darkness: Conversations about conquering depression.* New York: Dell Publishing.
Crosby, A. W. (1997) *The measurement of reality: Quantification and Western society, 1250–1600.* New York: Cambridge University Press.
Curtis, R. C. (2009) *Desire, self, mind, and the psychotherapies: Unifying psychological science and psychoanalysis.* New York: Jason Aronson.
Damasio, A., & Van Hoesen, G. W. (1983) Emotional disturbances associated with focal lesions of the limbic frontal lobe. In K. M. Heilman & P. Satz (Eds.), *Neuropsychology of human emotion.* New York: The Guilford Press.
Damasio, A. (1994) *Descartes' error: Emotion, reason and the human brain.* New York: G. P. Putnam and Sons.
Damasio, A. (1999) *The feeling of what happens: Body and emotion in the making of consciousness.* New York: Harcourt Brace and Company.
Damasio, A. (2010) *Self comes to mind: Constructing the conscious brain.* New York: Pantheon Books.
Darwin, C. (1965) *The expression of the emotions in man and animals.* Chicago: The University of Chicago Press.
Davidson, R. J., Pizzagalli, D., & Nitschke, J. B. (2002) Representation and regulation of emotion in depression: Perspectives from affective neuroscience. In I. Gotlib II & C. L. Hammen (Eds.), *Handbook of depression.* New York: The Guilford Press.
Davison, G. C. (2006) President's column. *The Clinical Psychologist*, 1–2, 1–3.
Dawkins, R. (2006) *The god delusion.* New York: Houghton Mifflin Company.
De Houwer, J., Fielder, K., & Moors, A. (2011) Strengths and limitations of theoretical explanation in psychology: Introduction to the special section. *Psychological Science*, 6, 161–162.
Deikman, A. J. (1982) *Observing Self: Mysticism and psychotherapy.* Boston: Beacon Press.
Dennett, D. C. (1981) Intentional systems. In J. Haugeland (Ed.), *Mind design: Philosophy, psychology, artificial intelligence.* Cambridge: MIT Press.
Dennett, D. C. (1991) *Consciousness explained.* Boston: Little, Brown and Company.
Dennett, D. C. (2006) *Breaking the spell: Religion as a natural phenomenon.* New York: Penguin Books.
De Oliveira, J. A., & Vandenberghe, L. (2009) Upsetting experiences for the therapist in-session: How they can be dealt with and what they are good for. *Journal of Psychotherapy Integration*, 19, 231–245.
Diamond, J. (1997) *Why is sex fun? The evolution of human sexuality.* New York: Basic Books.
Dijksterhuis, A., & Nordgren, L. F. (2006) A theory of unconscious thought. *Perspectives on Psychological Science*, 1, 95–109.
Dingfelder, S. F. (2007) More than a feeling. *Monitor on Psychology*, 38, 40–41.
Dingfelder, S. F. (2009) From the research lab to the operating room. *Monitor on Psychology*, 40, 40–43.
Doidge, N. (2007) *The brain that changes itself: Stories of personal triumph from the frontiers of brain science.* New York: Viking Press.
Duncan, B. L. (2002) The legacy of Saul Rosenzweig: The profundity of the dodo bird. *Journal of Psychotherapy Integration*, 12, 32–57.
Eagleman, D. (2011) *Incognito: The secret lives of the brain.* New York: Pantheon Books.
Eccles, J. (Ed.). (1982) *Mind and brain: The many-faceted problems.* Washington: The Paragon Press.

Edelman, G. M. (1989) *The remembered present: A biological theory of consciousness.* New York: Basic Books.
Edelman, G. M. (2004) *Wider than the sky: The phenomenal gift of consciousness.* New Haven: Yale University Press.
Ekman, P. and Davidson, R. J. (Eds.). (1994) *The nature of emotion: Fundamental questions.* New York: Oxford University Press.
Ekman, P., Friesen, W. V., & Ellsworth, P. (1972) What emotion categories can observers judge from facial behavior? What emotion dimensions can observers judge from facial behavior? In A. P. Goldstein & L. Krasner (Eds.), *Emotion in the human face: Guidelines for research and an integration of findings.* New York: Cambridge University Press, pp. 39–55.
Eliot, L. (1999) *What's going on in there? How the brain and mind develop in the first five years of life.* New York: Bantam Books.
Ellenberger, H. (1974) Psychiatry from ancient to modern times. In S. Arieti et al. (Ed.), *American Handbook of Psychiatry.* Vol. I. New York: Basic Books.
Estes, W. K. (1994) *Classification and cognition.* New York: Oxford University Press.
Feinberg, T. E. (2001) *Altered egos: How the brain creates the self.* New York: Oxford University Press.
Ferenczi, S. (1931) Child analysis in the analysis of adults. *Final contributions to the theory and technique of psychoanalysis.* London: Hogarth Press.
Fierman, L. B. (Ed.). (1965) *Effective psychotherapy: The contribution of Hellmuth Kaiser.* New York: The Free Press.
Fischer, R. (1971) Altered states of consciousness. *Science,* 174(4012), 897–904.
Flanagan, O. (1992) *Consciousness reconsidered.* Cambridge, MA: MIT Press.
Fletcher, G. J. (1984) Psychology and common sense. *American Psychologist,* 39(3), 203–213.
Forgas, J. P. (2002) Feeling and doing: Affective influences on interpersonal behavior. *Psychological Inquiry,* 13(1), 1–28.
Frank, J. D., & Frank, J. B. (1961/1993) *Persuasion and healing: A comparative study of psychotherapy.* Baltimore, MD: The Johns Hopkins University Press.
Freeman, L. (1994) *The story of Anna O.: The woman who led Freud to psychoanalysis.* Northvale, NJ: Jason Aronson Inc.
Freud, S. (1895) Project for a scientific psychology. In *The standard edition of the complete psychological works of Sigmund Freud.* Vol. 1. London: Hogarth Press, pp. 283–397.
Freud, S. (1949a) *Collected Papers: Volume I.* London: Hogarth Press.
Freud, S. (1949b) *Collected Papers: Volume II.* London: Hogarth Press.
Freud, S. (1927/1957) *The ego and the id.* London: The Hogarth Press Ltd.
Freud, S. (1962) *Three essays on the theory of sexuality.* New York: Basic Books.
Freud, S. (1997) *Dora: An analysis of a case of hysteria.* New York: Touchstone.
Friedman, R. E. (1987) *Who wrote the Bible?* New York: Summit Books.
Frijda, N. H. (2005) Emotion experience. *Cognition and Emotion,* 19, 473–497.
Fromm, E. (1941) *Escape from freedom.* New York: Farrar and Rhinehart.
Fromm-Reichmann, F. (1950) *Principles of intensive psychotherapy.* Chicago: University of Chicago Press.
Gabriel, R. (2014). *Acquittal: An insider reveals the stories and strategies behind today's most infamous verdicts.* New York: Berkley Books.
Gawande, A. (March 30, 2009) Hellhole. *The New Yorker,* 36–45.
Gay, P. (1988) *Freud: A life for our time.* New York: W.W. Norton and Company.

Gazzaniga, M. S. (2010) *Who's in charge? Free will and the science of the brain.* New York: HarperCollins Publisher.

Geary, D. C. (2005) *The origin of mind: Evolution of brain, cognition, and general intelligence.* Washington, DC: American Psychological Association.

Gendlin, E. T. (1978) *Focusing: A step-by-step technique that takes you past getting in touch with your feelings—to change them and solve your personal problems.* New York: Everest House.

Gergen, K. J. (1991) *The saturated self: Dilemmas of identity in contemporary life.* New York: Basic Books.

Gilbert, P., & Andrews, B. (Eds.). (1998) *Shame: Interpersonal behavior, psychopathology, and culture.* New York: Oxford University Press.

Gill, M. M. (1954) Psychoanalysis and exploratory psychotherapy. *Journal of American Psychoanalytic Association,* 2, 771–797.

Gill, M. M. (1982) *Analysis of transference: Vol. 1. Theory and technique.* Psychological Issues Monographs 53. New York: International Universities Press, p. 193.

Ginot, E. (2016) *The neuropsychology of the unconscious: Integrating brain and mind in psychotherapy.* New York: W.W. Norton and Company.

Gladwell, M. (2008) *Outliers: The story of success.* New York: Little, Brown and Company.

Goffman, E. (1959) *The presentation of self in everyday life.* New York: Anchor Books.

Goldberg, E. (2001) *The executive brain: Frontal lobes and the civilized mind.* New York: Oxford University Press.

Goldfried, M. R. (Ed.). (1982) *Converging themes in psychotherapy: Trends in psychodynamic humanistic and behavioral practice.* New York: Springer Publishing Company.

Goleman, D. (1995) *Emotional intelligence: Why it can matter more than IQ.* New York: Bantam Books.

Gouldner, A. W. (1965) *Enter Plato: Classical Greece and the origins of social theory.* New York: Basic Books.

Granit, R. (1977) *The purposive brain.* Cambridge, MA: MIT Press.

Graves, R. (1988) *The Greek myths.* Mount Kisco, NY: Moyer Bell Limited.

Greenberg, L. S. (2015) *Emotion-focused therapy: Coaching clients to work through their feelings.* Washington, DC: American Psychological Association.

Greenberg, L. S., & Paivio, S. C. (1997) *Working with emotions in psychotherapy.* New York: The Guilford Press.

Greenberg, L. S., & Safran, J. D. (1987) *Emotion in psychotherapy.* New York: The Guilford Press.

Greenwald, A. G. (1982) Is anyone in charge? Personal analysis versus the principle of personal unity. In J. Suls (Ed.), *Psychological perspectives on the self* (Vol. 1, pp. 151–181). Hillsdale, NJ: Lawrence Erlbaum Associates.

Griffiths, P. E. (1997) *What emotions really are: The problem of psychological categories.* Chicago: University of Chicago Press.

Gross, Z. (1952) *Learning and lobotomy.* Doctoral dissertation. University of California at Los Angeles.

Gross, Z. (1992) *A portrait of the person: A personality theory for the clinician.* Santa Monica, CA: Global Village Press.

Gross, Z. (1996) The "I" of the selves. *New Ideas in Psychology,* 14(3), 269–279.

Gross, Z. (2001) Two languages, one vocabulary. *Journal of Psychotherapy Integration,* 11(4), 481–505.

Gross, Z. (2002) Feelings are the self in equilibratory motion. *Constructivism in the Human Sciences,* 7.

Gross, Z. (2003) The structural dynamics of the psychotherapeutic relationship. *Constructivism in the Human Sciences*, 8, 91–104.

Gross, Z. (2003) *Different differences: A metatheoretical exploration*. Unpublished manuscript.

Hampden-Turner, C. (1981) *Maps of the mind: Charts and concepts of the mind and its labyrinths*. New York: Macmillan Publishing.

Haney, C. (2008) A culture of harm: Taming the dynamics of cruelty in supermax prisons. *Criminal Justice and Behavior*, 35, 956–984.

Harlow, H. F. (1974) *Learning to love*. New York: Jason Aronson.

Harris, D. (February 8, 2004) Repeating history's mistakes. *New York Times*.

Hawking, S. (1988) *A brief history of time*. New York: Bantam Books.

Hawkley, L. C., & Cacioppo, J. T. (2007) Aging and loneliness: Downhill quickly? *Current Directions in Psychological Science*, 16, 187–191.

Hebb, D. O. (1949) *The organization of behavior: A neuropsychological theory*. New York: John Wiley and Sons.

Heider, F. (1958) *The psychology of interpersonal relations*. Hillsdale, NJ: Lawrence Erlbaum Associates.

Heinsen, D. F. (1982) Husserl's theory of the pure ego. In H. L. Dreyfus & H. Hall (Eds.), *Husserl, intentionality, and cognitive science*. Cambridge: MIT Press.

Henry, P. J. (2008) College sophomores in the laboratory redux: Influences of a narrow data base on psychology's view of the nature of prejudice. *Psychological Inquiry*, 19, 49–71.

Herrigel, E. (1971) *Zen in the art of archery*. New York: Vintage Books.

Hertel, P. T. (2002) Cognitive biases in anxiety and depression: Introduction to the special issue. *Cognition and Emotion*, 16, 321–330.

Hill, C. E., Sim, W., Spangler, P., Stahl, J. Sullivan, C., & Teyber, E. (2008) Therapist immediacy in brief psychotherapy; Case study II. *Psychotherapy: Theory, research, practice, training*, 45, 298–315.

Hood, B. (2012) *The self illusion: How the social brain creates identity*. New York: Oxford University Press.

Horvath, A. O. (2006) The alliance in context: Accomplishments, challenges, and future directions. *Psychotherapy: Theory, research, practice, training*, 45, 258–263.

Ivins, W. M. Jr. (1953) *Prints and visual communication*. London: Routledge and Kegan Paul Ltd.

Izard, C. E., & Bartlett, E. S. (1972) *Patterns of emotions: A new analysis of anxiety and depression*. New York: Academic Press.

Izard, C. E. (1977) *Human emotions*. New York: Plenum Press.

Izard, C. E. (2007) Basic emotions, natural kinds, emotion schemas, and a new paradigm. *Perspectives on Psychological Science*, 2(3), 260–280.

Izard, C. E. (2010) The many meanings/aspects of emotion: Definitions, functions, activation, and regulation. *Emotion Review*, 2(4), 363–370.

James, W. (1890/1950) *The principles of psychology*. Boston: Dover Press.

Jaynes, J. (1976) *The origin of consciousness in the breakdown of the bicameral mind*. Boston: Houghton Mifflin Company.

Jerison, H. J. (1997) Evolution of the prefrontal cortex. In N. A. Krasnegor, C. R. Lyon, & P. S. Goldman-Rakic (Eds.), *Development of the prefrontal cortex: Evolution, neurobiology, and behavior*. Baltimore: Paul H. Brookes Publishing Co.

Jones, E. (1953) *The life and work of Sigmund Freud: Volume 1, 1856–1900: The formative years and the great discoveries*. New York: Basic Books.

Kagan, J. (1989) *Unstable ideas: Temperament, cognition and self.* Cambridge: Harvard University Press.

Kagan, J. (2011) Three lessons learned. *Psychological Science,* 6, 107–113.

Kahneman, D. (2011) *Thinking, fast and slow.* New York: Farrar, Straus and Giroux.

Kashima, Y., Kokubo, T., Kashima, E., Boxall, D., Yamaguchi, S., & Macrae, K. (2004) Culture and self: Are there within-culture differences in self between metropolitan areas and regional cities. *Personality and Social Psychology,* 30, 816–823.

Kasper, L. B., Hill, C. E., & Kivlighan, D. M. Jr. (2008) Therapist immediacy in brief psychotherapy: Case study I. *Psychotherapy: Theory, research, practice, training,* 45, 281–297.

Kasser, T., Cohn, S., Kanner, A. D., & Ryan, R. M. (2007) Some costs of American corporate capitalism: A psychological exploration of value and goal conflicts. *Psychological Inquiry,* 18, 1–22.

Krasnegor, N. A., Lyon, G. R., & Goldman-Rakic, P. S. (1997) *Development of the prefrontal cortex: Evolution, neurobiology, and behavior.* Baltimore: Paul H. Brookes Publishing Company.

Keil, F. C., & Wilson, R. A. (Eds.). (2000) *Explanation and cognition.* Cambridge, MA: MIT Press.

Kelly, G. A. (1955) *The psychology of personal constructs. Vol. 1. A theory of personality. Vol. 2. Clinical diagnosis and psychotherapy.* New York: W.W. Norton and Company.

Keltner, D., & Anderson, C. (2000) Saving face for Darwin: The functions and uses of embarrassment. *Current Directions in Psychological Science,* 9, 187–192.

Kendler, H. H. (2005) Psychology and phenomenology: A clarification. *American Psychologist,* 60, 318–324.

Kernis, M. H. (2003) Toward a conceptualization of optimal self-esteem. *Psychological Inquiry,* 14, 1–26.

Kimble, G. A. (2000) Behaviorism and unity in psychology. *Current Directions in Psychological Science,* 9, 208–212.

Koch, C. (2004) *The quest for consciousness: A neurobiological approach.* Englewood, CO: Roberts and Company.

Koestler, A. (1967) *The ghost in the machine.* New York: Macmillan Publishing.

Kohut, H. (1971) *The analysis of the self: A systematic approach to the psychoanalytic treatment of narcissistic personality disorders.* New York: International Universities Press.

Koole, S. L., & Kuhl, J. (2003) In search of the real self: A functional perspective on optimal self-esteem and authenticity. *Psychological Inquiry,* 14, 43–51.

Krasnegor, N. A., Lyon, G. R., & Goldman-Rakic, P. S. (Eds.). (1997) *Development of the prefrontal cortex: Evolution, neurobiology, and behavior.* Baltimore: Paul H. Brookes Publishing Company.

Kuhn, T. S. (1970) *The structure of scientific revolutions.* Chicago: The University of Chicago Press.

Kurzban, R., & Aktipis, C. A. (2007) Modularity and the social mind: Are psychologists too self-ish? *Personality and Social Psychology Review,* 11, 131–149.

Lakoff, G. (1987) *Women, fire, and dangerous things: What categories reveal about the mind.* Chicago: The University of Chicago Press.

Lazarus, R. S. (1991) *Emotion and adaptation.* New York: Oxford University Press.

Lazarus, R. S. (1994) Meaning and emotional development. In E. Ekman & R. J. Davidson (Eds.), *The nature of emotion: Fundamental questions.* New York: Oxford University Press.

Lecky, P. (1945) *Self-consistency: A theory of personality.* New York: Island Press.

LeDoux, J. (1996) *The emotional brain: The mysterious underpinnings of emotional life.* New York: Simon and Schuster.

LeDoux, J. (2002) *Synaptic self: How our brains become who we are.* New York: Viking.

Levi-Strauss, C. (1966) *The savage mind*. Chicago: The University of Chicago Press.
Levy, D. M. (1937) Primary affect hunger. *The American Journal of Psychiatry*, 94, 643–652.
Lewin, K. (1935) *A dynamic theory of personality*. New York: McGraw Hill Book Company.
Luchins, A. S. (1942) Mechanization in problem solving: The effect of Einstellung. *Psychological Monographs*, 54(6), i–95.
Luria, A. R. (1973) *The working brain: An introduction to neuropsychology*. New York: Basic Books Inc.
Lynch, J. J. (1977) *The broken heart: The medical consequences of loneliness*. New York: Basic Books Inc.
MacLean, P. D. (1949) Psychosomatic disease and the "visceral brain": Recent developments bearing on the Papez theory of emotion. *Psychosomatic Medicine*, 11, 338–353.
MacLean, P. D. (1952) Some psychiatric implications of physiological studies on frontotemporal portion of limbic system (visceral brain). *Electroencephalography and Clinical Neurophysiology*, 4, 407–418.
MacLean, P. D. (1970) The triune brain, emotion and scientific bias. In F. O. Schmitt (Ed.), *The neurosciences: Second study programs*. New York: Rockefeller University Press, pp. 336–349.
MacLean, P. D. (1973) *A triune concept of the brain and behaviour*. Toronto: University of Toronto Books.
MacLean, P. D. (1990) *The triune brain in evolution: Role in paleocerebral functions*. New York: Plenum Press.
Macmillan, M. (2001) Limitations to free association and interpretation. *Psychological Inquiry*, 12, 113–128.
Mahoney, M. J. (1991) *Human change processes: The scientific foundations of psychotherapy*. New York: Basic Books.
Mahoney, M. J. (1995) *Cognitive and constructive psychotherapies: Theory, research, and practice*. New York: Springer Publishing Company.
Mahoney, M. J. (2003) *Constructive psychotherapy: A practical guide*. New York: The Guilford Press.
Mahrer, A. R. (2000) Philosophy of science and the foundations of psychotherapy. *American Psychologist*, 56, 1117–1125.
Manstead, A. S. R. and Fischer, A. H. (2002) Beyond the universality-specificity dichotomy. *Cognition and emotion*, 16, 1–9.
Marks, C. E. (1981) *Commissurotomy, consciousness, and unity of mind*. Chicago: University of Chicago Press.
Martin, R., & Barresi, J. (2006) *The rise and fall of soul and self: An intellectual history of personal identity*. New York: Columbia University Press.
Masterson, J. F. (1985) *The real self: A developmental, self, and object relations approach*. New York: Brunner Mazel.
Matthews, G., Roberts, R. D., & Zeidner, M. (2004) Seven myths about emotional intelligence. *Psychological Inquiry*, 15, 179–196.
May, R. (1960) Personal communication.
McLean, K. C., Pasupahti, M., & Pals, J. L. (2007) Selves creating stories creating selves: A process model of self-development. *Personality and Social Psychology Review*, 11, 262–278.
McNaughton, B. L., Chen, L. L., & Markus, E. J. (1991) "Dead reckoning," landmark learning, and the sense of direction: A neuropsychological and computational hypothesis. *Journal of Cognitive Neuroscience*, 3, 163–182.

Menninger, K. (1958) *Theory of psychoanalytic technique*. New York: Basic Books.
Miller, A. (1981) *Prisoners of childhood: The drama of the gifted child and the search for the true self*. New York: Basic Books.
Miller, G. A., Galanter, E. H., & Pribram, K. H. (1960) *Plans and the structure of behavior*. New York: Holt, Rinehart and Winston.
Miller, M. (2009) *The tyranny of dead ideas: Letting go of the old ways of thinking to unleash a new prosperity*. New York: Henry Holt and Company.
Mischel, W., & Peake, P. K. (1982) Analyzing the construction of consistence in personality. In M. M. Page (Ed.), *Personality: Current theory and research. Nebraska symposium on motivation*. Lincoln: University of Nebraska Press.
Mitchell, S. A. (1993) *Hope and dread in psychoanalysis*. New York: Basic Books.
Mitchell, S. A., & Black, M. J. (1995) *Freud and beyond: A history of modern psychoanalytic thought*. New York: Basic Books.
Mizumori, S. J. Y. (1994) Neural representations during spatial navigation. *Current Directions in Psychological Science*, 3(4), 125–129.
Moffitt, T. E., Caspi, A., & Rutter, M. (2006) Measured gene-environment interactions in psychopathology: Concepts, research strategies, and implications for research, intervention, and public understanding of genetics. *Perspectives on Psychological Science*, 1, 5–27.
Montagu, A. (1971) *Touching: The human significance of the skin*. New York: Columbia University Press.
Morris, R. S. (1977) *The disconfirmation of self-presentation as a change agent in psychotherapy*. Doctoral Dissertation, California School of Professional Psychology.
Murphy, G. (1949) *Historical introduction to modern psychology*. New York: Basic Books.
Nathanson, D. L. (1992) *Shame and pride: Affect, sex, and the birth of the self*. New York: W.W. Norton and Company.
Natsoulas, T. (1998) Consciousness and self-awareness. In M. Ferrari & R. J. Sternberg (Eds.), *Self-awareness: Its nature and development*. New York: The Guilford Press.
Niiya, Y., Ellsworth, P. C., & Yamaguchi, S. (2006) Amae in Japan and the United States: An exploration of a "culturally unique" emotion. *Emotion*, 6, 279–295.
Norcross, J. C. (Ed.). (2002) *Psychotherapy relationships that work: Therapist contributions and responsiveness to patients*. New York: Oxford University Press.
Orange, D. M., Atwood, G. E., & Stolorow, R. D. (1997) *Working intersubjectively: Contextualism in psychoanalytic practice*. Hillsdale, NJ: The Analytic Press.
Oremland, J. D. (1991) *Interpretation and interaction: Psychoanalysis or psychotherapy?* Hillsdale, NJ: The Analytic Press.
Orenstein, R. E. (Ed.). (1973). *The nature of human consciousness: A book of readings*. New York: Viking Press.
Pagels, E. (1988) *Adam, Eve, and the serpent*. New York: Random House.
Pagels, E. (May 12, 1988) The origins of sin. *New York Review of Books*, 28–35.
Panksepp, J. (1998) *Affective neuroscience: The foundation of human and animal emotions*. New York: Oxford University Press.
Papez, J. W. (1937) A proposed mechanism of emotion. *Archives of Neurology and Psychiatry*, 38, 725–743.
Penfield, W. (1975) *The mystery of the mind: A critical study of consciousness and the human brain*. Princeton: Princeton University Press.
Piaget, J. (1971) *Structuralism* (C. Maschler, Trans.). New York: Basic Books.
Piaget, J. (1985) *The equilibration of cognitive structures: The central problem of intellectual development*. Chicago: The University of Chicago Press.

Pinker, S. (2007) *The stuff of thought: Language as a window into human nature.* London: Penguin Press.
Plato. (1984) *Great dialogues of Plato* (W. H. D. Rouse, Trans.). New York: Penguin Books.
Platt, J. R. (1970) *Perception and change: Projections for survival.* Ann Arbor: University of Michigan Press.
Polanyi, M. (1958) *Personal knowledge: Towards a post-critical philosophy.* New York: Harper and Row.
Pons, F., & Harris, P. L. (2005) Longitudinal change and longitudinal stability of individual differences in children's emotion understanding. *Cognition and Emotion,* 19, 1158–1174.
Pope, K. S., & Bouhoutsos, J. C. (1986) *Sexual intimacy between therapists and patients.* New York: Praeger.
Pope, K. S., Sonne, J. L., & Greene, B. (2003) *What therapists don't talk about and why: Understanding taboos that hurt us and our clients.* Washington, DC: American Psychological Association.
Posner, M. I., DiGirolamo, G. J., & Fernandez-Duque, D. (1997) Brain mechanisms of cognitive skills. *Consciousness and Cognition,* 6, 267–290.
Posner, M. I., & Raichle, M. E. (1994) *Images of mind.* New York: Scientific American Library.
Pribram, K. H., & Bradley, R. T. (1998) The brain, the me, and the I. In M. Ferrari & R. J. Sternberg (Eds.), *Self-awareness: Its nature and development.* New York: The Guilford Press.
Pritchard, R. M. (1961) Stabilized images on the retina. *Scientific American,* 204(6), 72–79.
Ramachandran, V. S. (2011) *The tell-tale brain: A neuroscientist's quest for what makes us human.* New York: W.W. Norton and Company.
Reddy, W. M. (2001) *The navigation of feeling: A framework for the history of emotions.* Cambridge: University of Cambridge Press.
Reich, W. (1933/1945) *Character analysis.* New York: Farrar, Straus and Giroux.
Reik, T. (1948) *Listening with the third ear.* New York: Farrar, Straus and Giroux.
Reis, H. T., & Collins, W. A. (2005) Relationships, human behavior, and psychological science. *Current Directions in Psychological Science,* 13(6), 233–237.
Richards, J. E. (Ed.). (1998) *Cognitive neuroscience of attention: A developmental perspective.* Mahwah, NJ: Lawrence Erlbaum Associates.
Riesen, A. H. (Ed.). (1975) *The developmental neuropsychology of sensory deprivation.* New York: Academic Press.
Roediger, H. L. (March 1, 2004) What happened to behaviorism? *Observer,* 17(5), 40–42.
Rogers, C. R., & Stevens, B. (1967) *Person to person: The problem of being human. A new trend in psychology.* Lafayette, CA: Real People Press.
Rosenthal, R. (2003) Covert communication in laboratories, classrooms, and the truly real world. *Current Directions in Psychological Science,* 12, 151–154.
Rosenthal, R., & Jacobson, L. (1992) *Pygmalion in the classroom: Teacher expectation and intellectual development.* New York: Irvington.
Rosenzweig, S. (1936) Some implicit common factors in diverse methods of psychotherapy. *American Journal of Orthopsychiatry,* 6, 412–415.
Roser, M., & Gazzaniga, M. S. (2004) Automatic brains—interpretive minds. *Current Directions in Psychological Science,* 13, 56–59.
Ryle, G. (1949) *The concept of mind.* New York: Hutchinson University Library.

Saarni, C. (1999) *The development of emotional competence*. New York: The Guilford Press.
Sabini, J., & Silver, M. (2005) Why emotion names and experiences don't neatly pair. *Psychological Inquiry*, 16, 1–10.
Safran, J. D. (1998) *Widening the scope of cognitive therapy: The therapeutic relationship, emotion, and the process of change*. Northvale, NJ: Jason Aronson.
Safran, J. D., & Greenberg, L. S. (Eds.). (1991) *Emotion, psychotherapy, and change*. New York: The Guilford Press.
Safran, J. D., & Muran, J. C. (2000) *Negotiating the therapeutic alliance: A relational treatment guide*. New York: The Guilford Press.
Sampson, E. E. (1988) The debate on individualism: Indigenous psychologies of the individual and their role in personal and societal functioning. *American Psychologist*, 43, 15–22.
Sampson, E. E. (2000) Reinterpreting individualism and collectivism: Their religious roots and monologic versus dialogic person–other relationship. *American Psychologist*, 55, 1425–1432.
Schore, A. N. (1994) *Affect regulation and the origin of the self: The neurobiology of emotional development*. Hillsdale, NJ: Lawrence Erlbaum Associates.
Schore, A. N. (2003) *Affect regulation and the repair of the self*. New York: W.W. Norton and Company.
Seigel, J. (2005) *The idea of the self: Thought and experience in Western Europe since the seventeenth century*. Cambridge: Cambridge University Press.
Shah, I. (1970) *The way of the Sufi: An anthology of Sufi writings*. New York: E. P. Dutton and Company.
Shah, I. (1977) *The veiled gazelle*. London: The Octagon Press.
Shakow, D. (1969) *Clinical psychology as science and profession: A forty-year odyssey*. Chicago: Aldine Publishing Company.
Shapiro, D. (1965) *Neurotic styles*. New York: Basic Books.
Shepard, R. N. (1990) *Mind sights: Original visual illusions, ambiguities, and other anomalies, with a commentary on the play of mind in perception and art*. New York: W.H. Freeman.
Sherif, M., & Cantril, H. (1947) *The psychology of ego-involvements: Social attitudes and identifications*. New York: John Wiley and Sons.
Shlain, L. (1991) *Art and physics: Parallel visions in space, time, and light*. New York: Harper Perennial.
Shneidman, E. S. (1996) *The suicidal mind*. New York: Oxford University Press.
Siegel, D. J. (1999) *The developing mind: How relationships and the brain interact to shape who we are*. New York: The Guilford Press.
Siegel, D. J. (2001) Toward an interpersonal neurobiology of the developing mind: Attachment relationships, "mindsight," and neural integration. *Infant Mental Health Journal*, 22, 67–94.
Skues, R. A. (2006) *Sigmund Freud and the history of Anna O.: Reopening a closed case*. New York: Macmillan Publishing.
Smith, E. W. L. (2003) *The person of the therapist*. Jefferson, NC: McFarland and Company.
Smith, E. W. L. (2004) Focusing on the person of the therapist. *Psychotherapy*, 39/2, 5–7.
Snell, B. (1982) *The discovery of the mind: In Greek philosophy and literature*. New York: Dover Publications, Inc.
Snibbe, A. C. (2003) Cultural psychology: Studying more than the 'exotic other.' *APS Observer*, 16(1), 30–32.
Snow, C. P. (1964) *The two cultures and a second look*. London: Cambridge University Press.

Sokolov, Y. N. (1963) *Perception and the conditioned reflex* (S. W. Waydenfeld, Trans.). Oxford: Permagon Press.

Solomon, A. (2001) *The noonday demon: An atlas of depression.* New York: Scribner.

Spitz, R. A. (1946) Hospitalism: A follow-up report on investigation described in volume I, 1945. In *The psychoanalytic study of the child* (1946 annual edition). New York: International Universities Press, pp. 2113–2117.

Stambor, Z. (2006) Stressed out nation. *Monitor on Psychology*, 37, 28–29.

Stein, R. (1991) *Psychoanalytic theories of affect.* London: Karnac Books.

Stern, D. N. (1985) *The interpersonal world of the infant: A view from psychoanalysis and developmental psychology.* New York: Basic Books.

Stern, D. N. (2004) *The present moment: In psychotherapy and everyday life.* New York: W.W. Norton and Company.

Stern, W. (1938) *General psychology, from the personalistic standpoint* (H. D. Spoerl, Trans.). New York: Macmillan Publishing.

Stolorow, R. D., Brandchaft, B., & Atwood, G. E. (1995) *Psychoanalytic treatment: An intersubjective approach.* Hillsdale, NJ: The Analytic Press.

Stone, H. (1985) *Embracing heaven and earth: A personal odyssey.* Marina del Rey, CA: DeVorss and Company.

Stricker, G. (1992) The relationship of research to clinical practice. *American Psychologist*, 47, 543–549.

Strunk, W. Jr., & White, E. B. (1972) *Elements of style.* New York: Macmillan Publishing.

Styron, W. (1951) *Lie down in darkness.* New York: Bobbs-Merrill.

Styron, W. (1992) *Darkness visible: A memoir of madness.* New York: Vintage Books.

Sulloway, F. J. (1979) *Freud, biologist of the mind: Beyond the psychoanalytic legend.* New York: Basic Books.

Swanson, D. (2010) *War is a lie.* Charlottesville, VA: Just World Books.

Swann, W. B., Jr., Stein-Seroussi, A., & Giesler. R. B. (1992). Why people self-verify. *Journal of Personality and Social Psychology*, 62, 392–401.

Tangney, J. P., & Dearing, R. L. (2000) Gilbert and Andrews take a new look at shame. *Contemporary Psychology*, 45, 628–630.

Teicher, M. (2002) Scars that won't heal: The neurobiology of child abuse. *Scientific American*, 286, 68–75.

Thayer, J. F., & Lane, R. D. (2000) A model of neurovisceral integration in emotion regulation and dysregulation. *Journal of Affective Disorders*, 61, 201–216.

Tolle, E. (1997) *The power of now: A guide to spiritual enlightenment.* Novato, CA: New World Press.

Tomkins, S. S. (1962) *Affect, imagery, consciousness: Vol. I. The positive affects.* New York: Springer.

Tomkins, S. S. (1963) *Affect, imagery, consciousness: Vol. II. The negative affects.* New York: Springer.

Turkle, S. (2011) *Alone together: Why we expect more from technology and less from each other.* New York: Basic Books.

Untermeyer, L. (Ed.). (1920) *Modern British poetry.* New York: Harcourt, Brace & Howe.

Uttal, W. R. (2001) *The new phrenology: The limits of localizing cognitive processes in the brain.* Cambridge: MIT Bradford Books.

Valenstein, A. F. (1962) The psycho-analytic situation: Affects, emotional reliving, and insight in the psycho-analytic process. *International Journal of Psycho-Analysis*, 43, 315–324.

Vaughan, S. C. (1997) *The talking cure: The science behind psychotherapy.* New York: Grosset, Putnam.

Viamontes, G. I., Beitman, B. D., Viamontes, C. T., & Viamontes, J. A. (2004) Neural circuits for self awareness: Evolutionary origins and implementation in the human brain. In B. D. Beitman & J. Nair (Eds.), *Self-awareness deficits in psychiatric patients: Neurobiology, assessment, and treatment*. New York: W.W. Norton and Company.

Von Senden, M. (1960) *Space and sight: The perception of space and shape in the congenitally blind before and after operation*. London: Methuen.

Wachtel, P. L. (Ed.). (1997) *Psychoanalysis, behavior therapy, and the relational world*. Washington, DC: American Psychological Association.

Wachtel, P. L. (2008) *Relational theory and the practice of psychotherapy*. New York: The Guilford Press.

Wager, T. D. (2006) Do we need to study the brain to understand the mind? *Observer*, 19, 25–27.

Wallerstein, R. S. (1995) *The talking cures: The psychoanalyses and the psychotherapies*. New Haven: Yale University Press.

Webbink, P. (1986) *The power of the eyes*. New York: Springer Publishing Company.

Westen, D. (2007) *The political brain: The role of emotion in deciding the fate of the nation*. New York: Public Affairs.

Westheimer, G. (2000) How we see things. *Science*, Vol. 288, 2324.

Weston, E. (May, 2009) Highlights and halftones. *Westways*, 101, 35–40.

Wiesel, E. (1960) *Night*. New York: Hill and Wang.

Wilkie, D. (2009) Coming soon a scanner near you. *Monitor on Psychology*, Vol. 40, 45–47.

Wilson, E. O. (1999) *Consilience: The unity of knowledge*. New York: Vintage Books.

Winnicott, D. W. (1972) *Holding and interpretation: Fragment of an analysis*. New York: Grove Press.

Wolf-Man. (1971) *The Wolf-Man by the Wolf-Man: The double story of Freud's most famous case*. New York: Basic Books.

Wundt, W. (1973) *An introduction to psychology*. New York: Arno Press.

Wyer, R. S. Jr. (Ed.). (1997) *The automaticity of everyday life: Advances in social cognition*, Vol. 10 (p. 1–61). Mahwah, NJ: Lawrence Erlbaum Associates.

Wynn, T., & Coolidge, F. L. (2008) A stone-age meeting of minds: Neandertals became extinct while Homo sapiens prospered. *American Scientist*, 96, 44–51.

Ying-yi, H., Morris, M. W., Chi-yue, C., and Benet-Martinez, V. (2000) Multicultural minds: A dynamic constructivist approach to culture and cognition. *American Psychologist*, 55, 709–720.

Zubek, J. P. (Ed.). (1969) *Sensory deprivation: Fifteen years of research*. New York: Appelton-Century-Crofts.

Zur, O. (2009) Power in psychotherapy and counseling: Exploring the "inherent power differential" and related myths about therapists' omnipotence and clients' vulnerability. *Independent Practitioner*, 29, 160–164.

Index

Page numbers in *italics* indicate a figure on the corresponding page. Page numbers followed by "n" indicate a note.

accommodation 69
acculturation 29
action 62
actors and therapists 195
adaptations 55, 124, 127; self-process 107; visual information 63
adult loving relationships 79, 92, 114–115, 147
affect hunger 47, 83, 114, 167; abuse in early childhood 169; for emotional intensity 155; heart of loneliness and love 80–82, 101–102, 145; and homeostasis 78–80; of NS 79–80, 95–96, 108, 129, 145; of prefrontal cortex 132
affection 80, 91
aging and loneliness 81
Aktipis, C. A. 47
alcoholism 72
alert state 85
Allman, J. M. 50, 87–88
Allport, G. W. 89, 115n1, 160
aloneness 195
alter ego 166
American Psychological Association 52
anger 30, 68, 141, 168
anguish 109–110, 131
Anna O/Breuer relationship 2–10
anterior cingulate cortex (ACC) 46, 62, 88, 207; classification 50; description 86; experiences of cognitions about 75; interactions with other brain systems 90; in orienting process 55, 67, 75, 84, 86; and prefrontal cortex 86–87; in psychological operations 86

anxiety 114, 136, 137, 173; and alcoholism 72; cause for 103; and depressions 139, 144; experience of 66, 71, 108, 133, 139–140, 151, 175, 189; and fear 30, 114, 125, 137, 203; finding neurological location for 33; intentional control failure 40; relief of 61, 62, 108; and self-presentations 22
apical communication 16–17
appearance 32, 41, 164
appraisals 100, 127
Aristotle 34
Armstrong, K. 54, 185
art of psychotherapy 180–209
assimilation 69
attachment, love and 200–201
attention 11, 16, 86–87, 113, 165
Atwood, M. 166
automaticity, interrupting 187–190
autoregulation 67, 90, 148
awareness 62–64, 90, 100, 163; consciousness 54; focal 66, 123, 130, 165; self- 31, 52–53, 56, 68, 97, 185

Baddeley, A. 87
Bargh, J. 41
Barrett, L. F. 31, 118, 122
baseline: communication 17–19; process 17, 19, 199, 203
Becker, C. L. 52
behavior 31, 35, 118–121, 133–134, 147, 207; and explanation 62; habituated 121; and "I" 97, 102, 103; and personality 28, 41, 52, 154; science of

Index   227

39; self-destructive 73, 84, 90; sexual 113; visual observations of 41
behaviorism 119–120
Beitman, B. D. 84, 87
Bettelheim, B. 149
body: mind and 48, 70, 77, 82, 107; soul and 51, 98
Bowlby, J. 200
Bradley, R. 89, 100
brain 47, *60*, 131; anterior and posterior areas of 15, 27, 57, 58, 60; -based definition of self-process 94–95; -based psychology 90; -based theory of the mind 44–74; biological task 70; encephalization quotient 49–50, 88; and human nature 131; imaging technology 28, 43n1, 84; and mind 27, 45, 48, 67–70, 83–84, 93, 207; and personality 14–15, 20, 23, 26–28, 59; phenomenal growth of 26, 42, 48, 124, 156–157, 207; purpose 48; volume 49–50
Breuer, J.: and Anna O relationship 2–10; case study 2; disagreement with Freud about repressed sexuality 7, 9
Broken Heart, The (Lynch) 81
Brothers, L. 100
Bryck, L. R. 169
Buber, M. 8, 13, 15, 25n3, 186

Cacioppo, J. T. 81
Cannon, W. B. 69
Cantril, H. 102
Casper the Friendly Ghost 54
caudate nucleus 84
centrality 102–105
cerebral evolutionary growth 49
cerebral nerves 131
change and growth 156–157
change resistant 83, 91, 107, 109, 114, 115n6, 124, 148
character structures 113–114, 130, 157; and emotions 134–136, 147; and personal identity 160–161, 165; private person of 168–169
children: attachment in 200; emotional skills practiced in 136; engagement with their feelings 18; personal growth of 157
cingulate cortex 87
cingulotomy 85, 86
Clever Hans effect 178

cognitions 55–57, 95, 127, 207; ACC 75, 86; body and 152; consciousness and 33, 52, 54, 55, 70, 84, 88; cortical regulation 96; emotional 91, 117, 200; as equilibrating process 35; feelings as 100, 130, 137, 153, 163; forms of 35, 61; fourfold classification of 31, 58–61; "I" and 97; mind 58–61, 62, 88, 118, 132, 162, 184; nonlinear/sensory 60–61; NS and 76, 95, 143, 163; personal reality 164; prefrontal cortex 67; self and feeling 143; simplification processes 45–46, 108
cognitive formatting 57–58
common sense 29, 36, 171; abandonment of 39–41; conversation 57; and logical thinking 59; paradigm 119
communication: baseline 17–19; covert 13, 22; *I-Thou* 8, 13, 15, *17*
complexity, hierarchy versus 32, 33
Conference on the Evolution of Psychotherapy (CEP) 181
Confucius 53
consciousness 21, 62–67, 95, 115n5, 132, 143; ACC and 86; automaticity and 76; awareness 54; characteristics 63–66; cognition and 33, 52, 54, 55, 70, 84, 88; as displaying information 45–46, 54, 108, 123, 164–165, 207; "I" and 97; as nonsensory phenomena 34; personal 34; as psychological function 107; self- 36, 53, 75; stream of 68
consultation 194
contact: Anna O. 3–5, 8; baseline 17; children 171; in conversation 16; definition 210; and depression 140, 146; deprivation of 71, 78; effects of inability to make 135; emotional 135, 140; emotional skill 147; with everyday living 171; eye 182; feed affect hunger 134; formation of personalities 134; human need 20; infant requires 134; lost ability to make 135; in marriage 150, 176; between mothers and daughters 135; negative effects of absence 134; not a "cure" 140; prisoners 71, 78, 79; stability of orienting system 148; therapists' effectiveness 181; therapists ix, 181, 182, 211; triggering childhood pain 176; validational feedback 79
control 102–105

Coolidge, F. L. 87
cortex 56
covert communication 13, 22
creativity 155
Crick, F. 64
Crosby, A. W. 33–34
cultural biases 29–30
cure 2–3
curiosity-terminating judgment 126

Damasio, A. R. 37, 84, 85, 89, 100
Davidson, R. J. 99
Dawkins, R. 31
death 76
Decade of Behavior 52
Deikman, A, J. 53
delusion of knowing 33–36
Dennett, D. C. 49
dependency, attachment and 201
depressions 110, 136, 151, 173; anxiety and 72, 114, 139–141, 144; experiences of 108; in infants 81; suicidal 70–72, 106, 151, 209; unhappiness and grief 140
deprivation 90, 148, 169; emotional 73, 78, 169; social 78–79, 134, 149; of validational feedback 80
Descartes' error 26, 39, 42, 100
diagnosis 193
dialogue 15, 57–58
dichotomy: and duality 32–33; and judgment 126
disequilibrium 72, 101–102, 108; information 45, 52, 55, 62, 69, 148, 162, 208; internal and external sources of 70, 102, 139, 140, 144–146; limbic system 18, 20; NS 75–76, 78, 80, 94, 109, 118, 122, 132–133, 137–139, 145, 148, 160, 163, 174–175, 200
disobedience 104, 168
display of information (DI) *see* consciousness
distress 132, 133, 192; and confusion 106, 155; emotional 136, 140, 141, 147, 150, 184, 197; and pain 72, 135, 136; personal 181
Ditchburn-Riggs experiments, on visual perception 63
Dodo Bird Verdict 181
double duality: of brain's information processing systems 58; of dialogue 15; of feelings 138–140; of personality 165–166
doubly dualistic brain *60*

Douglas, W. O. 103–104
drives 118
duality: versus dichotomy 32–33; of feelings 140–142; of personality 164–165
dyadic interaction theory, structural description of 15–17, *17*
dyadic triangle, attachments to 20–21

Eagleman, D. 103, 115n4
Edelman, G. M. 49
ego 37, 72, 77, 94, 97, 98, 99
Einstein, A. 34
Ekman, P. 99
Eliot, L. 81, 82, 92
Ellenberger, H. 53
Ellis, A. 182
embarrassment 100, 140–141, 197
emotional cognition 91, 200
emotional intensity 154–156, 188; affect hunger for 155; of infant 169; of private person 168
emotionalities/emotions 14, 18, 30, 34, 63, 100, 116–123, 129–131; and ACC 86; in Breuer and Anna O relationship 4–5, 7, 9; of character structure 134–136, 146, 147; dichotomous judgments 126; distress of 136, 140, 141, 147, 150, 184, 197; dyadic interaction 20; engagement 22, 24; evolutionary and cultural influences relating to 123–125; experiences 132–133; and feelings 32, 35, 48, 59, 78, 123, 127, 129–157; function of 127; hemispheric 151–153; idiosyncratic 197; interpersonal 117; natural kind of 118; neurological self and 27, 78, 102, 113; nonsensory experience of 31, 38, 52, 122; pain as 86–87; and personality 120, 144; and personal reality 164, 171; private person 168; as psychotherapeutic process 99; of public person 172; and rationality 40; reaction 72; self-conscious 100; and self-process 50, 86, 87, 105, 117–118, 126, 129; theory of 127; of therapeutic relationship 196–198; thinking of 60; transformational dynamics of 68
emotional skill, levels of 146–147
encephalization quotient (EQ) 49–50, 88
entropy resistant brain 207
equilibratory 7, 20, 61–62, 159

executive brain 42
executive functions 35, 58, 61, 85–86, 87
exercise 80
explanations 35–36, 104, 123, 193; and behavior 62; equilibratory nature of 61–62; projection as form of 95

face, of personal identity 160–161, 172
familiarity 21, 35, 36, 73, 119
fear 114, 137, 139, 140, 203
feedback, validational 19, 79–81, 109, 114, 149, 155, 171, 172, 177, 205
feelings 31, 36, 37, 68, 72, 123, 129–130, 136–138, 160, 174; of character structure 164; as cognitions 101, 130, 137, 163; cultural language of 172; dependency 201; double duality of 138–140; duality of 140–142; and emotions 32, 35, 48, 59, 68, 78, 100, 116–158, 123, 127, 129–157; engagement 18; experiences of 34, 35, 153–154; as explanations 125; of guilt 151; and "I" 97; idiosyncratic use of 138; interpersonal expression of 137; of loneliness 78, 81, 106; negative 154; nonsensory process of 61; and phenomenology of self 144; positive/negative 32, 154; as psychological things 40; remembering experiences of 163; and self-process 142, 145; and selves 142–144; social lexicon of 154, 171, 196–197; as systems of explanation 163; within the person 163–164; transformative nature of 149–151; and wedding of self 142–144
Ferenczi, S. 78, 80–81, 99, 177, 199
fighting 30
figure-ground illusion 23, 52, 64, 65
Fisher, P. A. 169
fixated personality structures 167
fMRI 84
focal awareness 66, 123, 130, 165
four F's of existence 133–134
Freeman, L. 7
Freud, S. 2–3, 33, 52, 109, 113, 144, 156, 199, 203; and Breuer 3, 7, 9; on emotionality 123–124; idea of "death instinct" 76; "I, the" 99; recognition of unconscious motivation 76–77; on self 143; theory of psychoanalysis 23; tripartite description of person 37, 39, 77, 94, 97, 125, 164, 171
Frijda, N. 117
Fromm, E. 113
frustration 111
fusion delusion 12, 80–81

Gage, Phineas 23
Galanter, E. H. 162
Galileo 29, 62
Gawande, A. 71, 79
Gay, P. 7
Gazzaniga, M. S. 64, 74n1, 115n4
Geary, D. C. 50, 88
Gendlin, E. 182
general relativity, theory of 34
ghosts, and souls 54
God 33, 185
Granit, R. 69
Greenberg, L. 182
Griffiths, P. E. 117
growth and change 156–157
guilt 31, 100, 140, 168

habits of mind 28–29; common sense 29, 36; cultural biases 29–30; delusion of knowing 33–36; duality/dichotomy confusion 32–33; hierarchy prejudice 32; about "I" and self-process 94; knowing as remembrance of past experience 37–39; projection 36–37; reification 30–32
habituated belief 121, 189
habituated personal systems 108, 157
Hampden-Turner, C. 44–45
happiness 39
Hawking, S. 34–35
Hawkley, L. C. 81
heart disease 81
Heider, F. 119
Heinsen, D. F. 98
"Hellhole" 71
hemispheric emotionality 151–153
hierarchy versus complexity 32, 33
History of God (Armstrong) 185
homeostasis 27, 32, 42, 47, 69, 84; and affect hunger 78–80; equilibration 67, 102; and personality systems 90–92, 208
Homo Sapiens 53, 87
homunculus 37, 44–45, 66, 94, 96–97, 120, 121
Husserl's theory of pure ego 98
hysteria 124

"I" 30, 33, 36, 44, 50, 53, 89, 115n3, 160; centrality of 102–103; constant presence of 99–101; as cursor 101–102, 160, 162; experience of 103, 107; in focal awareness 62; of intentionality 29; interaction of 107; as referencing/orienting device 102, 105; and self-process 55, 94; of selves 46, 54, 96–98, 107, 120, 162; *see also* Neurological Self (NS), the; self
id 37, 77, 94, 97
ideas 15, 62, 90, 100, 164
"I love you" phrase 143
immediacy 198, 204
Industrial Revolution 61
information: accommodation/assimilation 69; background display of 164–165; kinds of 63; processing 42, 76; sensory/nonsensory 15, 27, 57, 58–60, 64, 87
inside out approach 42
instinctual drives 113
instruments, use of 27
insula 84
"integrity of the NS" phrase 148–149
intellectualization 152
intentionality 28, 39–41, 86, 102–105, 114, 155, 158n6; associated with self-process 86; "I" of 29, 97; and pleasure/pain dichotomy 117; and self-hatred 106–107
internal cognitive processing 109
International Psychoanalytic Association 11
interpersonal emotionality 117
intersubjectivity 198–200
I-Thou dialogue 8, 13, 15, 17, 18, 21, 186, 187
Ivins, W. M. J. 61

James, W. 34, 36, 39, 96–98, 151
Jaynes, J. 115n5, 144
jealousy 140, 150
jinn/numina 75
Jones, E. 7
judgment, dichotomy and 126

Kagan, J. 72, 149
Kahneman, D. 37, 64
Kaiser, H. 11–13, 17, 73, 80
Kelly, G. 34
Kendler, H. H. 107
Kimble, G. A. 119–121
Kipling, R. 82

knower/doer 30, 36
knowing 29, 61–62, 99; delusion of 33–36; as remembrance of experiencing 37–39
Koch, C. 64, 84
Kuhn, T. S. 27, 118
Kurzban, R. 47

Lane, R. D. 86
Lazarus, R. S. 99–100
learning deficit 1
Levy, D. 169
liberation 111–112
limbic activity 27, 113, 130, 137, 207
limbic system 20, 50, 51, 76, 84, 91, 120, 122, 130, 133, 139, 207
linearity/nonlinearity, in human relations 57–58
Listening with the Third Ear (Reik) 13
localization 100
locus coeruleus 86
Loftus, E. 38
loneliness: of affect hunger 78, 101–102, 145; and aging 81; experience of 101; and love 80–82
loss of attachment 200–201
love 79; and art of psychotherapy 201–202; and attachment 200–201; experience of 117; and loneliness 80–82; pleasure of 30, 39–40, 90; and sex in psychotherapy 203–206
luxurious therapeutic dyad 181–186
Lynch, J. 81

Mahoney, M. J. 116
mating 30
May, R. 2
"me" 52, 53, 96; *see also* "I"
memories 36, 38, 45, 66, 87, 197
Menninger, K. 81
mentality: and personality 51; three processes of 54–58
midbrain systems 133
Miller, A. 183
Miller, G. A. 162
mind: and behavior 38–39; biological definition of 45–48; and body 48, 70, 77, 82, 107; and brain 27, 45, 48, 67–70, 83–84, 93, 207; cognition 58–61; definitions of 44–45; dynamics of 62; equilibratory nature of explanation 61–62; evolutionary development of 48–52; habits of

28–29; as homeostatic process 44; as homeostat of brain 67–70; mentality processes 54–58; and personality 77; sensory/nonsensory duality of 38; strength of 72–73; strong/weak 72; theory of 44–74, 89; tricks of 93; *see also* consciousness
"mind over matter" aphorism 40, 48, 70, 93, 208
mindstorms 70–73
Minuchin, S. 181
modularity, and mind 47
monitoring 86, 100
morality 28
motivation 37, 77, 90, 121
Murphy, G. 51, 98
music, listening to 22
mythologies 125

Nair, J. 84, 87
natural kind of emotion 118
Nature of Emotion: Fundamental Questions, The (Ekman and Davidson) 99
Neanderthals, the 87
neural self 89
neuroimaging technology 28, 43n1, 85, 121
Neurological Self (NS), the 46, 71, 75–78, 91, 92, 95, 98, 122, 143; affect hunger of 79–80, 95–96, 108, 129, 132, 145; of children 200; damage to 149; disequilibration of 75–76, 78, 80, 94, 109, 118, 122, 132–133, 137–139, 145, 148, 160, 163, 174–175, 200; and emotion 27, 78, 102; homeostatic process 74, 75; hypothesis of 88; integrity of 148–149; "I" of 162; limited orientation process 132–134; neurology of 84–89; orientation as 50, 76, 101, 132, 207; and prefrontal cortex 130–132, 144; and private person 169–170; self-presentation 148; self-process 94, 159; stability of 80, 102, 109, 124–125, 130–131, 155, 159, 201
neurology 67, 81–82, 84–89
Neuropsychiatric Institute 106
neurotransmitter 82
nonconscious: behavioral solicitations 178–179; habits 18, 28–29, 66; self-presentation 147–148
nonconsciousness 65, 77
nonlinear/sensory cognition 60–61

"nonsense" 52
nonsensory process 26, 28, 31, 38, 50, 52, 53, 54, 75
nonverbal communication 22

objects, movement between 34
observations 35, 52, 118
Occam's razor 35
Odyssey 53
orientation 54–55, 70, 88, 133; with ACC 84; as biological function of self-process 45–46, 50, 53, 85, 94, 149, 207; as homeostatic process 55, 67, 84; as mentality process 54–55, 107; as NS function 50, 76, 101, 132, 207; process 72, 75; psychological aspects of 77; recognition of 89; reflex 46, 84–85; sensory 51; survival system 55, 62, 71, 89, 132; visual 86
orienting network 85
outside in approach 41
overeating 30

pain 70, 135–136, 141, 173; associated with ACC 86; avoiding 39, 153; chronic 86; confusion and 57, 59, 162, 167–168, 174, 197; distress and 72, 135, 136; emotions and 86–87, 101, 126, 156, 169; love and 79, 90, 151, 162; reducing 44, 108; self-process and 86, 87; of social isolation 79; source of 162; suicidal 72; *see also* depressions
panics 72
Panksepp, J. 100
paradigmatic shifts 26–28, 42–43, 73–74, 118
paradigms 27, 90
parental attachment 200
Pavlov 84–85
perceptions 28, 31, 45, 50, 52, 53, 97
person: of character structure 160–161; definition 159–160; face 160–161; feelings 160, 163–164; "I" 160, 162; paradoxical nature of 166–168; personal reality 160, 164; portrait of *161*; psychological selves 160, 162–163; psychotherapeutic implications of 175–178; structural dynamics of 161–164
personal consciousness 34
personal duality 166
personal identity 130, 157, 157n2; character structure and 160–161,

165; cultural language of feelings 172; public person of 170–173
personality: and behavior 52; and brain 14–15, 20, 23, 26–28, 59; change 163; destabilizing systems of 159; disorder, origin of 173–175; double duality of 165–166; duality of 164–165; and emotionality 120, 144; and executive functions 58; growth of 157; habituation 113–115; homeostasis 70; investigation of 100; lens of neurological equilibration 93–94; and mentality 51; and mind 77; process 129; psychological theory of 67, 73–74; and reification 30; secure base 169; structures 21, 67, 72, 82, 83, 90–91, 105, 108, 109, 130, 149, 183, 188; styles 20; theories of 41–43
personal reality 91, 95, 116, 141, 160, 164, 171
personal structures 80, 109, 156
Pfungst, O. 178
phrenology 32
phylogeny 87
physical reality 31, 121
Piaget, J. 22, 69, 89, 114, 160
Pinker, S. 57–58
planning 61
Plato 26, 30, 40, 51, 52, 58, 98, 103, 124, 143
play and work 79
Play Mountain Place, in Los Angeles 25n4
pleasure: experience of 41, 201, 202; of love 21, 30, 39–40, 73, 90, 141; seeking 39; validating internal intensity 154
Pleasure/Pain dichotomy 73, 117
Pleasure Principle 23, 28, 32, 83, 91, 127, 206
Posner, M. I. 85–86
Power of Now, The (Tolle) 71
"practice makes permanent; not perfect" aphorism 46, 67, 82, 83, 189
prefrontal cortex 42, 46; ACC and 75, 86–88; adjustments to 68; affect hunger of 132; cognition 67; disequilibrated 57; disruption in 48; equilibratory dynamics of 122; evolutionary growth of 184; limbic system and 50, 120, 130, 139, 154, 160, 207; nonsensory processes in 26, 27, 50, 56, 58, 60, 61, 118–120, 130;

NS and 80, 101, 130–132, 139, 144, 154, 160, 162, 183
Pribram, K. H. 89, 100, 133, 162
printing, graphic 61
prisoners, at Pelican Bay 78–79
"Prisoners of Childhood" phrase 183
private person 160; of character structure 168–169; and NS 169–170
projection 36–37, 95
"proto-self" 84, 85, 100
pseudocyesis 7
psychoanalysis 1–2
psychological phenomena 26–28, 32, 36, 48, 51, 70, 82, 89, 95, 119, 143, 207
psychological self (selves) 71, 88, 101, 107, 157, 160, 162–163, 169
psychological structure: definition of 22, 89, 160; neurological underpinnings of 89–90
Psychology and Phenomenology; a Clarification (Kendler) 107
psychotherapeutic cure 10
psychotherapeutic dyad: dynamics of 21–23; uniqueness of 183–184
psychotherapeutic implications: of person 175–178; of personality habituation 113–115
psychotherapeutic journey 190–191
psychotherapists 129, 144, 197, 202–203, 205, 209
psychotherapy 3, 16, 22–23, 92; absence of dyadic reciprocity in 186–187; art of 180–209, 201–202; goals of 180–181; love and sex in 203–206; reason for success 140; relational 108; two-person psychology of 198
public person 160, 170–173
pure ego 98
Pygmalion Effect 178

qualia 31, 134

rationality 28, 77, 99
Real Self 53, 98
"reasoning part, the" phrase 40
recreational sex 154
Reddy, W. M. 34
regularity, visual experience of 119
Reich, W. 11, 113
reification 30–32, 119
Reik, T. 13, 177
reinforcement 83, 108
religion and science 61

remembering 38, 97, 102, 163
remembrances 37–38
repressed emotional experiences 3, 6, 197
repression 45, 66, 151, 158n5, 173
right/wrong judgments 32–33
Risk Management Program 204
Roediger, R. 38, 82
Rogers, C. 186
Rosenthal, R. 22, 178
Rosenzweig, S. 181

Schore, A. 134
secondary relationships, social contract of 19
secure base 169
"seeing is believing" phrase 52
self (selves) 32, 35, 40, 50–51, 75–76, 116, 130, 141; and body 98; and brain 93; as cognitive classifications of NS 95; and consciousness 36, 100; as controller behavior 143; dimensions of 89; Ego 77, 94, 99; and emotionality 100, 117, 125, 184; executive functions 86; experience of 33, 66, 84, 185; face as presentation of 172; and feelings 142–144, 183; finding neurological location for 33; and intentionality 40; "I" of/and 30, 46, 53–55, 95, 96–99, 100, 102, 107, 120, 162, 165; as knower/doer of person 36; and mind 44; neural 89; neurology of 90; nonsensory process 31, 38, 51, 53; orientation as 46, 55, 70, 90, 120; proto- 84, 85, 100; psychological 71, 88, 101, 107, 157, 160, 162–163, 169, 171; as source of action 60, 120, 121; as source of rational intention 39; spiritual 97–98; see also Neurological Self (NS), the
self-awareness 31, 52–53, 56, 68, 97, 185
self-blame 106
self-concepts 22, 96, 114, 138, 143, 162, 171
self-conscious emotions 100
self-consciousness 75, 131, 165
self-experience 52–54, 75, 185
self-hatred 40, 71, 106–107
self-observation 105
"Self of Selves" 96–97
self-phenomena 75, 94, 107, 118
self-presentations 17, 19–20, 22, 147–148, 176
self-process 66, 84, 86, 93, 95–96, 159, 207; autoregulatory relationship

with NS 93, 95–96; brain-based definition of 94–95; description 96; emotionalities and 50, 87, 105, 117–118, 126, 129; experiences of 75, 159; feelings and 142, 145; homeostatic function of 94; "I" and 55, 94; love and 117; nonsensory 38; orientation, as biological function of 45, 85, 94, 149, 207; pain and 87; structural dynamics of 107–109; tripartite theory of 94–95
sensory and nonsensory experiencing 26–28, 39, 42, 51, 54, 82, 104, 127, 207
separateness 169, 195
sex/love in psychotherapy 203–206
sexual behavior 113
sexuality 9, 17, 79, 168, 203–205
shame 100, 140
Sherif, M. 102
simplification (cognition) 45, 46
skills, automation of 30
smell 63
Snell, B. 51
social conduct 29
social deprivation 78–79, 134, 149
social environment 95
social feelings 140
social isolation 81
Society for the Exploration of Psychotherapy Integration (SEPI) 181
Socrates 29, 62
Sokolov, Y. N. 84
solitary confinement 78–79, 81
soul: and body 51, 98; and ghosts 54; and spirituality 116
sound 63
speech 50
spindle cells 88
spirituality and humanity 116
"spiritual self" 97–98
Spitz, R. 78
St. Augustine 33, 36, 97, 168
Stein, R. 124
Stern, W. 102, 133
stimuli 119, 120
"stimulus-response" paradigm 145
Stolorow, R. 199
stress 61, 135, 169; see also distress
subjectivity 200
subtext and text, difference between 13
suicidal depressions 70–72, 78, 106, 151, 209
superego 37, 77, 94, 95, 97, 171

superhero 166
suppression 45, 66, 173
synapses 81–82

talking cure phrase 2, 6, 8, 156
technological revolution 82
temperament 149
tension 108, 137
text and subtext, difference between 13
Thayer, J. F. 86
theory of general relativity 34
therapeutic dyad: intersubjectivity 198–200; luxurious 181–186; nonsensory/nonlinear nature of 184–186
therapeutic mode of engagement 193
therapeutic relationship: emotionality of 196–198; power of 23–25
therapist 99, 105, 122, 149–150, 157, 176, 198, 201–206; actor and 195; corrective emotional experiences 195; effectiveness of 181; patient/client and 13, 16–17, 24, 59, 114, 182–184, 186–188, 199, 202; in therapeutic process 191–196
"therapist immediacy" 204
things and processes 131–132
thinking 45, 59, 61
time, descriptions of 33–35
Tolle, E. 71
tonality, emotional 141, 147

touch and physical contact 134
Tulving, E. 38–39
two-person psychology 198

unconscious 65–67, 76–77
unhappiness 139–140
unintentional explanatory behavior 74n1
Upanishads 53
"use it or lose it" aphorism 47, 71, 80, 82

validational feedback 19, 79–81, 109, 114, 149, 155, 171, 172, 177, 205
visual experiencing 54, 119
visual information, display of 63–64, 164
visual sensory system 30–31, 57
vocabularies, of psychological process 54
von Osten, W. 178

Wachtel, P. L. 198
Wager, T. D. 86
Westen, D. 22
Wiesel, E. 149
Winnicott, D. W. 169
Wolf-Man 203
work and play 79
working memory 87
Wundt, W. 116
Wynn, T. 87

zero 53
Zeus 60

Printed in the United States
By Bookmasters